The Strength of Poetry

Terminal Moraine (1972)
Children in Exile: Poems 1968–1984 (1984)
You Were Marvellous (1983)
Partingtime Hall (with John Fuller, 1987)
All the Wrong Places: Adrift in the Politics of the Pacific Rim (1988)
Out of Danger (1994)
Leonardo's Nephew (1998)

The
Strength
of
Poetry

OXFORD LECTURES

JAMES FENTON

Farrar, Straus and Giroux
New York

Farrar, Straus and Giroux
19 Union Square West, New York 10003

Copyright © 2001 by Salamander Press Ltd.
All rights reserved
Distributed in Canada by Douglas & McIntyre Ltd.
Printed in Great Britain
Designed by Paul Cleal
Library of Congress Card Number: 00-110997
ISBN 0-374-22845-0
Originally published in 2001 by Oxford University Press,
United Kingdom
Published in the United States by Farrar, Straus and Giroux
First American edition, 2001

To John Fuller

Acknowledgements

I am grateful to Oxford University for giving me the platform for these lectures, and particularly to the President and Fellows of Magdalen College for their help and hospitality. Many of these lectures were subsequently printed in the *New York Review of Books*, and I am once again grateful to the Editors and staff for help in preparation for publication. I have dropped three of the lectures. The others are published in the order in which they were delivered, in the years 1995 to 1999.

Contents

1. A Lesson from Michelangelo

In old age, Giambologna used to tell his friends the story of how, as a young man, a Flemish sculptor newly arrived in Rome, he made a model to his own original design, finished it *coll'alito*, 'with his breath'—that is to say, with the utmost care, bringing it to the very peak of finish—and went to show it to the great Michelangelo. And Michelangelo took the model in his hands and completely destroyed it, and then remodelled it to his way of thinking, and did so with marvellous skill, so that the outcome was quite the opposite of what the young man had done. And then Michelangelo said to Giambologna: Now go and learn the art of modelling before you learn the art of finishing.[1]

One supposes from this terrible story that the model must have been made of wax. One supposes that, even on a hot summer's afternoon in Rome, it would have needed a certain amount of working before the wax became malleable enough for Michelangelo to shape according to his own wishes. Who knows, perhaps several minutes were involved. They must have seemed like hours, as the young sculptor watched, and the wrathful old genius, biting his lower lip, squeezed and squashed and pounded away at the model that had been so lovingly finished. And well before the new model began to emerge, and with it the ostensive reason for the exercise—learn to model before you learn to finish—another point was being made: See how I crush all your ambitions and aspirations, see how feeble your work is in comparison with mine, see how presumptuous you were even to dare to cross the threshold—*Thus I destroy you!*

There were compensations, of course, for the young Giambologna. He had walked in with a sample of his juvenilia, and he had left carrying a vibrant little Michelangelo. You might say that he was lucky the master had thought him worthy of the lesson, even if the lesson had to be delivered in such a devastating way. You might say this. Or you might argue that the ostensive lesson was only a pretext for the destruction of the young man's work.

There is no such thing as the artistic personality—not in poetry, not in the visual arts. Michelangelo's personality was just one of the colourful range on offer. He was paranoid about his productions, keeping his drawings secret not only from his contemporaries who might include potential plagiarists, but also from posterity itself. As his days drew to a close he made two large bonfires, and not a drawing or cartoon was found in his studio after his death.[2] And this paranoia extended to his relations with other artists. He did not 'bring on young talent'. He appears to have surrounded himself deliberately with no-hopers, and it was easy to imagine it was the skill, not the shortcomings, of Giambologna that drove him into such a rage.

But you don't have to be like that to be a great artist, or a great poet. If Michelangelo was both, so apparently, was Leonardo, of whom Vasari tells us that, in addition to his gifts as a musician, he was 'the most talented improviser in verse of his time'.[3] We are told by one scholar that while 'Michelangelo jealously guarded his artistic property against other artists, it was not in keeping with Leonardo's nature to trouble himself to preserve the authorship of the wealth of ideas which poured out of him', that he was

> amiable by nature, communicative and ready to be of help . . . when he turned to the greater themes of painting or sculpture, he was interested above everything else in the solution of some fundamental problem; when he

had succeeded to his own satisfaction, perhaps only theoretically, he liked to leave its execution to others; and what happened further to the work of art seems to have troubled him but little, much less did it occur to him to sign it. He was so independent and had so little vanity that in the execution of his work the identity of the patron had not the slightest influence with him.[4]

And yet there were, as Vasari makes clear, limits to Leonardo's lack of vanity: he did not tolerate insulting behaviour, he could not stand a foolish, ignorant patron, and he couldn't bear to remain in the same city as Michelangelo. Nor Michelangelo with him. So one went off to Rome, and the other to the court of the King of France, and thereby they put between themselves about as great a distance as they possibly could, without falling off the edge of what they deemed the civilized world.

But it does not follow from this that genius always repels genius. Verrocchio presents a further type; a teacher who was happy to surround himself with talent, who trained Lorenzo di Credi and loved him above all others. Verrocchio it was who took on the young Leonardo and who famously decided to renounce painting when he recognized that Leonardo's angel in the *Baptism* outshone his own work. He was ashamed to have been out-painted by a mere boy. But if this renunciation seems hysterical, I would say it is less so in Verrocchio's case than it would have been in others. Verrocchio had plenty of other fish to fry. He had begun life as a goldsmith. In Rome, he

saw the high value that was put on the many statues and other antiques being discovered there, and the way the Pope had the bronze horse set up in St John Lateran, as well as the attention given to even the bits and pieces, let alone the complete works of sculpture, that were being unearthed every day.[5]

So he decided to give up being a goldsmith and would be a sculptor instead. And when he had won honour as a sculptor so that 'there was nothing left for him to achieve', he turned his hand to painting.

I take these stories about artists, from Baldinucci and Vasari, because they date from a period when it appears that one could acknowledge straightforwardly motives of which we would today be obscurely ashamed. Verrocchio observes that there is much honour to be gained in the field of sculpture, so he becomes a sculptor, and when he feels he has won the honour that is going, he turns to painting with the same motive, but when he sees his way blocked by Leonardo he turns back to sculpture again. There is something equable about this temperament and something generous about the recognition of which it was capable. But this generosity was far from typical of its time and place. It was noteworthy. It was a cause célèbre.

Otherwise one feels that the Italy these artists worked in was a place of the most vicious rivalry and backbiting, manoeuvrings for commissions, angling for patronage, plots, triumphs, and disappointments. You had to wait literally for years to be paid. If your work was deemed ugly, you soon learnt about it from lampoons or pasquinades. You got stabbed in the back. Anonymous denunciations for sodomy would arrive, as regular as parking tickets.

Since your work, standing, and honour were all bound together, the award of a grand commission to a friend or rival would be a devastating blow. It would make you rethink your life, as—and this is the last of the Vasarian exempla— Brunelleschi and Donatello were forced to do when Ghiberti won the famous competition for the Florence Baptistery doors. The contest had taken a year. When the entries were exhibited, it was clear to the two friends that Ghiberti's work was better than theirs, and so they went to the consuls and argued that Ghiberti should get the commission. And for this,

Vasari says, 'they deserved more praise than if they had done the work perfectly themselves. What happy men they were! They helped each other, and they found pleasure in praising the work of others. What a deplorable contrast is presented by our modern artists who are not content with injuring one another, but who viciously and enviously rend others as well!'[6]

So Vasari praises the two artists, and he is not sentimental either, for he goes on to relate how the consuls asked Brunelleschi, who had clearly come a very good second, whether he would cooperate with Ghiberti on the doors, but Brunelleschi said no, since 'he was determined to be supreme in some other art rather than merely be a partner or take second place'.[7] Nor was this a passing fit of pique, although both artists eventually did return to Florence and did help Ghiberti. Perhaps the strength of their sense of failure may be gauged from the fact that Donatello, who had not done so well, took a year away from Florence, whereas Brunelleschi, the honourable runner-up, took at least five, and when he did return, he did so principally as an architect.

It's not enough to fail. You have to come to feel your failure, to live it through, to turn it over in your hand, like a stone with strange markings. You have to wake up in the middle of the night and hear it whistling around the roof, or chomping in the field below, like some loyal horse—My failure, my very own failure, I thought I'd left it behind in Florence, but look, it's followed me here to Rome. And the horse looks up at you in the moonlight and you feel its melancholy reproach. This is after all the failure for which you were responsible. Why are you neglecting your failure?

Many people live in such horror of failure that they can never embark on any great enterprise. And this inability to get going in the first place is the worst kind of failure because there is truly no way out. You can cover up. You can hide behind a mask of exquisite sensibility. You can congratulate yourself on the fact that your standards are so high that no human effort could possibly match up to them. You can make yourself unpleasant to your contemporaries by becoming expert on their shortcomings. In the end, nothing is achieved by this timidity.

Or you can permit yourself one failure in life, and devote your remaining days to mourning. 'Alas, alas, the critics panned my play.' 'When was this, friend?' 'In 1894!' This failure, it would seem, has been kept like a trophy, lovingly polished and always on display. But for a productive life, and a happy one, each failure must be felt and worked through. It must form part of the dynamic of your creativity.

The judgement on Donatello's competition entry was: Good design, poor execution. Donatello could decipher that from a message saying: You are not yet fully formed as an artist; you must study. But the message received by Brunelleschi was: You will never be as good as Ghiberti. This was a hard blow. Brunelleschi did what he felt necessary—sold a small farm and, with Donatello, walked down to Rome. And there something happened to them which I hope will happen to any poet reading this. Failure rewarded them a thousandfold.

For they came to a place, a sort of Land of Green Ginger, where every answer to every urgent enquiry lay literally at their feet. This, for a poet, would be like discovering voice, technique, and infinite subject matter, fresh and unused, and finding them all in a flash. The ruins of Rome were fresh and unused. You pulled back a caper bush and there lay an architrave. You peered behind the pigpen, and there was a sarcophagus. You dug a little and there was a bust, a capital, a herm.

And so they dug and drew and made measurements of the astonishing buildings all around them, and they went without food, and they got filthy, and people decided they must be geomancers in search of treasure. Which wasn't far wrong. For the secrets of the classical orders were revealing themselves, and the lost technology of the ancient world. But all this time

Brunelleschi never revealed to Donatello—especially not to Donatello—the scope of his ambition to revive the classical art of architecture and make that his bid for fame. They were friends. They were rivals. For the project to be worthwhile, it had to be the means whereby Brunelleschi would defeat not only Ghiberti, but also Donatello, his best friend from the Salon des Refusés.

Why should artistic ambition be like that? Why should a sculptor, a poet, feel the need to be the unique object of admiration, to create around himself an illusion of being quite the only pebble, the only boulder on the beach? Why should uniqueness itself be so closely involved with our definition of a work of art, so that we expect every performance to be unique, every hand, every voice, every gesture?

Without looking too far for an answer, we might say our efforts in the direction of art have something to do with a moment, or a period, in which we felt or knew ourselves to be unique. (I mean, normally speaking. We are not piglets. We weren't born in a litter.) Dandled on the lap we were unique, when our parents taught us all the things we could do with our lips and our limbs. And this was a time of pure inventiveness. Everything we did was hailed as superb. We leapt up and down and our innards went wild with surprise. And the palms of our hands were beaten together. We learnt about rhythm and we learnt new ways of making a noise, and every noise we made was praised. And we learnt how to walk, and all eyes were upon us, the way they never would be again.

Because there follows the primal erasure, when we forget all those early experiences, and it is rather as if there is some mercy in this, since if we could remember the intensity of such pleasure it might spoil us for anything else. We forget what happened exactly, but we know that there was something, something to do with music and praise and everyone talking, something to do with flying through the air, something to do with dance.

And during this period of forgetting we have been forced to take a realistic view of the world, and to admit that there are other people in it besides ourselves and our adoring audience. And in our various ways of coping with this fact we form the basis of our personality. And one will say through his art: There can be only me—the rest being counterfeits. And another will say: There is me, and my best friend, and we are the best. And a third version would be: There is me and my best friend, who (but don't tell him) isn't as good as me.

Auden wrote a wonderful thing to Stephen Spender in 1942—it is quoted in Auden's *Juvenilia*—when he said: 'You (at least I fancy so) can be jealous of someone else writing a good poem because it seems a rival strength. I'm not, because every good poem, of yours say, is a strength, which is put at my disposal.'[8] And he said that this arose because Spender was strong and he, Auden, was weak, but this was a fertile weakness.

And it would indeed be a source of fertility to be blessed with that attitude both to the living and to the dead, so that everybody's good poem is a source of strength to you, and the corpus of published poetry lies before you as the ruins of Rome appeared to Brunelleschi. One associates Auden's luck in this regard with his abiding conviction that in any gathering he was always the youngest person in the room.

An extreme case of the opposite attitude would be that of Wordsworth in old age, at least the attitude that Carlyle claimed to detect:

> I got him upon the subject of great poets, who I thought might be admirable equally to us both; but was rather mistaken, as I gradually found. Pope's partial failure I was prepared for; less for the narrowish limits visible in Milton and others. I tried him with Burns, of whom he had sung tender recognition; but Burns also turned out to be a limited inferior creature, any genius he had a

theme for one's pathos rather; even Shakespeare himself
had his blind sides, his limitations:—gradually it became
apparent to me that of transcendent unlimited there
was, to this Critic, probably one specimen known,
Wordsworth himself! He by no means said so, or hinted
so, in words; but on the whole it was all I gathered from
him in this considerable *tête-à-tête* of ours; and it was not
an agreeable conquest. New notion as Poetry or Poet I
had not in the smallest degree got; but my insight into
the depth of Wordsworth's pride in himself had consid-
erably augmented;—and it did not increase my love of
him; though I did [not] in the least hate it either, so quiet
was it, so fixed, *un*appealing, like a dim old lichened crag
on the wayside, the private meaning of which, in
contrast with any public meaning it had, you recognized
with a kind of not wholly melancholy *grin*.[9]

You notice how far we have come from the candid psychology
of ambition as perceived by Vasari to the uncandid, sly, deceit-
ful self-love as perceived by Carlyle, whose meaning,
unpacked, was—there is only me, *and there only ever has been
me.*

Nor was this simply something that Wordsworth came to
believe at the end of his life. There was a period when his
'intolerance of others', as Gittings tells us, 'was reported to
have reached alarming lengths'.[10] And it happened, that this
was the period in which Keats, who admired Wordsworth to
distraction, was ushered into his presence. He had sent a copy
of his 1817 *Poems* to Wordsworth, who, if he had read them,
had done so without cutting all the pages. But all went well
initially, and Wordsworth kindly asked what Keats had been
writing recently. And from this point I shall follow Haydon's
account, even though the detail has been disputed.[11] What
seems not in dispute is that Keats did a bit of a Giambologna.
Haydon says:

I said he has just finished an exquisite ode to Pan—and as he had not a copy I begged Keats to repeat it—which he did in his usual half chant, (most touchingly) walking up & down the room—when he had done I felt really, as if I had heard a young Apollo—Wordsworth drily said 'a Very pretty piece of Paganism'—This was unfeeling and unworthy of his high Genius to a young worshipper like Keats—& Keats felt it *deeply*—so that if Keats has said any severe thing about our Friend; it was because he was wounded—and though he dined with Wordsworth after at my table—he never forgave him.[12]

If it did not happen quite like this, something quite like this appears nevertheless to have happened, and Keats became aware of that quiet, fixed, unappealing, dim old lichened crag, and got a whiff of its meaning. Because his attitude does change, and it is not so long after this encounter that Keats writes his celebrated letter to Reynolds of 3 February 1818. Nothing from the surviving letters gives Keats's side of the encounter, unless we take this passage as a record of a man recovering from an insult.

It may be said that we ought to read our Contemporaries, that Wordsworth &c should have their due from us, but for the sake of a few fine imaginative or domestic passages, are we to be bullied into a certain Philosophy engendered in the whims of an Egotist—Every man has his speculations, but every man does not brood and peacock over them till he makes a false coinage and deceives himself.

And a few lines later:

We hate poetry that has a palpable design on us—and if we do not agree, seems to put its hand in its breeches pocket. Poetry should be great & unobtrusive, a thing which enters into one's soul, and does not startle it or amaze it with itself but with its subject.—How beautiful are the retired flowers! how they would lose their beauty were they to throng into the highway crying out, 'admire me, I am a violet! dote upon me I am a prim-rose!'[13]

Well, we hate an insult both for the evidence it gives us of another's malice, and for the way it finds us out, the way it gets at our self-esteem, or worse, if the insult thinks it can get at us, even though we feel passionately that we are not as base-minded as that. If Keats came from his encounter with Wordsworth insulted and disillusioned, it is not surprising that he should have refrained from saying so directly, for it is humiliating to admit that some trivial remark has cut us to the quick, humiliating further to give any evidence that the jibe has lodged with us, that it has arrived with all its luggage and intends to stay for a long time. Keats looked into Wordsworth's soul and saw something unexpectedly petty:

Modern poets differ from the Elizabethans in this. Each of the moderns like an Elector of Hanover governs his own petty state, & knows how many straws are swept daily from the Causeways in all his dominions & has a continual itching that all the Housewives should have their coppers well scoured: the ancients were Emperors of vast Provinces, they had only heard of the remote ones and scarcely cared to visit them—I will cut all this— I will have no more of Wordsworth or Hunt . . .[14]

It may be that there was something about Keats that created alarm in his contemporaries. Byron seems hysterical in his attack on Keats's 'piss-a-bed' poetry: 'No more *Keats* I entreat—flay him alive—if some of you don't I must skin him myself [:] there is no bearing the drivelling idiotism of the Mankin.—'[15] And 'Mr Keats whose poetry you enquire after— appears to me what I have already said;—such writing is a sort of mental masturbation—he is always f—gg—g his *Imagination*.—I don't mean that he is *indecent* but viciously soliciting his own ideas into a state which is neither poetry nor anything else but a Bedlam vision produced by raw pork and opium.'[16] Then he becomes a 'dirty little blackguard', simply for having been praised in the *Edinburgh Review*. And then, in death, he is assumed to be a person of 'such inordi- nate self-love he would probably not have been very happy'. Byron assumes it to be true, and becomes obsessed by the idea that Keats was killed off by a burst blood vessel after receiving a savage review in the *Quarterly*. He affects a kind of regret, but cannot conceal an illicit excitement at the story. It is hard not to conclude that Keats was seen as a threat by Byron, and that this was his greatest sin. As for Wordsworth, going through his impossible phase, Gittings says: 'From 1815 to 1820, the diffi- cult second half of a man's forties, Wordsworth showed at his worst, and his emergence at fifty to something like his normal self was greeted by all with relief. It is an irony that his malaise coincided precisely with the whole of Keats's writing life.'[17]

Irony doesn't seem quite strong enough a word to cover the implication of this passage: that one of the supremely gifted poets of the time should be driven into something that looked like a kind of mental illness, by the mere fact of another poet's existence; that Wordsworth could not be at ease with himself until he knew that Keats was dead.

But if it *were* true, and if it were true that Byron suffered something like the same disease, then one would suppose that what identified Keats as a threat was his aspiration for great- ness, rather than the greatness itself. It is not that either of the older poets had been put into a pother after reading the odes. It's the *Poems* of 1817, stuff that might strike us, for the most part, as not exactly threatening—and anyway Wordsworth hadn't even read all of it,[18] and there's no guarantee that Byron had either.

It seems unfair, excepting in this sense, that Keats's encounter with opposition, with envy perhaps on Wordsworth's part, and his disenchantment, seems to have benefited him, to have made him stronger, whereas it was nothing unless debilitating to Wordsworth. Keats had a strong and just sense of his own development, and he didn't mind taking a nosedive:

> The Genius of Poetry must work its own salvation in a man: It cannot be matured by law & precept, but by sensation & watchfulness in itself—That which is creative must create itself—In Endymion I leaped head-long into the Sea, and thereby have become better acquainted with the Soundings, the quicksands, & the rocks, than if I had stayed upon the green shore, and piped a silly pipe, and took tea & comfortable advice.—I was never afraid of failure; for I would sooner fail than not be among the greatest.[19]

So it might have been the aspiration that was the problem for anyone setting out in poetry. If I aspire to musicianship, I am at once set on a journey through a series of immensely complicated disciplines. It is extremely improbable that I will get anywhere without training. And it therefore does not happen that even a precocious musician seems pretentious. We feel, however much we envy the success, that it must have been earned. But it is far from clear how we are supposed to *earn* success in poetry. Poetry often seems unearned.

Nor is it at all clear how we could be delayed, held back from achieving our aim, if we looked like a bit of a threat. Verrocchio can always hold Leonardo back, keeping him grinding colours, or preparing panels, or busy at any number of prentice tasks. Or he could affect to bring him on, keeping him sketching from dawn till dusk, but always delaying the dread moment when he picks up the paintbrush. But in poetry there is really no equivalent for these intermediate disciplines. The way to learn to write poetry is: to write poetry. So we pass directly from the aspiration to the activity itself, and that leaves us at first vulnerable, because, looked at in a certain way, we have no *right* to be writing poems at this stage. But unfortunately we have no option *but* to give it a whirl. The old joke—Do you play the violin? I don't know, I've never tried—describes our predicament. We are in the position of someone who takes up a violin for the first time and has a go at giving a concert.

But you might object: surely there are things one can do, like writing parodies, like trying out the traditional forms, like studying other peoples' poetry, like going in for competitions. I would certainly say that people who have no interest at all in studying other peoples' poetry are unlikely to produce it themselves, although it is not at all uncommon for them to attempt to do so. As for parodies and the trying out of forms, these are things that some people do and find useful. In the case of parody, its chief usefulness is getting people to write poetry who are too shy or too sly to admit that that is what they want to do.

As far as the trying out of traditional forms is concerned, I have this to say: that there seems to me to be a fundamental difference between trying out a traditional form as an exercise, and writing a poem in a traditional form. It is true that, in the context of a workshop, structure may be given to a certain group's work by the trying out of certain famous forms, and it is true that such things can be fun as competitions or games among friends. But I do not think that the trying out of forms is an exercise that points in the direction of writing poems. Trying out the sonnet—taking the sonnet for a spin, putting the little filly through her paces—seems a rather different activity from the writing of poetry. The great questions of form go deeper than that, and the commitment implied is much more profound than the respectful nod in the direction of form-as-exercise would imply. Don't try out a sonnet. Try to *write* a sonnet. Try to write a *real* sonnet. But that's the whole aim. That's not an exercise.

Auden tried everything there was going, but his attitude was different. It was much more like Brunelleschi and Donatello going crazy among the ruins of Rome, digging things up, finding how they worked, imitating them. And imitating for Auden meant much more than the banal copying of metrical pattern and rhyme scheme. It meant a recapturing and reinterpretation of the quality of a thing—a madrigal, a calypso, whatever it was.

There is another form of activity, though, besides reading other peoples' work and trying perhaps to imitate it, and this is showing your work to other people. And this activity is of the essence. And of course it can be most devastating, usually because what one has written usually turns out to be a complete turkey, and we only realize this at the moment we hand the thing to our friends. We should all take heart though from the case of Flaubert, who put a phenomenal effort into the composition of the first version of his *Temptation of Saint Anthony* (one single episode involved him in the reading of sixty ancient texts, histories, and scholarly commentaries) and finally read it aloud to his friends Louis Bouilhet and Maxime DuCamp, who recalled later that

> the hours that Bouilhet and I spent listening to Flaubert chant his lines—we sitting there silent, occasionally exchanging a glance—remain very painful in my memory. We kept straining our ears, always hoping that the action would begin, and always disappointed, for the situation remains the same from beginning to end. St Anthony, bewildered, a little simple, really quite a blockhead if I dare say so, sees the various forms of temptation

pass before him and responds with nothing but excla-
mations: 'Ah! Ah! Oh! Mon dieu! Mon dieu!' . . . Flaubert
grew heated as he read, and we tried to grow warm with
him, but remained frozen . . . After the last reading [and
the whole thing had taken thirty-two hours] Flaubert
pounded the table: 'Now; tell me frankly what you
think.'
    Bouilhet was a shy man, but no one was firmer than
he once he decided to express his opinion; and he said:
'We think you should throw it into the fire and never
speak of it again.'
    Flaubert leapt up and uttered a cry of horror. . . . He
repeated certain lines to us, saying 'But that is beautiful!'
'Yes, it is beautiful. . . . There are excellent passages,
some exquisite evocations of antiquity, but it is all lost in
the bombast of the language. You wanted to make music
and you have made only noise.'[20]

I think we can assume that there was justice in what the
two friends said, rather than envy, which is what Flaubert's
mother thought. But there remains the problem first of daring
to show the work to your friends, next of bearing to listen to
what they say about it, but finally, finally and most impor-
tantly, there is the whole matter of interpreting what your
friends say, deciding whether to accept or reject their judgement, and figuring out where you are going to go from there.
And this is where the delicate matter of the relations between
poets comes in.
    Why should it be, for instance, that Coleridge wrote 'Kubla
Khan' in the late 1790s, say October or November 1797, that the
Wordsworths definitely knew it in 1798 because Dorothy says in
her Hamburg journal that she 'carried Kubla to a fountain',
meaning, we believe, that she carried her drinking can, which
she called Kubla, but that Coleridge is not recorded as reciting
the poem till 1811–12, and that it was not published until 1816.

If we had written the poem would we be so reticent?

I believe the answer is that Coleridge wrote the poem, much as one writes any poem, with a great deal of excitement, and that he put it in his pocket and went over to see the Wordsworths. Now the state of mind one is in after writing a poem is rather like the state of mind that continues in a waking person after a particularly vivid dream—but with this difference, that we are under the illusion, after such a dream, that it will be of interest to others. But very few dreams are. They might interest our lovers, and they are meat and drink to our analysts, but not to anyone else. But we don't know this, because the state of mind that produced the dream is still with us. Nor do we know, after we have written the poem, whether it will be of interest to others. Put it away for a while, and you can possibly tell, but at the moment of completion you merely hope that the thrill is not an illusion.

Coleridge came bounding over to see the Wordsworths, as he had often done, to read his latest work. And they sat in a rather damp parlour, and Coleridge launched into his reading, and while he was at it, full tilt, Dorothy was watching William, as she always did, for his reaction. And there was a little gesture which she knew well, which meant that his nose had been put out of joint. Keats noticed it too, and it survived in one of the passages I quoted. Wordsworth put his hand in his breeches pocket. And Dorothy knew that all was not well. Coleridge was in the process of committing an utter Giambologna.

The reading was over. Silence fell. And Coleridge, who was on a natural high not caused by anything remotely resembling substance abuse, thought—great, they're impressed. And he waited for a compliment or two. And nothing happened, and finally he too began to suspect that something was up. And then Dorothy said, in a bright voice, 'Well, at least I shall know what to call my drinking *can* now. Come along, Kubla, we're going to the well.' And Wordsworth suddenly burst out laughing in a rather horrible and forced way, and said, 'I say Dorothy, that's awfully good—Kubla Can—do you get it, Coleridge?' And Dorothy left the room, and silence fell again, punctuated occasionally by Wordsworth's chuckling over Dorothy's joke.

Finally, it was Coleridge's turn to say something, to cover up the dreadful Giambologna he appeared to have committed. And he began telling a story about how he had been taking opium and gone into a trance, and something about a person from Porlock and all of it made up. And Wordsworth turned to him and said: 'I think you should throw that poem in the fire Coleridge, and never speak of it again.'

Now if Coleridge had been Keats he would have fallen out of love with Wordsworth on the spot. But Coleridge was not Keats. He was absolutely convinced, and puzzled by the fact, that he had made a faux pas of the worst kind, because he could not recognize the thing that Keats and Carlyle recognized when they looked into Wordworth's soul—that unappealing, lichen-covered thing.

It was not that he was not sly. In his own way Coleridge was incredibly sly. He affected to like Southey's poetry, of which he had a low opinion. Same with Byron. He thought he was the warmest, the most discerning of Wordsworth's admirers, but he once went to great lengths to write a two-volume book, the *Biographia Litereria*, merely in order to be able to print a whole chapter on the defects of Wordsworth's poetry, which he knew would be enough to send Wordsworth *up the wall*. A whole chapter on Wordsworth's defects! And Byron read that chapter with particular interest. And Coleridge never knew what he, Coleridge, was up to.

If he'd been a character out of Vasari he could have understood that Wordsworth had to be the only one in his field, and he might even have done a better job of going off to Rome, or going to work at the court of the King of France, or whatever the equivalent would have been. But he couldn't manage to fall out of love with him. He couldn't leave him alone.

But 'Kubla Khan' wouldn't go away. Coleridge had improvised the story whereby he had turned it into a curiosity, and it was as a curiosity that he would recite it to his friends. One day in early April 1816 he did so in the company of Byron— Byron who, despite his views on the Lake Poets, always had time for Coleridge (his letters show this), always admired poems such as 'Christabel', and had even put work in Coleridge's way.

Byron was impressed and immediately asked why Coleridge had not published such a fine work. Coleridge shrugged and said that Wordsworth hadn't liked it. Thereupon my suggestion is that Byron set Coleridge right upon the character of his friend. When the poem saw print, it was with an acknowledgement of Byron's encouragement.

> The following fragment is here published at the request of a poet of great and deserved celebrity, and, as far as the Author's own opinions are concerned, rather as a psychological curiosity, than on grounds of any supposed *poetic* merits.

But Coleridge did not think Byron's celebrity as a poet was deserved. As Henry Nelson Coleridge reported in his *Table Talk* (2 June 1824),

> Nothing of Lord Byron's would live, not much of the poetry of the day. The *art* was so neglected; the verses would not scan.

This then is the essence of a true Giambologna. It is based on a gross misunderstanding of the actual state of affairs. Giambologna takes a statuette to show to Michelangelo, and he thinks he's just a poor Flemish nobody, wanting a pat on the head. But Michelangelo takes one look at Giambologna and what he sees is a threat. In fact Michelangelo hallucinates. What he sees is a gleaming, nude bronze warrior, striding into the studio with some kind of weapon in his hands, and he thinks: Oh, so I'm supposed to be Goliath, am I? And he seizes the weapon and crushes it with all his might. And the hallucination passes, and he sees that it's just that Flemish twerp who keeps pestering . . .

Giambologna emerges from his meeting with Michelangelo, with the wax model still warm from the worker's hand. He can't believe that Michelangelo, whom he had worshipped as a god, could have been so perfectly foul to him. He feels sorry for himself as a foreigner. He thinks: He wouldn't have behaved like that if I had been a Florentine; the bastard just said to himself, Who does this Flemish twerp think he is? And so he walks on through a Rome with which he is distinctly out of love, the Rome that had once seemed to him like the Land of Green Ginger, until he comes to the small tavern where he and several of his countrymen live. And it's evening, and his friends are at table and they call out to him: Hey, Jean, how did it go? And then they say: Oh, like that, was it? And Giambologna takes a taper and goes up to his room, lights a lamp, and places the little model on the table, the model that he had made to his own design and finished so beautifully.

And he thinks: it's so banal, that advice—learn first to model before you learn to finish. It's like saying learn to walk before you learn to run. Who needs it? What's the point? Why set yourself up as a genius if that's the best you can do?

And then he thinks: Who's he to talk about modelling anyway? The *Bacchus* looks as if it's going to fall over. The *David*'s got one leg longer than the other. Who's he to talk about modelling? And the thought of the injustice of it makes him throw his shoes across the room with such force that one of his countrymen comes up to see what's wrong.

And Giambologna says: 'Michelangelo's idea of modelling, I mean *his idea of modelling*, is sticking a couple of breasts on a bloke to make a woman. That's his idea of modelling!'

And the friend says: 'Yes, Jean, yes, come and have a drink.'

But Giambologna says: 'He talks about learning to model before you learn to finish. I mean—what does he know about finishing? When was the last time he ever finished anything? Tell me! When?'

'Sistine Chapel?' says the friend, but Giambologna doesn't hear.

'The façade of San Lorenzo is a disgrace. The tomb of Julius is just a fragment. He doesn't even bother any more, he thinks he's so clever he can leave half the block untouched.'

'You're right,' says the friend. 'He's a complete tosser. Now come on down.' But Giambologna stays upstairs, calmer now he has fallen out of love with Rome and out of love with Michelangelo, now the scales have fallen from his eyes. And from time to time he goes over to the table, and examines the little *bozzetto*, and really it's not entirely bad, it's just that it's full of all the things that Giambologna can't stand about Michelangelo.

And soon without knowing it he is biting his lower lip, and working away at the red wax, till it becomes malleable again. And now he begins to revise the figure according to his way of thinking, reducing the gigantism of the muscles, giving the features an elegance and brio, working away with his finest tools till every centimetre of surface is brought to the most beautiful finish he has ever achieved.

Dawn comes. He can hear the shepherds making their way up the Janiculum, singing their peasant songs to their clanking flocks. And now all the bells of Rome begin to ring. It sounds like the introduction to the last act of *Tosca*. It *is* the introduction to the last act of *Tosca*. Giambologna feels a surge of hope again. He thinks he will be able to excel anyone in his art.

And he is right to think so, for his mental apprenticeship to that angry genius has come to an end. Giambologna will become sculptor to the Medici. His works will be like a sort of diplomatic currency, given only to princes, distributed the length and breadth of Europe. He has taken Michelangelo's advice, but he has rejected the spirit of that advice. His works will be known, yes, for the bravura of their modelling, but they will be known above all for the brilliance of their finish.

2. *Wilfred Owen's Juvenilia*

A thousand suppliants stand around thy throne,
Stricken with love for thee, O Poesy.
I stand among them, and with them I groan,
And stretch my arms for help. Oh, pity me!
No man (save them thou gav'st the right to ascend
And sit with thee, 'nointing with unction fine,

—Excuse me: ''nointing with unction fine'—what's this
'nointing business? What is this 'nointing with *unction* fine?
Oh, this is what we permit ourselves, or what we used to
permit ourselves, in our juvenilia. This is the stuff we pray
desperately will not be found. This is what we later burn.

These are our first steps in poetry, and, surprisingly enough,
we tend to want those first steps to be giant strides. We do not,
as poets, start with humble studies, aiming to work our way
up towards the grand canvas. We start with the large gesture.
We sit down at our little tables, we chew our little pencils for
a while, we open our exercise books, and we write down the
most imposing title we can think of—'An Ode to the Sun',
'The Meaning of Life', or in this case, with a simple flourish,
'To Poesy':

No man (save them thou gav'st the right to ascend
And sit with thee, 'nointing with unction fine,
Calling thyself their servant and their friend)
Has loved thee with a purer love than mine.[1]

This is the teenage Wilfred Owen: no man, he says to Poesy,
no man if we exclude the 'nointing brigade (by which he

means all acknowledged poets) no man loves Poesy more
purely than I do. And he appears to mean this boast, for he
goes on to point out that other poetry-lovers tend to be half-
hearted, tend to turn to other goddesses, but he, Wilfred, is
absolutely single-minded:

> I neither cease to love,
> Nor am content to love but for the sake
> Of passing pleasures caught from thee above.

It is not that Poesy brings back gorgeous memories of the past,
although it does do this. It is not that she knows

> the unseen road
> Which leads unto the awful halls of Fame
> Where, 'midst the heapèd honours, thine the load
> Most richly prized, of all crowns the best!
> No! not for these I long to win thee, Sweet!

He is on intimate enough terms with Poesy to call her
Sweet.

> No more is this my fervent, hopeless quest—
> To stand among the great ones there, to meet
> The bards of old and greet them as my peers.

That's not what he wants. He calls that an impious thought.
But he wants to know the way to begin, he wants to know the
path to follow which will lead eventually to poetic achievement. And he sees straight away (because this poem is based
on his real thoughts, even if the language used is what was
once called Wardour Street[2]) that he lacks learning, but that
learning requires money as well as effort. A great part of the
pathos of Owen's early story comes from the future poet's

unhappiness at missing out on education. Should he go into a job? he asks. Or (translated into Wardour Street):

> What then? Dost bid me first seek out the Court
> Where this world's wretched god, the money-sack,
> Doles out his favours to the cringing herd,
> There slave for him awhile to earn his pelf?

His answer to this is that, even if he made money quickly, there is so much to be learnt that the thought of it fills him with fear. He would like a classical education. He would like to master several languages. He must of course have a faultless style in his own language, and must know all its authors. He must master the art of criticism—and this is interesting for he must do so both to defend his work and to strike at his enemies.

At the end of all this, there is still the fear that such a long training would destroy his 'simple ardent love', that (if he were not writing in Wardour Street) his spontaneity would be impaired. So he asks the goddess for a storm, a downpour of inspiration:

> So, midst long triumph-roars of awful sound,
> Flash thou thy soul to me at last, and roll
> Torrential streams of thought upon my brain,
> So give, yea give Thyself to me at last.

And if the goddess gives herself to him, she will find him 'a doting master.' This is to be, it would seem, a monogamous relationship, in which he asserts a beneficent male tyranny. The goddess will forget his youth and ignorance, the fact that he is somewhat lower class[3] and that he has no friends to assist him in his ambitions. If Poesy embraces him, he will not heed the world's mockery. Jeering won't get to him. He will sit alone with poetry in private, kissing by the light of the moon,

> Our faces pressing nigh
> Quietly shining in her quiet light.

The last line, adapted from Coleridge, reminds us that we are never such kleptomaniacs as in our juvenilia. We steal from our masters. We steal from our friends, from our enemies even. We try out tones of voice for which we are ill suited. We write as if we belong to some other period. We are suckers for gorgeous words such as nenuphar, asphodel, and pelf. And because we are not yet in command of our vehicle we get out of control. We reveal ourselves inadvertently and we inadvertently commit ourselves to some point of view that isn't really 'us' at all. As above, Wilfred Owen finds himself expressing at length the fantasy of being the only poet in the world. But little else in his short life would suggest that he truly, seriously was ever enslaved by this fantasy. Poetry was a club which he dearly wanted to join, a peerage by which he longed to be accepted. In that sense, the poem 'To Poesy' represents his state of mind. But he is so full of awe of others, one doubts that even in a long life he would have come to forget that he was one of many.

And so we are betrayed by our juvenilia, in both senses of the word. These poems give away what we are like. And they give an utterly misleading impression. In view of this, the benevolent practice of editors has been to rope the juvenilia off, to place it in a section of its own at the end of the volume, or in a separate volume, to avoid disappointing the reader.

But this handy convention of editorship is not mimicked by life itself. We do neatly pass through a discrete phase of juvenilia before entering adulthood. Nor are poets cheeses. You cannot prod us and say: yes, this one is now mature—this one needs another six weeks. When we write of people passing from a phase of immaturity to maturity, we are often guilty of tidying up reality, of simplifying experience.

Here is a passage from an otherwise excellent book by

Dominic Hibberd, in which the writing has over-tidied the facts which are being presented:

> But soon, somewhere near Beaumont Hamel, [Owen] found himself obliged to hold a flooded dugout in No Man's Land, where he endured the events described in 'The Sentry'; as his futile match burnt out in the darkness, leaving him with the mental picture of his sentry's 'huge-bulged' eyes, his training as an officer and as a poet came to an end. He had finally reached maturity, and the fixed, sightless eyes of nightmare had stared at him 'face to face' at last, a dream made real.[4]

Inadvertently Professor Hibberd here attributes to the experience of war something very like the popular view: it makes a man of you. Owen suffers a horrible experience. Of such experiences we can say for certain only one thing—they wound, they traumatize people. An experience of this kind does not necessarily project a man into maturity. It is just as liable to maim him for life. We would not say: 'At the moment Owen left his testicles on the barbed wire, he matured as an officer and as a poet.' Why should we say the same about a night in a flooded dugout?

Yet such is the power of the myth of war, it is particularly hard with Owen not to succumb to a false teleology, not to see the experience of combat as utterly decisive in the poetry, not to feel that the death of the poet sets its seal on the work, as if everything were leading up to this. Professor Hibberd himself, having said that Owen's 'training as an officer and a poet came to an end' at Beaumont Hamel, goes on to show how Owen later went through three different and significant kinds of training. Therapy is a training, so Owen trained as a patient at Craiglockhart. He trained as a poet under the influence of Sassoon. Finally, he was eventually retrained as an officer.

For it is Professor Hibberd who revives old suppressed stories about Owen having been accused of cowardice during his first spell at the front. It is he who goes on to describe Owen's retraining and his return to France, and nobody could be more aware that the poem 'The Sentry', although begun a few months after the events in January 1917, was only completed in France in September of the next year. It is one of Owen's last poems, number 175 out of the 177 poems and fragments in the Stallworthy edition.

It is a fallacy to imagine that his first intimate experience of war must turn a youth into a man. Behind it is the belief that maturity only comes with acts of military bravery, and it seems particularly inappropriate to associate such a criterion for maturity with Wilfred Owen, with Owen either as an officer or as a poet, or, generally speaking, as a man.

Take Ernest Hemingway as a counter-example. He worked in ambulances in the First World War, was wounded, indeed came near to facing life as a cripple. But this did not settle for him the question of his manhood. He had to go back to other wars. He had to pursue bloodsports and associate himself with bullfighters. During the Second World War he had to stick a machine-gun on his fishing boat and scout around the Caribbean pursuing enemy submarines and finally, during the German retreat in Europe, he had to slip out of his role as a war reporter and into a little semi-official military work (killing retreating soldiers).

One might speculate that what Hemingway had missed, what would have counted for him as the real test, was the life of a fighting soldier under orders. But there are so many other examples, most typically in the world of mercenaries, of men for whom fighting under orders only creates a further appetite for the fight. And so they roam the world, looking for the next scrap. One wouldn't call any of this mature.

One might on the other hand, if maturity is anything to do with self-knowledge, say that Dylan Thomas was mature, if unpatriotic, when he wrote, on 14 September 1939: 'I am trying to get a job before conscription, because my one-and-only body I will not give.' And: 'The Army Medical Corps is presumably admirable, but I don't want to help—even in a most inefficient way—to patch poor buggers up and send them out again into quick insanity and bullets.'[5] Perhaps Owen and Sassoon had done their bit. Certainly Thomas was perfectly clear about his own non-role in the coming war, although some of his objections are more convincing than others. I like the argument that the whole soldiering business is a bit too queer for him:

It's a temptation [Thomas judiciously allows], in the pubs, on Saturday nights, in the billiard saloon, to want to allow myself to get that fuggy, happy, homosexual feeling and eat, sleep, get drunk, march, suffer, joke, kill and die among men, comrades, brothers, you're my pal, I'm with you son, back to back, only die once, short life, women and children, here's a photograph of my wife, over the bloody, down the bloody, here's to the bloody, shit and blood. But the temptation's not too strong, and the sanity of the imagination is.[6]

The sanity of the imagination—Owen, as a teenager, fell upon a phrase like that, which he had found in Keats's preface to *Endymion*, where Keats excuses the mawkishness of some of his juvenilia. He says:

The imagination of a boy is healthy, and the mature imagination of a man is healthy; but there is a space of life between, in which the soul is in a ferment, the character undecided, the way of life uncertain, the ambition thick-sighted . . .[7]

And one can see only too well that Owen, then 18, thought of himself as going through this 'space of life between'. The evidence is that Owen experienced puberty as a devastating loss of innocence, and that this had two immediate effects for him. The first was that it destroyed his ability to subscribe to Christianity. I do not say that it knocked the religious sense out of him entirely, but it knocked his Christian orientation for a six. The second effect was that, at a time when male friendship was particularly important to him, the 'pureness' had gone out of it. Owen was left with a desperate vulnerability to male beauty and a nostalgic yearning for idealized child-companions, which was quite at odds with his developing sexual feelings. What was not destroyed, however, during the ferment of the soul, was his intimacy with his mother.

Owen developed a secret life, but he as good as told his mother that he had developed a secret life. He wrote in Letter 314:

> 'What you want' said John Balman to me, 'Is a course in the University of Life'. I have taken that Course, and my diplomas are sealed with many secret seals. . . .[8]

And again shortly afterwards, in Letter 319:

> My present life does not, as Father points out, lead to anywhere in particular; but, situated where I was, say in 1911, I don't think I could have done wiselier than I did. I have not struck out in any direction yet. I have made soundings in deep waters, and I have looked out from many observation-towers: and I found the deep waters terrible, and nearly lost my breath there.[9]

This is a long time before the trenches. Owen is talking about some emotional experience, and, if we follow Professor Hibberd in the suggestion that Owen's sexual adventures with men began in Bordeaux, and if we follow the indications in the poems that what he came to discover was a sexual under-world, then we can give content to the expression that he had found the deep waters terrible. It is likely that there would have been much fear and shame in the discovery.

Susan Owen worried that her son might form some attach-ment with an unsuitable woman. Owen is almost frank with her:

> If you knew what hands had been laid on my arm, in the night, along the Bordeaux streets, or what eyes play upon me in the restaurant where I daily eat, methinks you would wish that the star and adoration of my life had risen; or would quickly rise.

But after boasting like this that he has become the object of sexual attention, he goes on to say that 'All women, without exception, *annoy* me, and the mercenaries (which the inno-cent old pastor thought might allure) I utterly detest; more indeed than as a charitable being, I ought'.[10]

Owen does like to boast a little. When a woman whose daughter he is teaching goes so far as to propose a trip to Canada with him, he lets mother know. When he meets up with a French boy he has befriended, and finds that his post-card has been treasured among other billets-doux, he lets mother know. When he meets the celebrated poet Laurent Tailhade and calls at his hotel, he goes perhaps further than he intends in letting mother know:

> I saw him up at his window in shirt-sleeves, mooning. He received me like a lover. To use an expression of the Rev. H. Wigan's, he quite slobbered over me. I know not how many times he squeezed my hand; and, sitting me down on the sofa, pressed my head against his shoulder. [*two lines illegible*] It was not intellectual; but I felt the living

verve of the poet . . . who has fought *seventeen duels* (so it is said).[11]

And in a letter Susan Owen showed to Blunden (now lost), he said that Tailhade 'calls my eyes "So very lovely!!" etc and my neck "The neck of a statue!!!! Etc"—because he is a poet and unconsciously appreciates in me, *not* the appearance of beauty but the spirit and temperament of beauty, Tailhade says he is going to write a sonnet on me.'[12]

Thus the young aspiring poet meets his first real poet, who immediately makes the most frantic passes at him, but Owen can still feel able to report back to mother. One wonders whether Owen took a private delight in making a slight fool of his mother, telling her things that he felt she, in her innocence, would not fully understand. As in Letter 308, where he describes Midnight Mass 1914, and the attention he has paid to the 'dear, darling little acolytes', and all the candles and the incense. And he says:

How scandalized would certain of my acquaintance and kin have been to see me. But it would take a power of candlegrease and embroidery to romanise me. The question is to un-Greekize me.[13]

A remark that escaped the censorship of Susan and Harold Owen.

What's lacking from the letters and from the biographies, up to and including the first years of the war, is any evidence of Owen having been in love with any nameable human being. All the more striking then is the evidence from the poems themselves that the realm of Eros was what Owen felt to be his great subject, and that the experience of love was viewed as so devastating, such a prelude to shame or a dangerous occasion for people's mirth at his expense. In the Sonnet beginning 'Stunned by their life's explosion into love' Owen tells us that some people never get over their experience of the erotic, while others, dedicated to religion, become maimed by their chastity and lose touch with the natural world. But if, instead of falling either for religion or for lust, they had discovered Poesy, they 'Might yet have kept a whole and splendid heart'—a healthy imagination.

This hardly looks like the theory of a grown man, and although the poem was revised at Craiglockhart, it is probably quite early. While the choice it poses—either religion, or sex, or poesy—is wildly unrealistic, it gives evidence of their conflicting pulls at a certain point in Owen's life, as does poem number 62, 'The time was aeon'. Here we are introduced to an allegorical figure called the Flesh, which appears in the likeness of a boy who changes 'from beauty unto beauty':

> As change the contours of skin, sleeping clouds.
> His skin, too, glowed, pale scarlet like the clouds
> Lit from the eastern underworld, which thing
> Bewondered me the more.

But then a crowd comes along, 'maddened by the voice of a small Jew'

> Who cried with a loud voice, saying 'Away!
> Away with him!' and 'Crucify him! Him,
> With the affections and the lusts thereof.'[14]

Religion, or St Paul, tells us to crucify the Flesh. But religion is also the context of sexual events for Owen, as in the deliberately blasphemous 'Maundy Thursday', in which the poet watches a congregation going up to kiss the cross held by a boy server: the men, doing so, kiss the emblem of religion, the women are seen as kissing the body of Christ indeed, while the children are thought to kiss a doll. But when the first person of the poem goes up, he disdains to kiss the 'very dead'

Christ, and kisses the 'warm live hand' of the 'server-lad' himself. This is the Owen who is in no danger of being Romanized, but cannot be un-Greekized. In the sonnet 'Perversity' he sees

> More loveliness in Grecian marbles clear
> Than modern flesh

And he has a problem with inappropriate or unsubstantial love-objects:

> I fall in love with children, elfin fair;
> Portraits; dark ladies in dark tales antique;
> Or instantaneous faces passed in streets.[15]

That last line strikes one as the key to the matter, for it is quite clear that Owen sought love on the streets, and found it, to the extent that he found it, in sordid rooms. In 'A Palinode', written or revised after his return from teaching in Bordeaux, in London in October 1915, Owen tells us something of a change that has come over him. Before, he says, he preferred nature to society, and kept his solitude, hating 'men and all their ways' because he felt hated and unneeded. But men did not leave him alone in his reverie, so he 'took antidotes'. Here, in the last three stanzas of the poem, we see the first glimmering of the poet's gifts:

> But in my error, men ignored not me,
> And did not let me in my moonbeams bask.
> And I took antidotes; though what they be
> Unless yourself be poisoned, do not ask.

> For I am overdosed. The City now
> Holds all my passion; these my soul most feels:
> Crowds surging; racket of traffic; market row;
> Bridges, sonorous under rapid wheels;

> Pacific lamentations of a bell;
> The smoking of the old men at their doors;
> All attitudes of children; the farewell
> And casting-off of ships for far-off shores.[16]

A picturesque version of the city, of dockland (Bordeaux perhaps), is what we are given, after a hint of an initiation into some poisonous practices which somehow are also antidotes. In other poems, London's dockland is the backdrop, and the city is seen as sordid rather than picturesque. The incoherent draft 'Lines to a Beauty seen in Limehouse' seems to be about a foreigner, perhaps a sailor (since there were seamen's hostels in Limehouse). The beauty of the loved one is contrasted with the dirt of the city.

A poem of 1918, written somewhat in the manner of Wilde, evokes an East End creature of the night:

> I am the ghost of Shadwell Stair.
>   Along the wharves by the water-house,
>   And through the cavernous slaughter-house,
> I am the shadow that walks there.
>
> Yet I have flesh both firm and cool,
>   And eyes tumultuous as the gems
>   Of moons and lamps in the full Thames
> When dusk sails wavering down the Pool.
>
> Shuddering, a purple street-arc burns
>   Where I watch always. From the banks
>   Dolorously the shipping clanks.
> And after me a strange tide turns.
>
> I walk till the stars of London wane,
>   And dawn creeps up the Shadwell Stair.
>   But when the crowing sirens blare,
> I with another ghost am lain.[17]

Professor Hibberd tells us two interesting things about this poem. The first is that the somewhat bold rhyming of water-house with slaughterhouse reflects Owen's knowledge of the East End, since there was indeed a waterworks and a slaughterhouse in the neighbourhood of Shadwell Stair. Secondly he gives us a French rhymed prose translation of the first verse, made by Owen's friend C. K. Scott Moncrieff in 1918. Scott Moncrieff wrote shortly after the war that Owen had welcomed the last word of this first verse 'rather as tho' it put a key in the lock of the whole':

Je suis le petit revenant du Bassin; le long de quai, par l'abreuvoir, et dans l'immonde abbatoir j'y piétine, ombre fantassin.

The speaker of the poem is, in this version, male and an infantryman—it is Owen looking for someone, 'another ghost', like himself.[18]

Of course it is possible that Scott Moncrieff was deluded by vanity into thinking that Owen approved of his rewriting of his poem. It is perfectly possible that Owen was describing someone he had seen, or some type he had seen, hanging around the docks. But it is hard not to read this poem, the best of Owen's attempts at the erotic, as an evocation of an anonymous homosexual encounter.

A part of the interest of reading Owen's poems chronologically and in full (with all the fragments and drafts) is that the chronology preserves the oddity and uncertainty of the poet's development. Owen's first experiences of the war came in the first half of 1917. Then came the treatment at Craiglockhart, near Edinburgh, and the meeting with Sassoon. We imagine that it was here that Owen 'came of age'. But actually among what Owen was working on at Craiglockhart and subsequently at Scarborough were some of his most mawkish expressions of sexual confusion. Of the

177 poems and fragments numbered by Stallworthy, 110
count as finished poems, and of these about 30 poems are
what Owen's reputation rests on—I should say that the first
of the mature poems is number 90, 'Inspection', a work in
the manner of Sassoon. 'Anthem for Doomed Youth' is
number 96. But the next section of the book, the early 100s,
is taken up with a portfolio of juvenilia, and it is really not
till the late 130s that the almost straight run of war poems
begins.

The chronological approach both conceals and reveals. It
makes some poems seem later than they probably were,
because Owen was revising them; at the same time it shows us
that Owen was slow to abandon a bad poem. A document
reproduced by Hibberd in *Wilfred Owen: The Last Year*, entitled
'*Projects.* (May 5. 1918. Ripon)' makes the point most forcibly.
This is what Owen was planning:

1. To write blank-verse plays on old Welsh themes.
   Models: Tennyson, Yeats, 1920.
2. Collected Poems (1919)
3. Perseus
4. Idyls in Prose[19]

So much for our handy teleologies, which would have led us
to construct an Owen shocked into the twentieth century by
the war. The war was contingent. The war was here and now.
But the future in 1918 held out a pale scarlet vision of blank-
verse plays on old Welsh themes in the manner of Tennyson.
The future held out a Collected Poems (1919) which would
doubtless have included reams of the verse that I have been
innocently referring to as juvenilia. The future held a return
to the 'Perseus' draft:

> O Eros Eros . . . thy dart!
> Poisoned also and keen: O merciless and might . . .
> I entered hell's low sorrowful secrecy—

The Perseus fragment being a sprawling, now indecipherable mess of a poem full of gender confusion and invented mythology. Owen only shocks me, when he shocks me, by these wilful nippings-back in style, as if he couldn't stay out of the shops of Wardour Street.

> Nay, light me no fire tonight,
> Page Eglantine;
> I have no desire tonight
> To drink or dine;
> I will suck no briar tonight,
> Nor read no line;
> An you be my quire tonight
> And you my wine.

A pipe-smoking knight from days of yore proposes a cosy evening with his page. And this seems to have been written in Scarborough some time between November 1917 and February 1918.

A few weeks before, as a climax to all the help and encouragement he had given Owen at Craiglockhart, Sassoon devised a good send-off for his friend: dinner in a quiet club, over a bottle of burgundy. At the end of the evening, he read from a volume he had brought with him of portentous poems by a certain Aylmer Strong, called *A Human Voice*. And the two men were reduced to convulsions by lines like:

> Oh is it true I have become
> This gourd, this gothic vacuum.

And:

> What cassock'd misanthrope,
> Hawking peace-canticles for glory-gain,
> Hymns from his rostrum'd height th'epopt of Hate?

It was good, I think, to encourage Owen to see how funny bad poetry could be. But it did not stop him writing 'Page Eglantine'.

At the end of the evening Sassoon handed Owen a sealed packet which Owen assumed to contain some 'holy secret' concerning Sassoon himself, but which turned out to be a sort of rebus. It contained a ten-pound note, Robert Ross's address in London, and a note which read simply: 'Why *shouldn't* you enjoy your leave? Don't mention this again or I'll be very angry.' Owen's thank-you letter to Sassoon recalls the language of Aylmer Strong. He writes:

> When I had opened your envelope in a quiet corner of the Club Staircase, I sat on the stairs and groaned a little, and then went up and loosed off a gourd, a Gothic vacuum of a letter, which I 'put by' . . . until I could think over the matter without 'grame'.[20]

'Grame' is an obsolete word meaning either anger or sorrow. (A word revived by Swinburne and Rossetti, which is probably how it entered the Sassoon–Owen private language.) Owen 'groaned a little' because ten pounds was a lot of money—it would have taken Owen five weeks' work in Bordeaux to put away that sum—and because the gift no doubt reminded him of the difference in class between himself and Sassoon. Taken together, the contents of the package said: don't be afraid to enjoy yourself in the way you want; here are the means; and here is your introduction to the milieu, Robbie Ross's address.

It is one of those fascinating moments in the history of private life, and it took place in the Conservative Club in Edinburgh, exactly a year before Owen's death. Ross, the friend and champion of Oscar Wilde, the publisher of *De Profundis,* was, to be sure, someone who could give Owen an entry into London literary society; and he did so immediately, introducing him to such figures as H. G. Wells and Arnold

Bennett. But the significance of Ross's address in Half Moon Street was that it was also a centre for Ross's own milieu, and even a place to stay, for it was a rooming house with an understanding landlady.

One does not have to believe that Sassoon and Owen had talked completely frankly about sexual matters. Sassoon, you will recall, had been shown Owen's juvenilia and must have been well acquainted with his turmoil. And he was no fool. As a fellow officer (who hardly knew him) later said of Owen: 'I always suspected him of having an extra soft spot for Tommy, although he never allowed it to interfere with discipline.' Owen's gratitude to Sassoon was boundless. As he said in his thank-you note:

> Know that since mid-September, when you still regarded me as a tiresome little knocker on your door, I held you as Keats + Christ + Elijah + my Colonel + my father-confessor + Amenophis IV in profile.
> What's that mathematically?
> In effect it is this: that I love you dispassionately, so much, so *very* much, dear Fellow, that the blasting little smile you wear on reading this can't hurt me in the least.

So the place of the mysteriously absent, although physically present, father had been filled. Sassoon had confirmed Owen's belief in himself—had approved of him, had removed the fear of parental wrath. Sassoon had, Owen told him,

> *fixed* my Life—however short. You did not light me: I was always a mad comet; but you fixed me. I spun round you a satellite for a month, but I shall swing out soon, a dark star in the orbit where you will blaze. It is some consolation to know that Jupiter himself sometimes swims out of Ken![21]

At which point he gives up trying to keep any further control on this astronomical image.

The sense that one's life might be going to be short—that of course would be a material consideration, an effective force in moving one from phase one (juvenilia) to whatever phase two is going to be. But Owen, in common with many a soldier, had another strong sense, a strong sense of what life might be for him *after* the war. We have seen this already in his confident list of literary priojects. We see it in apocalyptic form in the terrifying letter (no. 510) that he sends to Colin, his brother, after going over the top.

The letter begins with a description of the action, including the sensation of being under a storm of shells. Then, in a paragraph that begins 'Now write soon something about your new Farm' we sense the tone changing and going dangerous. Colin was working on a farm. That too was necessary war work, and it would hardly have been kind of Wilfred to stress the difference between their two conditions. But he was not in his right mind. Here's how it goes:

> Now write soon something about your new Farm. Sketch me a plan of it. Have you a pleasant room of your own? Most of the gentlemen here seem keen on farming after the war. The musician is going to farm, having not practised the piano since 1914; the aviator is going to farm; the undergraduate is going to farm.

That is, all our careers have been wrecked. After the war, we're going to go in for your cushy life. The farmer Colin works for is Mr Bather:

> Some day I will arise and go unto Mr. Bather, and will say unto him 'Bather, I am no more worthy to be called thy son than Colin; but make me as one of thy hired servants.' But his brother was wrath and would not let

him in, and began to beat him and entreat him shame-
fully.

He is saying to Colin: even if I survive the war, you will not let
me into your privileged existence. You will treat me like the
Prodigal Son.

But this Bather came out and said unto him 'Why beat-
est thou the ass? Be gentle with my servant, lest he fall
on good soil, and make it like the wilderness of Judea,
which is a great wilderness.[22]

There follows a page and a half more of this, a mosaic of
passages taken from Scripture, and more or less incoherent.
The contemplation of what he might do after the war was
enough to turn a man's mind.

In his recovered state, Owen was relieved of one particular
burden. He learned that the erotic problems that tormented
him were really not that important. Sassoon told him: 'Why
shouldn't you enjoy your leave?' And he learned too that he
had an important task in the here and now: the task of warning and being truthful about the war. And somehow it was
possible to divide off that task from the task of Poesy, as
outlined in the poem with which we began. We could easily
imagine that Poesy was still enthroned in his imagination, but
that it was possible for him to put it in that highly charged
emotional category of things that he would do *after* the war,
while for the here and now there was this other immediate
task. War now. Wardour Street later. Warning now. Truth-
telling now. Fanciful dramatic rewrites of the Mabinogion
later.

This is not to imply that Owen's career would have taken
such a shape, had he survived—that he would as it were have
reverted to the status of poetaster. It is only to say that a
complicated set of forces combined to release him from the

spirit of his juvenilia. When reasoning about our creativity, we cannot assume that causality is going to behave in the way causality normally behaves. There must *be* such a thing as causality, we assume; but we cannot expect to understand its workings. In the writing of poetry we may say that the thing we predict will not happen. If we can predict it, it is not poetry. We have to surprise ourselves. We have to outpace our colder calculations.

It took all that war and all that suffering to distract Owen from poetry, to make him say that he (of all people) was not concerned with it. And it was only when he was no longer concerned with it that he could be surprised, that he could be exalted by his gift.

3. *Philip Larkin: Wounded by Unshrapnel*

It is often casually said of Larkin's poetry that it expresses common experience, that it has its origin in the commonplace, or even—I have seen this in newspapers—that the famous catchphrases that have been drawn from it ('What will survive of us is love', 'Books are a load of crap', 'Life is first boredom, then fear', 'They fuck you up, your mum and dad') express a common point of view. But what strikes us most about Larkin is not the commonness but the singularity of the point of view.

It is true perhaps that the last of these quotes may command common assent. Parents do fill children with the faults they had—or so we may often feel. But the whole poem (often parodied and for many years commonly known by heart without having been consciously committed to memory) derives its notoriety from the fact that it goes much further than common consent can bear: die young, it commands, and stay childless. We wouldn't go as far as *that*. Just as we wouldn't go so far as to say that life really *is* first boredom, then fear. As for 'Books are a load of crap', this is what a certain character in a poem ('A Study of Reading Habits') concludes when he finds himself unwillingly identifying with the failures in the fiction he reads. It was never remotely intended as expressing a common truth, while the beautiful 'What will survive of us is love' is not a view to which Larkin assents, but an untruth, identified as such—something which our almost-instinct is tempted to find almost true.

And just as the lines that have stuck in people's heads tend not to be truths but untruths, so the 'common' experiences out of which the poems grow seem on closer examination to be highly specialized. How many people do you really think allow their earnings to pile up, while reproaching themselves with a mysterious inability to spend more on themselves. Yet this is the point of departure for the poem 'Money':

> Quarterly, is it, money reproaches me:
>   'Why do you let me lie here wastefully?
> I am all you never had of good and sex.
>   You could get them still by writing a few cheques.'

This attitude is surprising coming from Larkin's provincial middle-class background, where timidity about spending money (particularly 'eating into capital') might be common, but where few (at least in my experience) would imagine that the kind of sex they wanted could be had simply by paying for it.[1] I know that there is an aggressive intention behind the flatness of the rhythms and the banality of the sex/cheques rhyme. Larkin's poems do sometimes start off aggressively ugly and then pull a beautiful stunt, as this one is going to do. But it seems crass of the poet to suggest (if he is talking about himself) that if he'd only spent more on, as it were, fast cars, he would have had fabulous blondes crawling all over them. And he could have. But somehow he didn't.

So he looks around him and sees that money has something to do with life, namely that just as you can't save up your youth for your old age, so, however you organize your savings, they won't have any value by the time you retire. Then comes the beautiful stunt

> I listen to money singing. It's like looking down
>   From long french windows at a provincial town,

The slums, the canal, the churches ornate and mad
In the evening sun. It is intensely sad.[2]

The scene comes at you out of nowhere, conjured by words
that are poised halfway between the general and the particular. (The idea of money singing was perhaps borrowed from
Auden's poem 'They'.) What sort of ornate churches—are they
Gothic Revival ornate? The madness sounds baroque, but that
would shift the scene abroad, whereas the slums and the canal
seem English. Just enough is given to make the scene grip-
ping, and indeed saddening. Convinced by the last stanza,
one tries in retrospect to give some credence to its predecessors. Yes, you think, it must be sad to be a miser with yourself,
sad to have missed out on the bubbly, the fast cars, and the
floozies. Instead of running a library, you could have been
prancing around in the pit stop at Monte Carlo, or cutting a
dash on the slopes of Aspen.

Except that the whole reasoning is preposterous, and the
whole set-up, apart from the sadness, a wild misrepresenta-
tion. The money was never there, unspent, in such vast quan-
tities as would achieve some great materialist fantasy. And as
for sex, Larkin's act was to repeat that he never got it, but the
likely truth is that he got as much as he could put up with. His
problem seems to have been that he didn't want a sexual partner near enough to be a bother. But he arranged a solution to
that problem in the form of a sexual partner at a distance, a
non-sexual partner close by, and a magazine collection to
bridge the gap. Women ministered to him. He had no reason
to feel neglected.

But Larkin was sly and perverse, and the poems that issue
from this perversity are full of sly tricks. 'I Remember, I
Remember', one of the earliest classically Larkinesque poems
(completed in January 1954) describes being on a train which
stops in Coventry. The I of the poem exclaims to a friend: 'I
was born here.' Then he finds, looking out, that he cannot

even remember which side of the station is which. He has forgotten all about Coventry. His friend asks whether this is where he 'has his roots'. But the Larkin figure is thinking of all the things that never happened in his childhood, the anecdotes or significant episodes that would be the stock in trade of other people's memoirs or novels. And when the friend says to him, 'You look as if you wished the place in Hell', he replies that he supposes it's not the place's fault, concluding with the celebrated line, 'Nothing, like something, happens anywhere.'[3]

Taken as an aesthetic gesture, one of the famous gestures of the Fifties, Larkin's poem seems to say: I detest dishonesty in writing; I detest self-mythologizing; if nothing of note happened in my childhood, I'm the kind of guy who's prepared to say so, rather than dress up non-events as events. Taken as lyric, the poem asserts its own right. It stands alone, as any lyric stands alone, to convince us, or not, on its own terms. And I for one can easily be convinced that this is what one may, in a certain mood, feel about one's childhood: the childhood other people describe, I never had.

But when one sets the poem against the biography, it becomes, to an intriguing degree, an act of concealment. In the poem, the city of Coventry is drained of historical significance. The poet does not choose to go into the most obvious explanation for his inability to recognize the place, namely that it was under reconstruction having being flattened in 1940 during the Blitz. Yet Coventry is clearly intended to be the actual, observed city: the men with numberplates who sprint down the platform in the first stanzas are returning from having delivered cars (a typically specific, local Larkin detail, like the many little details in *Jill*, from which you can work out, if your memory is long enough, exactly where you are in Oxford). Yet the actual Coventry is deprived of its actual past.

And we might add that, if we are talking about the actual

Coventry and the actual Larkin, that he could have told a most striking story, that his father, the city's treasurer, had been an admirer of Hitler, to the extent of having attended the Nuremberg rallies (this is what Larkin later told the historian John Kenyon). At home, he could have said, his father kept 'a statue of Hitler on the mantelpiece, which at the touch of a button leapt into a Nazi salute', and that he kept Nazi regalia in his office up to the outbreak of war.

Then he could have mimicked his father's attitude in 1939, as expressed in the letter reproduced as the front endpaper of the *Selected Letters*: 'The British govt. have started this war . . . Hitler has done all he could for peace . . . Well, all I hope is that we get smashed to Hades . . . Our army is useless . . . A.R.P? Ha ha! This is the end of civilisation . . . after all, man has to be superseded sooner or later . . . we're only a stage in the earth's development . . . a very unimportant stage too . . .'.[4]

According to Andrew Motion's biography, Sydney Larkin did not change his tune during the war. Instead, when Coventry was blitzed in 1940, he congratulated himself on his foresight in having ordered one thousand cardboard coffins the previous year, and continued to praise 'efficient German administration' while nevertheless disparaging Hitler.[5]

Auden said somewhere that if you grew up as he did in Birmingham it was absurd to talk about having your roots in Birmingham. The friend in Larkin's poem shares this sense of absurdity:

'Was that,' my friend smiled, 'where you "have your roots"?'

The answer the poem gives is that, if you grow up in Coventry (not that it is necessarily Coventry's fault) you can expect nothing to 'happen' to you.

But plenty 'happened' to Larkin. For two days after the bombing of Coventry, he waited in Oxford without word of his family, then set out with a friend, Noel Hughes, to find out what had happened to both of their homes. Larkin drew on this experience for one of the most important passages in *Jill*, describing how his friend hears the news of the Huddlesford raid, which is said to be like the Coventry raid. John Kemp asks immediately whereabouts was damaged:

> 'Residential areas . . . I expect they went for the station and the factories and the centre of the city . . .' He looked doubtfully at John. 'Do you live anywhere near the station?'
> 'No, not at all.'
> John got up, leaving his food, and went trambling out into the sun. They said a thousand people were killed outright in a raid like that, not counting the wounded and those that died afterwards. It was not possible for his parents to have escaped.

John becomes certain that his parents are dead:

> it was obvious, he deserved to be punished in this way. Since leaving them, he had pushed them to the back of his mind, had sometimes felt ashamed of them, had not bothered to write to them regularly, had done things they would have been sorry at.

He blames himself for his parents' death. He believes they have been killed 'because he treated them lightly'. So he goes back to his home filled with dread and praying they will be all right, and praying for enough strength to stand it if the worst has happened. But he finds his home intact and a note pinned to the door saying his parents have gone away. He peers into the house.

> It was strange, like looking into a doll's house, and putting his hands against the window frames he felt as

protective as a child does feel towards a doll's house and its tiny rooms.

But when he finally leaves the town by train the destruction of the city he had known so well has a new effect on him:

> It no longer seemed meaningless: struggling awake again, rubbing his eyes with chilled hands, he thought it represented the end of his use for the place. It meant no more to him now, and so it was destroyed: it seemed symbolic, a kind of annulling of his childhood. The thought excited him. It was as if he had been told: all the past is cancelled: all the suffering connected with that town, all your childhood, is wiped out. Now there is a fresh start for you: you are no longer governed by what has gone before.
>
> The train ran on, through fields lying under the frost and darkness.
>
> And then again, it was like being told: see how little anything matters. All that anyone has is the life that keeps him going, and see how easily that can be patted out. See how appallingly little life is.[6]

The experience of John Kemp differs from that of Larkin himself in two respects: Larkin went back to Coventry in the company of his friend Noel Hughes, but there was no note on the door, and it wasn't till he returned to Oxford that he was reassured that his family had survived. Hughes later described the desolate experience of Larkin hanging around in the hope of finding someone who knew where his parents were:

> For at least the seven years that I had known him, Philip lived at the same house, but at only one other house had he felt able to call for news of his missing

parents. That done, he had shot his bolt . . . Later, as I got to know, and to know more about, Philip's father . . . I could imagine how Philip could have lived for years in a neighbourhood and yet be reared in almost total isolation from it.[7]

What nobody seems to have quite described is the full impact on Larkin of the father who, in a manner of speaking, calls down a curse on the city, which curse is fulfilled, although his parents and their house are spared. The elegant censorship at work in 'I Remember, I Remember' (which might as well have been entitled 'I Suppress, I Suppress') shows up as the subject of 'Forget What Did':

> Stopping the diary
> Was a stun to memory,
> Was a blank starting,
>
> One no longer cicatrized
> By such words, such actions
> As bleakened waking.
>
> I wanted them over,
> Hurried to burial
> And looked back on
>
> Like the wars and winters
> Missing behind the windows
> Of an opaque childhood.[8]

This torn-up childhood, this so-called 'forgotten boredom'— this never leaves Larkin alone. It will be with him in his work to the last years of his life. Yet paradoxically the urge to destroy his past (in his psyche) coexisted with the archivist's urge to preserve it. Motion found shoeboxes full of carefully stored incoming letters, together with 'memorabilia of all sorts—his parents' jam recipes, for instance' together with a comprehensive set of papers (minus the diaries which had been shredded). Larkin's will, found by Queen's Counsel to be contradictory on the question of the destruction or preservation of his papers, was declared 'repugnant'. Larkin's mind was repugnant in the same legal sense. The late poem, 'Love Again', which shocks with its intimate description of sexual jealousy, ends on an urge to 'say why it never worked for me'—presumably why love never worked for him:

> Something to do with violence
> A long way back, and wrong rewards,
> And arrogant eternity.[9]

'The Winter Palace', a poem written a year earlier in November 1978, expresses a desire to forget not just his childhood but everything else—literally:

> Most people know more as they get older:
> I give all that the cold shoulder.
>
> I spent my last quarter-century
> Losing what I had learnt at university
>
> And refusing to take in what had happened since.
> Now I know none of the names in the public prints
>
> And am starting to give offence by forgetting faces
> And swearing I've never been in certain places.
>
> It will be worth it, if in the end I manage
> To blank out whatever it is that is doing the damage.
>
> Then there will be nothing I know.
> My mind will fold into itself, like fields, like snow.[10]

Defiant, self-obliterative rage—something to do with violence and wrong rewards, long ago—something that goes on doing the damage, that can't be blanked out except by an act of self-annihilation: we stand very little chance of discovering what this was all about. One might guess though that the role of the father comes into it in no small measure.

A strange thing about Larkin is that, though he had the perfect father for a son to defy, he never seems to have rebelled against him. On the basis of what we read in the letters, Larkin's attitude to Germany seems to have been a watered-down version of his father's. If the son rebelled, it was not against his father so much as against the war itself and the orthodoxy surrounding it. He was about as ungungho as you can get, writing in 1940 soon after the Coventry raid:

> My bloody uncle is convinced that the invasion will start tomorrow . . . Shouldn't be at all surprised. Germany will win this war like a dose of salts, and if that gets me into gaol, a bloody good job too. Balls to the war . . .[11]

And in 1941:

> I feel the war must be over this year if Hitler does his job in his accustomed way. My only fear is he'll do it messily—gas, etc. And that I will be called up to be mown down, while the real army arranges itself behind me.[12]

And in 1942, to a friend who wanted to become a conscientious objector, he wrote:

> I should like to say how much I admire your fight against the bleeding army. I don't think I should have the courage myself, but I might, and anyway I admire your actions very greatly. It seems logical to me that the men who can see the right must hold clear from the mass of writhing filth that threatens to engulf us all. The ethics of the thing are difficult: but I think one must stand by one's innermost feelings. If you can get out of their grip, gently, without tearing yourself in the

process, but gently, I think you should, and guard any new life that may have chosen you as a sprouting-ground. If there is any new life in the world today, it is in Germany. True, it's a vicious and blood-brutal kind of affair—the new shoots are rather like bayonets. It won't suit me.

Note the tense. He is still expecting Germany to win. And he goes on:

By 'new' life I don't mean better life, but a change, a new direction. Germany has revolted back too far, into other extremes. But I think they may have valuable new habits. Otherwise how could D.H.L. be called Fascist.[13]

By January 1943, Larkin has changed his mind about Germany, and believes 'externally' that Britain must win the war.

But I don't think it will do any good. And I have no driving power to bring it about. Men must abide by their feelings—I can't help it if everyone were like me we s'd all be hung.[14]

So the war has become a spiritual issue, over which he has nothing to contribute. He had half admired Hitler, saying of his speeches in 1941: 'I looked into them and felt the familiar sinking heart when I saw how *right* and yet how *wrong* everything had been. The disentanglement of this epoch will be a beautiful job for someone.'[15]

But he would undoubtedly have fought if told to do so. What he says of the army shows an unremarkable young man's natural apprehension:

I want to pretend it isn't there: that there's no war on. When I do get into it, it will be a hell of a struggle of readjustment. I dare say I shall get over it in about 5 months. But they'll be a dose of hell.

I wonder if Suicide is *very* easy? (Patient dragged away howling by airmen—in the Orator sense.)[16]

And:

I have a strong presentiment I shall get killed in this war—not that I am resigned to it, far from it.[17]

And:

We all have a hell of a way to go, both as artists and as human beings. And I sometimes don't think the army will help, except in the purely negative way of steering you clear of the war complex.[18]

After which he curses the war in his usual way.

On New Year's Day 1942, according to Motion, Larkin learned that he had failed his army medical, that his eyes had been graded four, and that he would not be called up. But the letter to Norman Iles dated 8 January says: 'My position is—I am Grade IV. What this implies I don't know, & can't find out, but I think it releases me from most of the carnage even if it doesn't let me stay at Oxford.'[19] If the army's letter was as specific as Motion says, then the subsequent alleged uncertainty might indicate shame at admitting he had been rejected. Larkin later made an attempt at doing war work, applying to Bletchley, and again being turned down. He later said he found the whole thing 'very odd' although one suspects that in the case of Bletchley it might just have crossed his mind that, having a father who was pro-Hitler, he might not have been the kind of person they wanted, from a security point of view.

Perhaps this speculation strays too far ahead of the facts.

The facts are that Larkin suffered two rejections, and that for the rest of the course of the war—a war which was of a character that tended to include civilians, offering a number of ways of coming to feel part of the war effort—Larkin kept up that pose of studied indifference. My belief is that he was wounded by rejection. Those who were actually wounded, wounded with shrapnel, years later might find pieces of the shrapnel working their way to the surface. Larkin seems to have been wounded by unshrapnel, and in later life little pieces of unshrapnel began to emerge, in his poems, squibs, letters and reviews. Decades after the all-clear had sounded, Larkin's patriotism crawled gingerly out from under the kitchen table. Decades after Lawrentian truth-to-feeling and indifference to the war, Larkin began to notice that the empire was being wound down and that troops were being brought home.

> Places they guarded, or kept orderly,
> Must guard themselves, or keep themselves orderly.

Larkin makes as little sense as an imperialist as he did as a pale Nazi-symp. He did not want Aden as a base; he just thought it shameful that Aden should be abandoned for lack of money:

> Next year we shall be living in a country
> That brought its soldiers home for lack of money.
> The statues will be standing in the same
> Tree-muffled squares, and look nearly the same.
> Our children will not know it's a different country.
> All we can hope to leave them now is money.[20]

The later gloss he gave on this—'I don't mind troops being brought home if we'd decided this way the best thing all round, but to bring them home because we couldn't afford to keep them there seemed a dreadful humiliation'[21]—blithely ignores the fact that the Labour government of the time, and the Labour movement as a whole, did indeed think that the winding up of imperial commitments was the 'best thing all round'.

The victim of unshrapnel, the patriot after the event, was able to tax Auden with having 'abandoned his audience together with their common dialect and concerns' by departing for America shortly before the war. 'For a different sort of poet this might have been less important', he concedes. 'For Auden it seems to have been irreparable', because Auden's 'key subject and emotion' were 'Europe and the fear of war'.

Larkin's essay, 'What's Become of Wystan?', which values only the first decade of Auden's work, is the enduring written expression of an argument which used to be commonplace. One doubts, however, that Auden could have earned Larkin's approval if he had remained in Britain, or even enlisted (supposing that had been possible). Because there was always the opposite argument to resort to:

> A 'war' poet is not one who chooses to commemorate or celebrate a war but one who reacts against having a war thrust upon him: he is chained, that is, to a historical event, and an abnormal one at that. However well he does it, however much we agree that the war happened and ought to be written about, there is still a tendency for us to withold our highest praise on the grounds that a poet's choice of subject should seem an action, not a reaction. 'The Wreck of the Deutschland', we feel, would have been markedly inferior if Hopkins had been a survivor from the passenger list. Again, the first-rank poet should ignore the squalid accident of war: his vision should be powerful enough to disregard it. Admittedly, war might come too close for this vision to be maintained. But it is still essentially irrelevant.[22]

This comes apropos Wilfred Owen, when Larkin reviews what he believes will be the definitive edition of his poems, the Day-Lewis one. But, while Larkin refuses quite properly to give Owen poetic stature simply on the grounds of his war record, and while he wishes to hold on to the idea of the irrelevance of war, he is nevertheless preparing to offer Owen an extraordinary compliment—that he is 'the only twentieth-century poet who can be read after Hardy without a sense of bathos'.[23]

This high praise, this distinguished service order, Owen was allowed to wear for a good dozen years, between 1963 and 1975, when Jon Stallworthy published his biography of Owen. At that point Larkin, taking his cue from some evidence in Stallworthy, did a little detective work and came to the conclusion that Owen had, in the last years of his life, been associating 'with (I take it) not only practising but proselytising homosexuals: it seems to me that if he didn't like that sort of thing he could easily have given them the brush off'.[24] Larkin was shaken by this discovery, and his review shows that he was beginning to revise his opinion of Owen in a downward direction, on the grounds that he had a 'private involvement' in the war.

Which would be convenient, because that would leave the twentieth century bare of any poetic talent at all that could be read after Hardy without a sense of bathos. Or none until you reach you know who.

Such laying waste of the poetic landscape, such a critical scorched-earth policy—this is not the product of a passing mood. This is of a piece with the rest of Larkin. Everything that is good is either dying or doomed. Nothing but bathos in poetry after Hardy. Nothing but cacophony in jazz after Charlie Parker. Jazz began to die 'when the Negro stopped wanting to entertain the white man', or when it acquired some tinge of the Black Power movement. Negroes were moving to hate the white man with their jazz: 'The post-war Negro was better educated, more politically conscious and culturally aware than his predecessors, and in consequence the Negro jazz musician was more musically sophisticated. He knew his theory, his harmony, his composition: he had probably been to the Juilliard School of Music'[25] and so on. If the Negro progressed, jazz had to die. And there was no telling what would rob Larkin of his musical pleasures. He tells us that the advent of the long-playing record 'deepened his isolation'; not surprising then that when the American Negro looked beyond the confines of his bondage, Larkin felt that he had lost his potency.

And he finds nothing to take the place of jazz. There is no sense of moving on, only a furious nostalgia for something irrevocably destroyed. The decline of poetry left him, in some moods, indifferent. He wasn't, he said, particularly interested in other people's poetry. But the decline of jazz was taken as a personal insult.

The decline of Britain was absolute, as the Jubilee poem for the Queen makes clear:

> In times when nothing stood
> but worsened, or grew strange,
> there was one constant good:
> she did not change.[26]

Larkin would have made a good poet laureate: he rose to the public role of poet on certain occasions, producing, in addition to this about the Queen, poems for a university library and a bridge. But he was not a good political poet. He was not even reliable Conservative Party material, and he sort of knew this. He has the distinction of being the only poet who censored his own work under pressure from the Department of the Environment, or, more accurately, under pressure from Lady Dartmouth, who chaired a committee which produced a report called *How Do You Want to Live?* Larkin, on request, wrote 'Going,Going' as a preface to the report:

> I thought it would last my time—
> The sense that, beyond the town,
> There would always be fields and farms,
> Where the village louts could climb . . .

Lady Dartmouth objected to the word 'louts', and so Larkin changed the line (he later undid all his changes, when he reprinted the poem in *High Windows*) to 'Where sports from the village could climb'. A later passage had to be cut:

> On the Business Page, a score
>
> Of spectacled grins approve
> Some takeover bid that entails
> Five per cent profit (and ten
> Per cent more in the estuaries): move
> Your works to the unspoilt dales
> (Grey area grants)!

None of this would do for Lady Dartmouth, for of course it apeared to attack both capitalism and the government. 'Going, Going' is a poem of feeling rather than thought, and it evokes feelings we might indeed all share. I would be happier with it, though, if its thoughts were clearer:

> And that will be England gone,
> The shadows, the meadows, the lanes,
> The guildhalls, the carved choirs.[27]

Surely at the time Larkin was writing the actual guildhalls and carved choirs were safer than they had ever been. Betjeman would not have played so free with history. He was too interested in specifics:

> The Church's restoration
> In eighteen-eighty-three

> Has left for contemplation
> Not what there used to be.
> How well the ancient woodwork
> Looks round the Rect'ry hall,
> Memorial of the good work
> Of him who planned it all.[28]

Larkin's poem is about a feeling that the country is going to the dogs—'I just think it will happen, soon': whether or not it's going to happen, he seems to insist, I *feel* it's going to happen.

This feeling of transience, this is the great Larkin feeling. And thinking about Larkin and reading him again, I have often turned to an essay of Freud's, no more than four pages, which is called 'On Transience'. Freud describes a trip to the mountains with a friend and an unnamed poet, whose identity has not been revealed.

> The poet admired the beauty of the scene around us, but felt no joy in it. He was disturbed by the thought that all this beauty was fated to extinction, that it would vanish when winter came, like all human beauty and all the beauty and splendour that men have created or may create. All that he would have loved and admired seemed to him to be shorn of its worth by the transience which was its doom.

Freud tries to argue with his friends that, while the beauty they admire is indeed transient, the thought of its transience should not interfere with their joy in it. And that this applies not only to beautiful objects such as flowers or a human form, but that also

> A time may indeed come when the pictures and statues which we admire today will crumble to dust, or a race of

men may follow us who no longer understand the works of our poets and thinkers, or a geological epoch may even arrive when all animate life upon the earth ceases; but since the value of all this beauty and perfection is determined only by its significance for our own emotional lives, it has no need to survive us and is there-fore independent of absolute duration.

Freud has no success in convincing his friends of this argu-ment, and his failure to do so leads him to ask himself whether there might not be some powerful emotional factor disturbing their judgement. And he comes to think (this was written about the time of his work on mourning and melan-cholia) that

> What spoiled their enjoyment of beauty must have been a revolt in their minds against mourning. The idea that all this beauty was transient was giving these two sensi-tive minds a foretaste of decease; and, since the mind instinctively recoils from anything that is painful, they felt their enjoyment of beauty interfered with by thoughts of its transience.[29]

This reminds one of the lines in 'The Trees', where Larkin says of them 'Their greenness is a kind of grief'. His emotions seem to work in a different time-frame to ours in this poem, because it is the sight of the new buds which says to him: 'Last year is dead.'[30] Most people, I think, would have noticed that in the autumn.

Freud's essay talks about the cycle of love and loss and mourning, and the mystery of how mourning comes sponta-neously to an end, leaving us with the capacity to love afresh, without thereby devaluing what we once loved. And under love he is including love of country, pride in its values, its works of art, the achievement of its civilization. If, say, I loved a certain kind of music, but in the course of time that infatuation came to an end, and I couldn't listen to it any more, then time would pass and I would discover other music that I could enjoy. This is better than spending the rest of my life grieving like a loyal dog over the corpse of my beloved music. And better, too, than saying to any new music that came along: no, I have been betrayed once; I shall never allow myself to be taken in again.

Larkin is justly famous for his poems about old age and death. But he also wrote a poem deploring his prime of life (it is called 'Maturity') and one called 'On Being Twenty-six' which begins:

> I feared these present years,
> The middle twenties,
> When deftness disappears . . .[31]

He was always anticipating transience, afraid to let himself in for a loss that would really matter. And he was always looking back in rage, on what he claimed to have forgotten, and wondering what it was that kept leaking this poison into his life, trying to blank out whatever it was that was doing the damage. But it was the looking ahead that was doing the damage. *That* was Larkin's problem.

4. *Goodbye to All That?*

I

The first paragraph of Dryden's *Essay of Dramatic Poesie* records the great imperial moment in what the English call the Second Dutch War, and what the Dutch call the Second English War. A naval battle is taking place off Lowestoft, more than a hundred miles from London, but the sound carries as far as the capital. Dryden recalls:

> It was a memorable day, in the first Summer of the late War, when our navy engag'd the *Dutch*: a day wherein the two most mightly and best appointed Fleets which any age had ever seen, disputed the command of the greater half of the Globe, the commerce of Nations, and the riches of the Universe. While these vast floating bodies, on either side, moved against each other in parallel lines, and our Country men, under the happy conduct of his Royal Highness, went breaking, little by little into the line of our Enemies; the noise of the Cannon from both Navies reach'd our ears about the City: so that all men, being alarm'd with it, and in a dreadful suspense of the event, which they knew was then deciding, everyone went following the sound as his fancy led him; and leaving the town almost empty, some took towards the park, some cross the river, others down it: all seeking the noise in the depth of silence.[1]

That the battle of Lowestoft could be heard in London is confirmed by Pepys, whose diary for this day, 3 June 1665, records:

All this day, by all people upon the River and almost everywhere else hereabout, were heard the Guns, our two fleets for certain being engaged; which was confirmed by letters from Harwich, but nothing perticular; and all our hearts full of concernment for the Duke, and I perticularly for my Lord Sanwich and Mr. Coventry after his Royal Highness.[2]

And Pepys's editors tell us that the sound of the gunfire was probably reflected by the stratosphere—'hence it was possible for guns firing in a s.-w. gale 120 miles to the n.e. to be heard in London'. But the battle was heard not only in London and Cambridge. It was also heard in The Hague. This was one of those intimate wars. Dryden uses the event in order to give a familiar historical setting for his fictional dialogue, much in the same way that Boccaccio evokes the plague in Florence at the opening of the *Decameron*. In both cases, it is the specificity of the description that makes it so riveting, and makes one wish that both authors had written more in that vein.

At that period, the river Thames at low tide formed rapids under London Bridge (a detail confirmed by Pepys), and in order to pass downriver the boats had to shoot these rapids, at some danger. This is what is meant by the expression 'shooting the bridge' in the next passage.

Taking then a barge which a servant of *Lisideius* had provided for them, they made haste to shoot the Bridge, and left behind them that great fall of waters which hindered them from hearing what they desired: after which, having disengag'd themselves from many Vessels which rode at Anchor in the *Thames*, and almost blockt up the passage towards *Greenwich*, they order'd the Watermen to let fall their Oares more gently; and then every one favouring his own curiosity with a strict silence, it was not long ere they perceiv'd the Air to break about them like the noise of distant Thunder, or of Swallows in a Chimney: those little undulations of sound, though almost vanishing before they reach'd them, yet seeming to retain somewhat of their first horrour which they had betwixt the Fleets.[3]

It has been argued that what people were hearing in London on that day was indeed distant thunder, that they were victims of a mass delusion. But I have to say that I don't believe this. Dryden seems quite right about the acoustics—one had to get away from the narrow streets of pre-Fire London, out onto the river or into the park; one had to get away from any other noise, one had to stop talking, and *then* one might begin to hear it, and it sounded like thunder but it didn't only sound like thunder—it sounded 'like swallows in the chimney', that beautiful image which almost forces our assent.

We are reminded that in times of war, when life depends on it, the ear very quickly learns to make the most astonishingly fine distinctions between noises made by friend and foe, between types of weaponry, between warlike and unwarlike bangs. The people of London go out to listen to the noises, because their prosperity depends on it. If the noises get louder, that could spell defeat. But even if the Dutch retreat, as Pepys noted, it might be by cunning. Pepys is so cautious it takes him five days to believe that the Dutch have indeed been defeated. Then he gets a full report:

> The earl of Falmouth, Muskery, and Mr. Rd. Boyle killed on board the Dukes ship, the *Royall Charles*, with one shot. Their blood and brains flying into the Duke's face— and the head of Mr. Boyle striking down the Duke, as some say.[4]

The last incident, the flying head of the son of the Earl of Cork hitting the future James II, found its way into a poem formerly attributed to Marvell, called 'Second advice to a painter':

> His shatter'd head the fearless Duke distains
> And gave the last first proof that he had Brains.[5]

But to return to Dryden and his wits on the river at Greenwich. They hear the noise receding and conclude that the English have won, which in turn is the cue for their dialogue to begin, which it does with the observation that the price of military victory is the amount of bad verse that will be written about it, that 'no Argument could scape some of those eternal Rhimers, who watch a Battel with more diligence than the Ravens and birds of Prey; and the worst of them surest to be first in upon the quarry, while the better able, either out of modesty writ not at all, or set that due value upon their Poems, as to let them be often desired and long expected!'[6]

The last remark seems to cover the case of Dryden himself, who, with admirable forbearance, waited more than a year before publishing his account of the Battle of Lowestoft in *Annus Mirabilis*. And here is how it begins, the same imperial moment evoked in poetry, after the vivid anxiety of the prose:

> In thriving Arts long time had *Holland* grown,
> Crouching at home, and cruel when abroad:
> Scarce leaving us the means to claim our own.
> Our King they courted, & our Merchants aw'd.
>
> Trade, which like blood should circulatory flow,
> Stop'd in their Channels, found its freedom lost:
> Thither the wealth of all the world did go,
> And seem'd but shipwrack'd on so base a Coast.
>
> For them alone the heav'ns had kindly heat
> In Eastern Quarries ripening precious Dew:[7]
> For them the *Idumaean* Balm did sweat,
> And in hot *Ceilon* Spicy Forrests grew.

The sun but seem'd the Lab'ror of their Year;
Each wexing Moon suppli'd her watry store,
To swell those Tides, which from the Line did bear
Their brim-full Vessels to the Belg'an shore.

Thus mighty in her Ships stood *Carthage* long,
And swept the riches of the world from far:
Yet stoop'd to *Rome*, less wealthy, but more strong:
And this may prove our second Punick War.

Imperialist poetry was never clearer than this, never less drawn to circumlocution. Holland is doing very well, says Dryden, and therefore, like Carthage, it must be destroyed. And he goes on to give an account of that same battle of Lowestoft—excepting that the word 'description' means something else, in the context of this kind of poetry:

Lawson amongst the formost met his fate,
Whom Sea-green *Syrens* from the Rocks lament:
Thus as an offering for the *Grecian* State,
He first was kill'd who first to Battel went.[8]

This from the same pen that brought us those swallows in a chimney! Sea-green Syrens on the rocks off Lowestoft! And what makes this description so impressively distinct from the facts as known is that Sir John Lawson didn't even die in the battle—didn't even earn that Homeric distinction of dying like Protesilaus, the first Greek to step onto the Trojan shore. He was wounded in the leg, and died a couple of weeks later in Greenwich. And he died, rather unpoetically, of gangrene. But since he was 'vice-admiral of the Red', and the senior officer to be killed in the engagement, Dryden drags him back through history to be the 'precious thing' that is thrown into the sea when Britain, in the style of Venice, weds the Main.

The Dutch commander, Opdam as he is known in English (Jacob Obdam, Heer van Wassenaer), gets his in the next stanza:

> Their Chief blown up, in air, not waves expir'd,
> To which his pride presum'd to give the Law:
> The Dutch confess'd Heav'n present, and retir'd,
> And all was *Britain* the wide Ocean saw.

This is the imperial moment—it's like lining up the three oranges. The money pours out of the machine and it's all for *me*. Opdam is blown up. The Dutch see the hand of God in this and call it a day. Britain gains control of everything, the whole Ocean becomes Britain, and with it all the jewels ripening in the east, all the aromatics, and the teacups that survive the attempt at Bergen when

> Amidst the whole heap of Spices lights a Ball,
> And now their Odours arm'd against them flie:
> Some preciously by shatter'd Porc'lain fall,
> And some by Aromatick splinters die.[9]

In this kind of poetry, everything is at the disposal of the imperial purpose: teacups, chronology, spices, mythology. Reason itself lies down to have its tummy tickled.

And I think that in any company, even in Holland and even with descendants of Admiral Opdam in the audience, I could bring all this up without offence. It is baroque. It is preposterous. But it is not by any stretch of the imagination controversial. These barges shooting the rapids under London Bridge, these men in wigs straining for sounds of war, these square-rigged ships all belong to another age. To the extent that they arouse our sentiments, they do so irrespective of national or imperial aspiration. I do not experience a flutter of the heart at the news of the success of the Duke of York at

Lowestoft, any more than I feel outrage or shame or loss of honour at the sight of one of our ships' prows, displayed as a trophy in the Rijkmuseum. The relics of these wars are part of a heritage we *share* with the Dutch.

Indeed, for the collector of medals who wishes to illustrate British history of this period, it is necessary to turn to the medals struck by the Dutch, which are anyway often superior to ours. *The Embarcation of Schevingen, Admiral de Ruyter, Admiral Tromp, Ships Burnt in the Medway near Chatham, The Peace of Breda,* and many more—these are the names by which desirable Dutch medals are known to British collectors, who treasure those poetic inscriptions which give a somewhat different spin to, for instance, the *Action at Bergen* already mentioned:

> Dus wort Brittanjes Trotz gestuÿt,
> die zelfs bÿ Vriendt vaert op vrÿbuÿt;
> en tergt de Noortsche Wallen.
> Hÿ schaekt Vorÿt Fredricks haven recht
> dog krÿgt Sÿn loon, door boeg en plecht
> van Neerlandts donderballen.

(Thus we arrest the pride of English, who extend their piracy even against their friends, and who, insulting the forts of Norway, violate the rights of the harbors of King Frederick; but, for the reward of their audacity, see their vessels destroyed by the balls of the Dutch.)[10]

And those silver discs, with their remarkable evocations of the sea, those precious little Drydens in relief, lead up, of course, to *The Embarkation of William of Orange at Helvoetsluys* and in next to no time to *The Battle of the Boyne* of 1690 and the *Pacification of Ireland* and *Ireland Subdued* of the same year. And suddenly we find ourselves in a controversial world, the world that has been at bloody issue for the last quarter of a century. It was made by those same men in wigs, those same square-rigged ships, that same Duke of York, that same baroque, and it leads us, with one giant stride, straight into the millennium. When will Ireland be reunited? When and how will the conflict cease?

And this sudden controversy, this sudden baroque ambush of the modern, reminds us that there is always a nasty surprise in store for the imperial mind. It is typical of the imperial point of view that it is ignorant of, or blind to, the other. The imperial mind keeps missing the point. It fails to appreciate, for all its benevolence, why it might come under attack, why it might, for instance, be worth a nation's while to rise up against it. The imperial mind has to be shocked out of its daydreams. It has to be subjected to some kind of demonstration that it cannot ignore.

This ability to look straight through a whole people, to fail to notice an indigenous population (as in the turn-of-the-century Zionist slogan which referred to Palestine as 'a land without a people for a people without a land'), is on perfect display in Robert Frost's 'The Gift Outright', a modern imperialist poem:

> The land was ours before we were the land's.
> She was our land more than a hundred years
> Before we were her people. She was ours
> In Massachusetts, in Virginia,
> But we were England's, still colonials,
> Possessing what we still were unpossessed by,
> Possessed by what we now no more possessed.
> Something we were withholding made us weak
> Until we found out that it was ourselves
> We were withholding from our land of living.
> And forthwith found salvation in surrender.
> Such as we were we gave ourselves outright
> (The deed of gift was many deeds of war)
> To the land vaguely realizing westward,

> But still unstoried, artless, unenhanced,
> Such as she was, such as she would become.[11]

The repeated assertion of the colonials' right to the land goes well with the sublime vagueness that anybody else's right might be involved. Yes, there had to be deeds of war—'The deed of gift was many deeds of war'—but why or against whom we need not, on this occasion, consider. The point is rather to wallow in the metaphysics of the conceit that Americans, in order to become truly American and truly strong, had to yield to the land, surrender to it, instead of what you would expect from an account of a pioneering society—that they had to seize the land and bend it to their will.

What seduced Frost into writing such egregious rubbish, was the urge to assert the arrival of a new Augustan age, spelled out in the poem called 'Gift Outright of "The Gift Outright" ':

> It makes the prophet in us all presage
> The glory of a next Augustan age
> Of a power leading from its strength and pride,
> Of young ambition eager to be tried,
> Firm in our free beliefs without dismay,
> In any game the nations want to play.
> A golden age of poetry and power
> Of which this noonday's the beginning hour.[12]

One has to resist the thought that poetry like this represents its era. The desire to be the distinguished representative of the Golden Age is too high on the poet's agenda. These lines were palpably foolish when written and remain so today. Nevertheless one can say for certain that Frost himself, had he miraculously hung on and been invited back, instead of Maya Angelou, for the Clinton inauguration, would have been alert enough to have sung a different tune. Something in time divides us from those days and from that rhetoric:

> We see how seriously the races swarm
> In their attempts at sovereignty and form.
> They are our wards we think to some extent
> For the time being and with their consent,
> To teach them how Democracy is meant.[13]

This goes well with the Peace Corps, so well with the spirit which took responsibility for the destiny of South Vietnam, that I cannot help but match it with the quotation I saw on the wall of the American Embassy in Saigon as the embassy was being sacked. It was a line from Lawrence of Arabia, framed above the desk of someone who had been given that task of teaching the Vietnamese 'In their attempts at sovereignty and form': 'Rather let them do it imperfectly than try to do it perfectly yourself. For it is their country, their war, and your time is short.'

If I ask myself what the last convinced imperialist poem might have been, taking the British Empire as its theme (and excluding Larkin's 'Homage to a Government'—which is an expression of *unconvinced* imperialism), I turn to a poem Eliot places among his 'Occasional Verses', with the following modest disclaimer:

> *To the Indians Who Died in Africa* was written at the request of Miss Cornelia Sorabji for *Queen Mary's Book of India* (Harrap & Co. Ltd., 1943). I dedicate it now to Bonamy Dobree, because he liked it and urged me to preserve it.

> A man's destination is his own village,
> His own fire, and his wife's cooking;
> To sit in front of his own door at sunset

And see his grandson, and his neighbour's grandson
    Playing in the dust together.

Scarred but secure, he has many memories
Which return at the hour of conversation,
(The warm or the cool hour, according to the climate)
Of foreign men, who fought in foreign places,
    Foreign to each other.

A man's destination is not his destiny,
Every country is home to one man
And exile to another. Where a man died bravely
At one with his destiny, that soil is his,
    Let his village remember.

This was not your land, or ours: but a village in the
    Midlands,
And one in the Five Rivers, may have the same
    graveyard.
Let those who go tell the same story of you:
Of action with a common purpose, action
None the less fruitful if neither you nor we
Know, until the judgement after death,
    What is the fruit of action.[14]

Or: If you should die, think only this of *you*, That there's some
corner of a foreign field, that is for ever both Birmingham and
the Punjab (the Five Rivers Eliot refers to). You have a destiny,
which happens, by some mysterious linguistic trick of mine,
to take precedence over your destination. You must die at one
with your destiny. I don't know why this is, and nor do you,
but we shall both find out the moment *after* our death.

    The vein of preposterousness runs deep here—nothing in
Dryden can match it—as an Anglican American addresses an
audience, very few of whom would have been his co-religion-
ists, and informs them that their deaths are required of them
for reasons only his God can reveal. And for Eliot to write this

at a time when the struggle for Indian independence was reaching its peak! Indeed, a part of the argument for independence after the Second World War was based on the fact that India had done its bit defending Britain and now it deserved something in return. So this adamant, metaphysical imperialism appears at the very moment of the Empire's decline, and from the pen of an assimilated Briton, writing to please a Queen.

Now imperialism, which may be described as an immense intrusion into other people's business, does not end when the imperialist decides to call it a day. One cannot simply announce: Okay chaps, the empire's over now, and it's time *to put all that behind us*. Much as everyone might like it, the empire does not simply collapse overnight. It collapses once. Then it continues to collapse. It breaks up once, then it breaks up again and again, and again. People's lives are ruined by it. Nations are ruined by it. People are still on the move, because there was once an empire and now that empire is no more.

And this state of being forever on the move will not end just because, say, Hong Kong is returned to China or the few last outposts are closed down. It goes on and on. It has its own great scale, its epic proportions. What will happen to the Chinese empire itself is an added conundrum. The Indians who died in Africa take their place alongside the Indians who lived in Africa, until fairly recently thrown out. And they become, of course, the Indians who live in England, whose destiny, or destination, or both, is Birmingham.

Then there were the Indians who arrived in Fiji in 1879 on the *Leonidas*. Fiji at that stage had only been part of the Empire for five years. It had been offered to Queen Victoria as a way of resolving internal conflicts which looked as if they were going to lead to endless tribal bloodshed, and the British accepted the offer, not with great alacrity but as a way of forestalling the interest of any other great power. The administration of Fijian traditional society was carried out in a comparatively enlightened way—traditional landholdings were preserved and remain intact to this day. But there were also sugar estates, and these were in desperate need of labour.

The Indians who arrived in Fiji, mostly young Hindu men, had undertaken an agreement, or *girmit*, that they would work for five years, after which they became *khula*, free, but had to wait another five years before receiving their ticket home. And it is said that in many cases these young men were tricked—they had not realized, they hadn't the remotest idea, how far Fiji was from Calcutta, where they embarked. They found that they had gone over the great sea, they had 'crossed the black water', and that in doing so they had lost caste and could never return. And certainly one might feel, after a ten-year wait, that there wouldn't be much to return to.

This form of indentured labour, this euphemistic slavery, this shipping of Indians to Fiji, lasted until 1916—the year before 'Prufrock'. But one wouldn't say that the story of the Indians who went to Fiji ended there. From independence in 1970 until the late Eighties, the politics of Fiji was dominated by ethnic Fijians. Then for a brief time, a matter of weeks, a government was elected in which Indian and ethnic Fijian might share power. But the Fijian military put a stop to that experiment, and the Indians of Fiji were left under no illusions that any step they took to improve their lot made them that bit less welcome. And so they began to look, if they had resources or qualifications to do so, in the direction of, say, Vancouver. Their journey, they perceived, was not yet over. Where they lived, they lived only on tolerance, and that tolerance had worn thin and they began to be afraid.

At that time, when I was working in Fiji, I came across a group of ethnic Fijian soldiers and was invited to drink with them. They had a toast which went: 'To the green grass of Fiji, which grew over the Great Wall of China, and fucked the Queen of England.' It occurred to me, as I contemplated this example of South Seas surrealism, that these people had a remarkable capacity to take the long view. The British had come and stayed a century. Now they were gone. The Indians were what was left, and might be expected, if suitably encouraged, to drift away before long. In the end it was the green grass of Fiji that would triumph over all.

2

I've taken this single strand of the imperial story simply as an illustration of the unfinished nature of imperial business. If business is unfinished in people's daily lives, how can we expect it to be finished in our culture, in our literature, in our poetry in particular? The word 'post-imperial' is easy and comforting to use, since it seems to draw a line under an episode, to say That was Then and This is Now. But one supposes in fact that the nature of the post-imperial is only just unfolding, that there is more to this story than has yet been told. We should not expect to be entirely clear what this unfolding Now is like, or how it is going to behave in the future. We shall discover that in many ways we have been blind, or that we are still blind, to the most surprising number of interests and considerations, that our past, viewed from one angle as a boon, turns baneful with the very slightest shift of the light source.

The events of this late or post-imperial world have a habit of appearing in a rather puzzling order. It is not the case that the British Empire triumphed first, then collapsed in scandal and controversy, and that this controversy gradually died away as the years progressed. The British Empire triumphed and collapsed simultaneously; it was buried with full honours by the Commonwealth; then this dead empire went off to fight in the South Atlantic. We declared recently that we have no selfish or strategic interest in Northern Ireland. But we do have a selfish and strategic interest in Antarctica. We are a puzzling people, a puzzle to ourselves.

That sense, to use a phrase of Larkin's from another context, 'of failure spreading back up the arm' comes to us when we contemplate the shrinking *patria* to which we were born. We wonder: Where will the shrinking end? What will the real post-imperial country turn out to be? My guess is that it will correspond roughly to that part of the country which was conquered by the Romans, up to Hadrian's but not the Antonine Wall. Until we see what will happen, though, how can we know how to describe ourselves? How can we define the cultural unit to which we belong?

For we live in an age in which the pressure is all toward self-definition, self-description of some kind. It wasn't always like this. The poets who grew up on *The Waste Land* thought of themselves as urban, restless, international. The notion that he might have his roots in Birmingham struck Auden as absurd. He has his mythic *patria* in the wilds of a mythic Cumberland, but he knew this to be a fiction of his own making. As for turning his verse out for the sake of the Empire, nothing could have struck Auden—or his generation—as more ludicrous.

Well, events in this case took that typically puzzling order, for after his resounding success as Mr Rootlessness, Eliot racinated himself. He found his metaphysical centre:

> ... A people without history
> Is not redeemed from time, for history is a pattern
> Of timeless moments. So, while the light fails
> On a winter's afternoon, in a secluded chapel
> History is now and England.[15]

And this, rather than his advice to the Indians, was Eliot's true spiritual contribution to the war effort. One wonders whether, for Eliot's American readers, such lines do not somehow smack of a kind of treachery. Certainly *Four Quartets* was not taken to heart in America as a supreme achievement in the way that it was, perhaps still is, in this country. People of my age were brought up on stories of the excitement felt as each of the *Quartets* came out in pamphlet form. And I suppose that a line such as 'History is now and England' has a rhetorical force that lifts it, naturally, out of its context in the poem, and gives it a function as a slogan for the war. One notices that the line would never have worked if it had been 'History is now and Britain', or if Little Gidding had shifted a few miles and Eliot had been obliged to write 'History is now and Wales'. In rhetoric, England could stand for the whole political, cultural unit. This is what hegemony is all about.

Today's poet will be alert to the great problem of deploying the word 'England', or 'English', in such a rhetorical way. Such words are hedged around with taboo, and if we use them we expect to check very carefully for nuance. And if we do not know for sure what is the future of Britain, we will take care over 'Britain' and 'British' as well. But it was not always thus. There was a time when, given the belief that empire was an absurdity and 'all that was in the past', a poet like Douglas Dunn could write his 'Poem in Praise of the British' confident that his ironies were shared:

> The regiments of dumb gunners go to bed early.
> The soldiers, sleepy after running up and down
> The private British Army meadows,
> Clean the daisies off their mammoth boots.
> The general goes pink in his bath reading
> *Lives of the Great Croquet Players.*
> At Aldershot, beside foot-stamping squares,
> Young officers drink tea and touch their toes.
>
> Heavy rain everywhere washes up the bones of British
> Where did all that power come from, the wish

To be inert, but rich and strong, to have too much?
Where does glory come from, and when it's gone
Why are old soldiers sour and the banks empty?
But how sweet is the weakness after Empire
In the garden of a flat, safe country shire,
Watching the beauty of the random, spare, superfluous,

Drifting as if in sleep to the ranks of memorialists
That wait like cabs to take us off down easy street,
To the redcoat armies, and the flags and treaties
In the marvellous archives, preserved like leaves in
    books.
The archivist wears a sword and clipped moustache.
He files our memories, more precious than light,
To be of easy access to politicians of the Right,
Who are now sleeping, like undertakers on black
    cushions.

That comes from Dunn's first book, *Terry Street,* published in
1969.[16] One could say of it that it takes nothing seriously, is
unshockable and untroubled. The past is this wonderful
absurdity. The politicians of the Right are not to be feared. We
are living in this wonderful afterglow, and all is well.

One of the things one would not have guessed about *Terry
Street* when it came out was that its author was Scottish. In
fact, given that most of the poems in the book are about a
working-class district in Hull, one might perhaps have
supposed him English. 'A Poem in Praise of the British' was
untypical of its volume, but not untypical of the way Dunn
later wrote at times, when he wrote *as if he were expressing
himself in French*, in an easygoing, dandyish way which sometimes tempted him. But what is absolutely untypical of the
later Dunn is the insouciance with which he treats the subject
of empire. Within ten years, in the volume called *Barbarians,*
which shows the influence of the hard, revolutionary Left,

you find a poem called 'Empires' which might almost have
been written to remedy the defects in seriousness of the earlier
one:

> . . . They interfered with place,
> Time, people, lives, and so to bed. They died
> When it died. It had died before. It died
> Before they did. They did not know it. Race
> Power, Trade, Fleet, a hundred regiments,
> Postponed that final reckoning with pride,
> Which was expensive.[17]

And so on. Soldiers are no longer funny. Empire is no longer
an amusing mystery. By now, Dunn has begun to think of
himself as a barbarian to identify with the victims of empire.
And this phase gives way to a further phase in which, to a
great extent, his Scottishness becomes his subject matter. He
returns to his roots.

And one cannot help thinking that his increased emphasis
on his nationality (if that is what Scottishness is), and on the
seriousness of his history, comes not only as a result of the
general rise of Scottish nationalism in the period, but also in
part from a looking across the water at what was happening in
Northern Ireland, both at the revived Troubles and at the
assertive self-expression and self-definitions of the Northern
Ireland poets. What had seemed to the young Dunn a natural
way to begin—writing in England about England—had indeed
once been natural. That was where he happened to live and
work. Evident too in Dunn's early work—on the surface, not
buried obscurely—is the sense that the divide for him was
between provincial life as a whole and that of the cultural
metropolis, which was quite definitely London. But within a
decade this had come to feel like a form of self-censorship or
a suppression of one's origins.

Now if the unfolding post-imperial *patria* were to turn out to be England alone as geographically defined—still no one would say that the clock had been turned back on the Empire, that all those stitches had been unpicked. The England that was left would contain the whole history of Empire within it, just as the history of the French empire has been incorporated within the map of France. An Irish nationalism or a Scottish or Welsh nationalism might have its vices as well as its virtues, but an English nationalism, when it raises its head above the level of absurdity, can only be sinister. We can remember that Rupert Brooke sitting in the Café des Westens in Berlin in 1912, and longing to go for a swim *à la nature*—and this already seems so sad, because Brooke was only a few stops on the S-Bahn from bathing places where he could easily have thrown off all his togs and leapt into 'cleanness'—Brooke was depressed because he was surrounded by *'Temperamentvoll German Jews'*. Grantchester, the countryside around Cambridge, was longed for as being *Judenrein*. One can detect, in so many professions of love for England, some sinister implication of hatred for something else—hatred of other peoples, hatred of the world as it is becoming.

If one cannot live without a sense of nationhood, one can love England for the complex thing it is and is becoming, not for some vicious conception of what it once might have been. The Dutch schoolchildren have a playground rhyme which goes:

> Witte zwanen, zwarte zwanen.
> Wie wil er mee naar Engeland varen?
> Engeland is gesloten,
> De sleutel is gebroken.
> Is er dan geen smid in het land
> Die de sleutel maken kan?

> (White swans, black swans.
> Who wants to join the boat trip to England?
> England has been locked.

> The key is broken.
> Isn't there any smith in the land,
> Who could mend the key?)

But if that question once had an answer, it seems to have been lost long since.

5. *The Orpheus of Ulster*

In 1982, when Blake Morrison and Andrew Motion published their *Penguin Book of Contemporary British Poetry,* Seamus Heaney exploded. He had had enough. He was not British, and he was fed up with being called British, or anything other than Irish. But since his work had first appeared with Faber in 1966, it had regularly been called British, and it had appeared in such anthologies as Edward Lucie-Smith's *British Poetry Since 1945* (1970), Jeremy Robson's *The Young British Poets* (1971), Michael Schmidt's *Eleven British Poets* (1980), and even, in 1968, Karl Miller's *Writing in England Today: The Last Fifteen Years.* It was time to set the record straight.

Heaney's riposte to Morrison/Motion took the form of a 198-line poem, *An Open Letter,* headed by a quotation from Gaston Bachelard: 'What is the source of our first suffering? It lies in the fact that we hesitated to speak . . . It was born in the moment when we accumulated silent things within us.' And the poem itself tells us that Heaney had thought about this matter for weeks, months, that he was embarrassed to bring the whole thing up because Morrison had been his 'good advocate' in writing a book on him, that he was disappointed particularly because he had understood that the anthology was going to be called *Opened Ground,* a phrase from one of his poems. He had wondered whether to let the matter drop:

> Anything for the quiet life.
> Play possum and pretend you're deaf.
> When awkward facts nag like the wife
> Look blank, go dumb.

> To greet the smiler with the knife
> Smile back at him.[1]

But Heaney felt that if he dithered, Hamlet-like, he would pay for it in Act Five, that silence was an abdication, that he had to refuse the adjective 'British'. And so he administered a 'simple lesson':

> Caesar's Britain, its *partes tres,*
> *United England, Scotland, Wales,*
> *Britannia* in the old tales,
>   Is common ground.
> *Hibernia* is where the Gaels
>   Made a last stand
>
> And long ago were stood upon—
> End of simple history lesson.
> As empire rings its curtain down
>   This 'British' word
> Sticks deep in native and *colon*
>   Like Arthur's sword.

Heaney was unhappy with the Burns stanza he had chosen, which leads him into many awkwardnesses, as here where he seems to overlook the fact that there were also Gaels who made their last stand in Scotland. And do we imagine that, writing in prose, he would have distinguished Catholic from Protestant by calling one lot native and the other *colon*? It seems unlikely.

There were twenty poets in Morrison/Motion, six of whom came from Northern Ireland. Heaney specifically says that he is speaking only for himself, not on behalf of the whole group:

> (I'll stick to *I*. Forget the *we*.
> As Livy said, *pro se quisque.*

> And Horace was exemplary
> At Philippi:
> He threw away his shield to be
> A naked *I*.)

This has more grandeur and passion than the context might
seem to justify, but the decision to speak only on his own
behalf was an important one for Heaney in another respect.
For years he had been resisting pressure to speak for the
Republican movement. In his new collection, a poem called
'The Flight Path' recalls meeting a Republican on a train in
1979 during the 'dirty protest' at Long Kesh and being challenged with:

> 'When for fuck's sake, are you going to write
> Something for us?' 'If I do write something,
> Whatever it is, I'll be writing for myself.'[2]

He will not, he is saying, put his poetry at the service of the
cause. He will only speak as an individual. Nevertheless, in
'An Open Letter', he comes close to flag-waving when he says:

> be advised
> My passport's green.
> No glass of ours was ever raised
> To toast *The Queen*.

The vehemence of this refusal to be called British took
many people by surprise and made Morrison/Motion look a
little foolish. Heaney was the star show in their anthology, the
one they deliberately placed first, the one they hailed as the
most important new poet of the previous fifteen years. Nor
was it the only time that Morrison had written of Heaney as
being British. In his book, also published in 1982, he said that
Heaney 'grew up in Northern Ireland, which technically at

least makes him British'. He calls his blend of sexual passion and domestic affection 'unique in modern British poetry' and, writing about *Field Work* (1979), he says the sequence 'marks Heaney's return not just to the countryside but to the mainstream of English Poetry: having begun in imitation of Ted Hughes and then looked more to his own countrymen, he now takes his place in an English lyric tradition that includes Wyatt at one end and Wordsworth at the other'.[3]

Morrison and Motion had naturally hoped that their anthology would be seen as a kind of landmark. They wanted it to be, for its time, what Al Alvarez's *The New Poetry* had been in its day. 'British poetry,' they said in their introduction, had taken 'forms quite other than those promoted by Alvarez', and part of the reason for this was the 'emergence and example of Seamus Heaney. . . . Heaney is someone Alvarez could not foresee at the time and someone he has attacked since.' And they contrasted the nakedness of the style of poetry Alvarez admired with the obliquity they detected in Heaney.

One turns to Alvarez's review of *Field Work*,[4] which was not only an attack on Heaney but also an attack on his English admirers in academe, people like Christopher Ricks and John Carey, who had recognized Heaney's gifts from the beginning of his career (I think that what they were recognizing was a successor to Ted Hughes) and were now declaring that in Heaney 'Britain has, at last, another major poet'. This seemed grossly disproportionate to Alvarez. Heaney's current reputation amounted to

> a double betrayal: it lumbers him with expectations which he may not fulfill and which might even sink him, if he were less resilient; at the same time, it reinforces the British audience in their comfortable prejudice that poetry, give or take a few quirks of style, has not changed essentially in the last hundred years.

And now comes the passage which, if he read it, would most have stuck in Heaney's craw:

> If Heaney really is the best we can do, then the whole troubled, exploratory thrust of modern poetry has been a diversion from the right true way. Eliot and his contemporaries, Lowell and his, Plath and hers had it all wrong: to try to make clearings of sense and discipline and style in the untamed, unfenced darkness was to mistake morbidity for inspiration. It was, in the end, mere melodrama, understandable perhaps in the Americans who lack a tradition in these matters, but inexcusable in the British.

In other words, Heaney's 'abrupt elevation into the pantheon of British poetry' was a symptom of what was wrong with British culture. Our critics were dedicated to 'safety, sweetness and light'. They showed 'a curiously depressing refusal of everything that is mysterious and shaking and renewing in poetry'. And they reminded Alvarez of Ophelia:

> Thought and affliction, passion, hell itself,
> She turns to favour and to prettiness.

There is an interesting example, in what Alvarez says, of the use of Eliot for purposes of cultural intimidation: if it is right to admire Heaney, then Eliot must have lived in vain, and not only Eliot but Lowell and Plath as well. This is the line. This is the tradition. This is the canon being wheeled into action. Astonishingly absent is any interest in the Irish dimension, except in this: Alvarez tells us that 'since Congreve and Sterne there has always been at least one major Irish star on the British literary scene'. At the time he is writing, it should be Beckett, but Beckett is too radical and experimental. Heaney is 'far less unsettling'.

The implication seems to be that that is therefore all Heaney is—an Irish entertainer on the British cultural scene, a symptom of what is wrong with British culture. It must have been exasperating to Heaney. If you look at what Alvarez had recommended, in the influential introduction to *The New Poetry*, as a 'new seriousness'—defined as 'the poet's ability and willingness to face the full range of his experience with his full intelligence'—and you see how Alvarez preferred the example of Hughes to that of Larkin, you might well have expected him to recognize in Heaney the sort of poet he had had in mind, had campaigned for. One might have predicted that *North* at least would have appealed to him.

Most exasperating of all, though, would be to feel that these misapprehensions about your nationality were, in part, your fault. For it would never have been so easy for the British to take whatever they liked from Ireland and call it British if a protest had been lodged a little earlier. That was the significance of the quote from Bachelard. Heaney was in a weak position, and knew it, which is one reason why *An Open Letter* is not a good poem (the other being that its versification is atrocious).

An Open Letter was a poor poem but an important event. It made its point and its point was not forgotten. It made its point on behalf of one writer, but established that point on behalf of a whole group. One no longer assumes—this is the crucial difference between then and now—that the political geography of the United Kingdom is coterminous with the cultural geography.

In the last of his Oxford lectures, given in 1993, Heaney says

I wrote that my passport was green, although nowadays it is a Euro-, but not an imperial, purple. I wrote about the colour of the passport, however, not in order to expunge the British connection in Britain's Ireland but to maintain the right to diversity *within* the border, to be understood as having full freedom to the enjoyment of an Irish name and identity within that northern jurisdiction. Those who want to share that name and identity in Britain's Ireland should not be penalized or resented or suspected of a sinister motive because they draw cultural and psychic sustenance from an elsewhere supplementary to the one across the water.[5]

This represents a considerable rewriting of *An Open Letter*. The notion that there might be such an entity as Britain's Ireland was specifically ruled out by the insistence that Britannia is Britannia and Hibernia is Hibernia and that's that. The lines 'No glass of ours was ever raised | To toast *The Queen*' have an aggressive Republican tone quite different from the statement: I draw cultural and psychic sustenance from an elsewhere supplementary to the one across the water, as if, for the Northern Ireland Catholic, his Irishness were a kind of wheatgerm which he sprinkled every morning on his—what would it be? on his Britishness?

The embarrassment behind the rewrite, so many years later, of a poem which he published only in pamphlet form, is indicative perhaps of a lingering sense that, though he had no alternative but to make his stand, the stand itself was some kind of betrayal, or some kind of slap in the face of people to whom he was, in various ways, obliged. 'Now they will say I bite the hand that fed me' is a Heaney line in a slightly different context—a bitter anticipation of reproach. But Heaney as a person and as a poet has a terrific sense of obligation and often expresses guilt that he might not have lived up to the clearly impossible standards he set for himself or that others have been happy to set for him.

The general praise that greeted his being awarded the Nobel Prize last year might tempt one to forget that this immensely popular poet has often had a bumpy ride, that he has not been short of critics, not least among his fellow poets. 'Certainly,' says the Protestant Ulster poet James Simmons, 'it began long ago. In those old gatherings under the auspices of Philip Hobsbaum in Belfast it was obvious that Seamus was being groomed for stardom.'[6] I would put this differently— not that I was over at those old gatherings (in which Hobsbaum, the English poet, gave encouragement and criticism to a generation of young Ulster writers). The fact is that no poet gets 'groomed for stardom'. What on earth would the process be? But that he was *tipped* for stardom, that he gave, somehow, warning of the talent to come—that I can believe.

And behind this tipping for stardom lurked the awesome thought: Who will inherit the mantle of Yeats? And it appeared that Yeats had only one mantle, and that it was not to be divided. Certainly in Heaney criticism there is a topos: Why does Heaney get all the attention, when poet X or Y is so much more this, so much more that? It seems Heaney was thought to have had a knack of soaking up all the available attention.

Here is Simmons again, in the same, avowedly Cassius-like essay:

> I remember feeling curiously angry and betrayed when I first reviewed *Wintering Out*. I had thought of Seamus as an ally in the general struggle to liberalise and reform Ulster, but he seemed to be retreating into the tribe, excluding Protestants, fostering resentment, betraying the tougher Catholic spokesmen of previous generations such as O'Faolain, O'Connor and Kavanagh. So many of the resentments he presents as specifically Catholic and Ulster are applicable to the poor universally, and there is a positive left-wing movement in which the human race has been trying to pull itself up by its bootstraps for centuries. Heaney's feelings seem to operate in isolation from this.

Two betrayals here—betrayal of the joint political effort to liberalize Ulster, and betrayal of the tougher old Catholic writers of yore. Nor are these going to be the last betrayals on the list.

It is astonishing how often in the poetry of this century this theme of betrayal crops up. Pound of course is the big one—lucky to get away with his life. Then Auden was bitterly accused of betrayal when he moved to America. And was not Eliot's espousal of England as a cause seen as a kind of betrayal? Sassoon betrayed his class, or wanted to. Lowell did betray his class, and in stirring style, when he refused to serve in a war whose prosecution, he thought, constituted a betrayal of his country (because the original war aims had been perverted to encompass the total destruction of Germany and Japan). He had his ancestors on parade when he announced his betrayal to no less a person than the President of the United States.

Heaney, so far in this story, has betrayed nationalism as represented by the IRA, liberalism as represented by Simmons, the tougher Catholic writers of yore, modernism as represented by Eliot, Lowell, and Plath—an impressive list of stabbings in the back. And it doesn't end there. His move South was a betrayal of the North. Working in the States was Yankification. Everything turns out to be a betraying of something.

But I suppose that one is not accused of betrayal unless one is recognized as a leader, and behind many of these attacks there is a recognition of pre-eminence either presaged or already gained. The attacks were certainly not afraid to wound. Ciarán Carson, another Ulster poet, wrote that in *North* Heaney seemed 'to have moved—unwillingly, perhaps—from being a writer with the gift of precision, to become the laureate of violence—a mythmaker, an anthropologist of ritual killing, an apologist for "the situation," in the last resort, a mystifier'.[7] One is curious, coming across such a passage, to look up where it comes from. 'Laureate of violence' is a killing phrase, and one expects a sustained argument to support it. But the review turns out to be as much an attack on the Faber publicity machine as on Heaney: it is the usual fraternal animus against an excessively hyped book.

The other often-quoted passage from Carson's review discusses the poem 'Punishment' and the lines:

> I who have stood dumb
> when your betraying sisters,
> cauled in tar,
> wept by the railings,
>
> who would connive
> in civilized outrage
> yet understand the exact
> and tribal, intimate revenge.[8]

This comes at the end of one of the 'bog poems' which form the first section of *North* in a description of a presumed adulteress drowned in a bog at some time in prehistory. Carson says that Heaney seems to be offering his 'understanding' of the situation almost as a consolation. He goes on:

> It is as if he is saying, suffering like this is natural; these things have always happened; they happened then, they happen now, and that is sufficient ground for understanding and absolution. It is as if there never were and never will be any political consequences of such acts; they have been removed to the realm of sex, death, and inevitability.[9]

That might be fair criticism—of a passage which caused consternation among numerous critics, among them Blake Morrison and Edna Longley—but it does not make the case that he was a 'laureate of violence'. Simmons goes much further:

> The poet's tenderness is troubled by the thought that he would have done nothing to save her had he been there: as he has not saved the local Catholic girls tarred and feathered for going out with soldiers; but suddenly we find he is on the side of the torturers. The 'little adulteress' whose 'tar-black face was beautiful' has 'betraying sisters,' and the poet writes of his own public words condemning the torturers as 'conniving.' He leaves us with the statement that he understands 'the exact/and tribal, intimate revenge.' He does not seem to be confessing or apologising. That's where it stands. This is very exciting and interesting. You wish he would say more.[10]

Note, with this piece of malicious provocation, how astonishingly far we have come from the Heaney depicted by Alvarez, the safe Irish entertainer playing to an essentially timid British audience. Here we have a laureate of violence who is on the side of the torturers. And Simmons's malice is revealed by his affecting to welcome this revelation of the real, hitherto unsuspected Heaney—as if it would simply be healthier to thrash all this out in public. This is one of those 'open minds as open as a trap' at work. Simmons knows perfectly well that Heaney is not on the side of the torturers. If the poems in the first part of *North* were worrying to his genuine (as opposed to ironical) admirers, it must be because they sometimes failed to reassure the reader about the difference between understanding the processes at work (understanding them, with a full sense of the terror involved) and understanding-as-forgiving or even as conniving.

Nothing would have been easier for Heaney, had he bought the Provisional IRA line, than to put his Muse at the service of the cause. As a young man, at the beginning of the civil rights protests, he wrote a ballad against the use of violence by William Craig, the head of the Black & Tans:

> Come all ye Ulster loyalists and in full chorus join,
> Think on the deeds of Craig's Dragoons who strike
>   below the groin,
> And drink a toast to the truncheon and the armoured
>   water-hose
> That mowed a swathe through Civil Rights and spat on
>   Papish clothes.
>
> We've gerrymandered Derry but Croppy won't lie
>   down,
> He calls himself a citizen and wants votes in the town.
> But that Saturday in Duke Street we slipped the velvet
>   glove—
> The iron hand of Craig's Dragoons soon crunched a
>   croppy dove . . .
>
> O William Craig, you are our love, our lily and our
>   sash.
> You have the boys who fear no noise, who'll batter and
>   who'll bash.
> They'll cordon and they'll baton-charge, they'll silence
>   protest tunes,
> They are the hounds of Ulster, boys, sweet William
>   Craig's dragoons.[11]

Stirring stuff. One can almost smell the rain on the Aran sweaters of the protesters who would have sung it. And I do hope that when Heaney produces his collected poems he will allow us to see more of his work in that vein, including the song he wrote after Bloody Sunday in Derry, 30 January 1972, which has apparently never seen the light of day. But the point was that times changed, changed and grew worse, until to write that sort of stirring stuff was no longer an option.

Here is Heaney, in his Nobel address, published as *Crediting Poetry*, looking back on the days of internment:

> I remember . . . shocking myself with a thought I had about [a] friend who was imprisoned in the Seventies on suspicion of having been involved with a political murder; I shocked myself by thinking that even if he were guilty, he might still perhaps be helping the future to be born, breaking the repressive forms and liberating new potential in the only way that worked, namely the violent way—which therefore became, by extension, the right way. It was like a moment of exposure to interstellar cold, a reminder of the scary element, both inner and outer, in which human beings must envisage and conduct their lives. But it was only a moment.[12]

Only a moment, and if it was the *only* such moment then Heaney was lucky, since the situation was such as to provoke many such moments in many such people. And Heaney chooses to describe this particular moment immediately after recounting that unforgettable, one hates to say classic, story of the recent Troubles. Here it is as he tells it:

> One of the most harrowing moments in the whole history of the harrowing of the heart of Northern Ireland came when a minibus full of workers being driven home one January evening in 1976 was held up by armed and masked men and the occupants of the van ordered at gunpoint to line up at the side of the road. Then one of the masked executioners said to them, 'Any Catholics among you, step out here.' As it happened this particular group, with one exception, were all Protestants, so the presumption must have been that the masked men were Protestant paramilitaries about to carry out a tit-for-tat sectarian killing of the Catholic as the odd man out, the

one who would have been presumed to be in sympathy with the IRA and all its actions. It was a terrible moment for him, caught between dread and witness, but he did make a motion to step forward. Then, the story goes, in that split second of decision, and in the relative cover of the winter evening darkness, he felt the hand of the Protestant worker next to him take his hand and squeeze it in a signal that said no, don't move, we'll not betray you, nobody need know what faith or party you belong to. All in vain, however, for the man stepped out of the line; but instead of finding a gun at his temple, he was pushed away as the gunmen opened fire on those remaining in the line, for these were not Protestant terrorists but members, presumably, of the Provisional IRA.[13]

In that same Oxford lecture which I have already quoted from, Heaney describes his mixed feelings of guilt at attending a formal dinner in Oxford in 1981 at the time that Bobby Sands, the IRA hunger striker, had just died. Sands's family had been friendly with the Heaneys, and though he would not, had he been in Ireland at the time, have joined Bobby Sands's wake, yet he still felt it was a betrayal to be enjoying such hospitality at such a time. He was in, he said, 'the classic bind of all Northern Ireland's constitutional nationalists', since his cultural and political ideas were 'fundamentally Ireland-centred', but at the same time he was always obliged to distinguish his aims from the *means* used by the IRA. And he compares his position, very properly, to that of John Hume (another Irishman deserving of a Nobel), who may well today be generally credited with brokering the recent ceasefire, whatever its current ambiguous state.

The difference is, of course, that Hume's work has kept him largely on a shuttle between Ulster and London, while Heaney's procedure has been parabolic: from Belfast and

Dublin via County Wicklow, from Ulster to Stockholm via California and Harvard—rather in the manner of the Voznesensky poem in which Gauguin, in order to get from Montmartre to the Louvre, makes a detour through Java, Tahiti, and the Marquesas. And just as it turned out recently that one part of the solution to the Ulster peace process (assuming that that is what it is) lay in the United States, so it has turned out, for Heaney, that an important part of his becoming a major Irish poet took place in the environs of Harvard Yard. Engagement and flight—the twin subjects of 'The Flight Path', the recent poem already quoted—have been simultaneously necessary for him.

He often writes of the dissident poets of Russia, calling himself an inner émigré, in comparison with Mandelstam. It is an analogy boldly made, which works only in certain senses of the metaphor. That Heaney felt under unbearable pressure at times in Ireland, we can easily believe—but it would not have been a pressure from either government or party. I could imagine it, though, in either Belfast or in Dublin, as a ghastly encouragement of something false, an egging on to make your poetry instrumental. The problem would not be censorship or suppression. It would feel, rather, like an insistent urging not to let people down in their proper (improper) expectations.

Again and again in Heaney you will find him returning to the myth of Orpheus. In the Nobel lecture he tells us that the day before his prize was announced he was sketching a votive relief, in the small museum in Sparta, in which Orpheus charms the beasts. But it is not only Orpheus the exerter of the magic power of music that draws Heaney to the myth. Not long ago I heard him read his translation of Ovid's account of Orpheus being torn to pieces—and what came across most vividly was that he was utterly outraged that *Orpheus* (as if this had happened yesterday) had been torn to pieces.

Perhaps the feeling is that if you possess that power, you are going to have to pay for it. Certainly he possesses that power.

I went to the reading he gave in Oxford, with Ted Hughes, at the end of his professorship and thought it the most exciting reading I had heard. It was exciting before it began, and it just went on from there. And now, with his new collection, *The Spirit Level*, he keeps up the provision of pleasure.

I don't feel obliged to take all of Heaney (for instance, I like Part Two better than Part One of *North*; my loss, no doubt, but I don't much care for what he fishes out of bogs). I didn't like what I conceived to be writing *as if* living under an Eastern European censorship. But 1989 seems to have put a stop to all that.

The poem which provides the title for the new collection, 'The Errand', arrived in proof form with an erratum slip. Originally it had read simply:

> 'On you go now! Run, son, like the devil
> And tell your mother to try
> To find me a bubble for the spirit level
> And a new knot for this tie.'

It's an evocation of one of those paradoxical injunctions that adults used to give children, teasing their intelligence with an impossible order. A drearier form was 'Go and ask for a long stand.' You were supposed to go down to the shop and say, 'Can I have a long stand please?' and they would keep you standing until you got the joke.

I guess Heaney had thought that the idea of finding a bubble for the spirit level was a good metaphor for writing a poem, and that, having written the single stanza, he was under the impression that the poem was finished. But then he realized that the pleasure he was getting from the memory these lines evoked was all the more intense because of what was still going on inside his head, which the rest of us would not be able to intuit. The poem was, in other words, only half written. So he added:

But still he was glad, I know, when I stood my ground,
Putting it up to him
With a smile that trumped his smile and his fool's
      errand,
Waiting for the next move in the game.[14]

The erratum slip was inserted and uncorrected proofs dispatched. I shan't be selling my copy in a hurry, because there is great delight in seeing the way the whole meaning of the poem shifts. Now it is about father and son, the father taking pride in the son's refusal to obey a nonsensical order, even as the son is foxed over what to do next. The notion of finding the bubble for the spirit level as finding the way to write the next poem has disappeared from sight. It is visible only in the title of the collection.

And here's a poem which went straight into my personal anthology of the best of Heaney. It is called 'The Butter-Print':

Who carved on the butter-print's round open face
A cross-hatched head of rye, all jags and bristles?
Why should soft butter bear that sharp device
As if its breast were scored with slivered glass?

When I was small I swallowed an awn of rye.
My throat was like standing crop probed by a scythe.
I felt the edge slide and the point stick deep
Until, when I coughed and coughed and coughed it up,

My breathing came dawn-cold, so clear and sudden
I might have been inhaling airs from heaven
Where healed and martyred Agatha stares down
At the relic knife as I stared at the awn.[15]

'The pleasure and surprise of poetry', says Heaney, is 'a matter of angelic potential' and 'a motion of the soul'. When I look at a poem like this for the first time, I ask myself: How did it do that? How did we get from the butter-print to heaven and back down to the 'awn' so quickly? It's like watching the three-card trick in Oxford Street. Suddenly the table is folded up under the arm and the trickster vanishes in the crowd—excepting that, when you tap your pocket, you find you have something valuable you could have sworn wasn't there just a moment before.

6. *Becoming Marianne Moore*

Something held women back when it came to the writing of poetry, and since whatever it was that held them back failed to hold women back from writing novels, we must suppose that the inhibition had something, at least, to do with the antiquity and prestige of the art. Certainly the social disadvantages under which women laboured will not, taken alone, explain the conundrum away. I follow Germaine Greer in this when she writes: 'Homer and Milton were blind; can we claim that being female is a worse handicap than being blind?' And when she says that

> In large measure it is women who have deified the poet; it was women who fainted when Byron came into a room, who looked for signs of superhumanity in the brow of Wordsworth and grieved over the world-woe engraved in Tennyson's cheeks. The more women adored poetry, the less able they were to write it. From being practical and external, the obstacles in the path of the woman who wanted to write songs for others to sing became progressively internalised. It is less crucial for women to work out how men did this to women than it is to assess the extent to which women did this to themselves.[1]

That line—'The more women adored poetry, the less able they were to write it'—leads us straight to the case of Marianne

Moore, who claimed of poetry that she too disliked it and implied that the best way to read it was with perfect contempt for it. She wasn't quite telling the truth, on this as on many other matters. We always expect her to be telling the truth, because we see her as a fearless old lady of an utterly independent mind. But we look at her, as it were, through the wrong end of her biography. It wasn't the old lady who wrote the poems that made Moore's reputation, that caused her to be recognized as one of the very best writing in America. It was a young woman, already possessed of a trick of sounding quite definite whenever she opened her mouth, but in fact cautious and elusive and quite capable of changing her mind.

Everyone with any interest in Moore would like a new edition of her poetry, one which would bring back rejected poems, show the history of her revisions, and above all make chronological sense. What we have in the first section of the *Complete Poems* is a reprise of Eliot's arrangement made for the *Selected Poems* of 1935. It was a good arrangement in its day, since it began with her most recent work, the poems like 'The Steeple-Jack' which she resumed writing in the early thirties, after an eight-year silence, during much of which she had been editing *The Dial*. But Moore was 45 when she first published 'The Steeple-Jack'. The early poems don't begin until page 31 of the *Complete Poems*, and of course many other early poems have been dropped altogether, and the executors of Moore's estate refuse to allow them to be revived. Moore had written the sentence 'Omissions are not accidents'. This was taken to be an expression of her editorial wishes, in perpetuity.[2]

And just as it is hard to unravel the chronology and textual history of Moore's poems, so it is easy to find oneself thinking of Marianne Moore, the famous old lady in Brooklyn, as being the definitive version—as it were, the text in its final form. And this leads us straight into error. The American poet April Bernard describes attending Elizabeth Bishop's modern poetry seminar at Harvard in 1977:

One poor girl announced that she had read somewhere
that Marianne Moore wasn't a 'feminist.' Miss Bishop
replied: 'My goodness, you don't know what you're talking about at all, do you?' Then after a pause, she growled:
'Feminists!' We were all vaguely scandalised and didn't
know whether she thought Moore was so obviously a
feminist that one shouldn't have to ask such a stupid
question, or whether Miss Bishop (who, after all, did
insist on the 'Miss') herself disliked feminists. Later I was
to learn it was both.[3]

Moore was a member of the Women's Suffrage Party of
Pennsylvania and worked for its Committee to organize
Cumberland County. Bishop says in her memoir that she
paraded with the suffragettes led by Inez Mulholland on her
white horse down Fifth Avenue and that she had 'climbed a
lamppost' in a demonstration for votes for women. That
would seem to make her unequivocally a feminist—but that
was in 1915. The poor girl who was slapped down by
Elizabeth Bishop was not necessarily misinformed. Moore
had had time to change. Feminism too had changed. In 1957,
Moore was asked by the *Encyclopaedia Britannica Year Book*
whether the net result of women's 'coming out of the
kitchen' had been helpful or detrimental to society. She
replied that she thought it had been helpful, citing the activ-
ities of a long list of women including Florence Nightingale,
Helen Keller, Marie Curie, and the suffragist Susan B.
Anthony. But she goes on:

> With regard to careers outside the home, delegated
> motherhood can be a threat, for I believe that our
> integrity as a nation is bound up with the home. Good
> children are not the product of mothers who prefer
> money or fame to the well-being of their families. Did
> not the Apostle Paul, in his ardour to afford Timothy a

steadying influence, bid him remember his mother, Eunice, and his grandmother, Lois?

We dare not regress by suppressing intelligence or forbidding women to be useful. But steadfastness, conscience, and the capacity for sacrifice, on the part of both parents, are basic to good family relations which, in turn, are basic to the well-being of society in general.

Women have the right to be useful, in the highest sense. That is a term that would have been familiar to the feminists at the turn of the century. The lecture halls would have resounded with talk of usefulness, and it is a high moral quality Moore attached to poetry: 'These things are important,' she said of certain qualities in poetry ('hands that can grasp, eyes | that can dilate | hair that can rise | if it must'), '. . . because they are useful.'[4] But the ambition to be useful and the call to make a sacrifice—to sacrifice all hope of marriage, for instance, if a useful career was in prospect—all this is rather foreign to the feminism of the Seventies. I suspect that the reason why Elizabeth Bishop bit that student's head off was that she foresaw that the young women might have difficulty in recognizing Moore's attitudes (as they came to be) as having anything to do with real feminism. How could a feminist base an argument on St Paul's epistle to Timothy?

Marianne Moore was, however, a feminist, a sometime socialist and Irish nationalist, a tennis player till her fifties, and a lifelong Presbyterian. She was born in 1887, in a suburb of St Louis, Missouri, a year before T. S. Eliot, whose grandparents knew hers. Her father went briefly mad after losing his fortune in the development of a smokeless furnace, and her mother, Mary Warner Moore, left him before Marianne was born. Later, John Moore recovered sufficiently to work for the mental home in which he had been placed, but Mrs Moore never had anything to do with him again, and lived in dread of his family bringing pressure for a reconciliation. Moore's biographer, Charles Molesworth, has concluded that Moore never enquired after her father.[5] Mrs Moore kept quiet on the subject, excepting on one of the many occasions when her older child, her son Warner Moore, looked like marrying against her wishes. Then, in a manoeuvre that strikes one as almost wicked, she told Warner that, before proposing to the girl in question, he had better inform her that there was a history of mental instability in the family, which might possibly reassert itself. The engagement didn't go ahead.

Moore published a poem in 1924 called 'Silence'. It goes:

> My father used to say,
> 'Superior people never make long visits,
> have to be shown Longfellow's grave
> or the glass flowers at Harvard.
> Self-reliant like the cat—
> that takes its prey to privacy,
> the mouse's limp tail hanging like a shoelace from its
>   mouth—
> they sometimes enjoy solitude,
> and can be robbed of speech
> by speech which has delighted them.
> The deepest feeling always shows itself in silence;
> Not in silence, but restraint.'
> Nor was he insincere in saying, 'Make my house your
>   inn.'
> Inns are not residences.[6]

This is a fictional father. The first part is attributed in a later note to a Miss A. H. Homans. The last—'Make my house your inn'—comes from a biography of Burke. Randall Jarrell took issue with the notion that 'The deepest feeling always shows itself in silence,' countering it with the line from Spenser 'Entire affection hateth nicer hands.' One has to say, though, that he is here taking issue with one of the profound tenets of

Moore's aesthetic—and he is at liberty to do so. Meanwhile we may note that Moore has, in her imagination, equipped herself with a father who was a connoisseur of the behaviour of 'superior people'—much like her mother, and like what her brother became—a muscular Christian with an alert sense of the social standing of the members of his congregation.

Mrs Moore took her children to live in Carlisle, Pennsylvania, where she worked as a teacher in the Metzger Institute, a high school for young women founded by a local Presbyterian, which was where Marianne received the free education which prepared her for Bryn Mawr in 1905. And that was where the feminism was drummed into her, by Bryn Mawr's redoubtable president, M. Carey Thomas, a figure of such unimpeachable rectitude that she was able to live with her lady friend on campus. 'When I was in college,' Moore later wrote, 'feminism was not taken for granted; it was a cause. It was ardently implemented and fortified by Miss Thomas.'[7] And this feminism was derived from the Quaker tradition, which, as Moore understood it, had always given women the right of leadership. Bryn Mawr was supposed to prepare women to exercise that right.

There is more than one view whether it did so. Moore herself always remained an enthusiast. H.D., who was Moore's college contemporary but left early, having flunked her exams, believed that Bryn Mawr destroyed the spirit of women. Here she is, in barely disguised fictional form, in Bryher's novel *West*. Bryher, born Annie Winifred Ellerman, the daughter of a rich English shipping magnate, met Moore in New York with H.D., shortly after Moore and her mother had moved to Greenwich Village. Her novel was published in 1925, but is set very much in the aftermath of the First World War. *West* is a short novel, and much of it is concerned with the question: What is wrong with Anne Trollope, the Marianne Moore character? 'Why is she so averse to life?' Helga, the H.D. character, says:

'She has never achieved any liberty of conscience. It may be some inherent weakness of will, but I think it is due to her education. None of the girls who did the full course at that college achieved anything. They were bled of will, Anne among them, and set in a groove until they feel unhappy out of narrow limits.'

'Modern education is mechanical, crushing. When it ought to be the way to independence.'

'I dare not think of it. And Anne is really a young Byzantine scribe, all strange colours and angles. Her mind was a bright mosaic.'

'Mosaic is not marble.'

'That would not matter. But her thoughts are still now, they glitter but have no roots. No roots in the earth. It is too late to alter her, I fear. Only I ask always and always, why did no one save her from being blunted?'

'I should like to cut her hair short, her wonderful hair. Break her from everything to which she is accustomed and plunge her into a new world.'

'Too late now. She would only run back to her rock the moment your back was turned, but I wish you could try the experiment.'[8]

And later in the book Bryher complains of 'Anne' that 'duty serves for an emotional outlet'.

That Quaker sense of duty to prepare a woman for a leading role in the world was one of the many duties which to us would appear civic but which had their origin in religion. The duty to end slavery was one, and thereafter to work to improve the lot of the Negro. Another, which affected Moore closely, was the duty to educate the Indians. You have to remember she was born only a decade after the Indian campaigns of 1874–6. A familiar figure in Carlisle when she was growing up was General Richard Henry Pratt, who had fought alongside Custer. 'Both General Pratt and his wife were very substantial and imposing', Moore remembered much later. 'They were romantic figures, always dashing up with their horse and carriage.'

Pratt had been left in charge of a group of Plains Indian prisoners, in St Augustine, Florida, where they arrived 'half naked, wild, dirty, vermin-ridden, crazed and in chains'. He taught them English and turned them into a tourist attraction, selling bows and arrows to support themselves. He inserted several of the cleverest of them into Negro schools, and then sent this vanguard back to the West, to persuade the chiefs to send their children to Carlisle to be educated at the establishment he had founded in the old barracks there, the United States Indian Industrial School. Shortly before the Moore family arrived in Carlisle, someone had undertaken to coach the Indians in the complexities of American football, and they soon began to produce a series of remarkable players like Isaac Seneca, Brave Thunder, Fast Bear, and Frank Mt Pleasant. The greatest of all was Jim Thorpe, whom she taught, along with his wife, Ida Miller, who was in her typing class.

All this comes from an article in *Sports Illustrated*, in 1960, written by an astonished Robert Cantwell, who went to interview the aged Marianne Moore about her recent poem in honour of the Brooklyn Dodgers, and discovered that not only did she remember all the great Indian athletes of the early part of the century—she had their photographs in her scrapbooks. They had been the heroes of her youth. Carlisle, having at first been apprehensive at the thought of housing the Indian School, started to take an intense local pride in it, as it began to produce the most extraordinarily successful football teams. The school received insufficient help from the Indian Bureau in Washington, but it began to be able to boost its finances from the high gate receipts at its games.

Graduating from Bryn Mawr in 1909, Moore went first to business college. The Presbyterian circles in which she moved were particularly keen on the Indian School, and when the commercial English teacher left, and no replacement could be found, she was offered the job. It was more than a job, it was part of a cause. It involved not just the teaching of secretarial skills and maths, but also instruction on how to read and draw up a contract—the idea being that when the Indian students went back to the reservation they could avoid being cheated.

Moore remembered pacing up and down the tennis court, wondering whether to take the job. Her maths, her simple arithmetic, wasn't up to it, and she was about to decide against. But then her brother Warner reminded her of her duty, and how their mother had taught to support their education, and Moore accepted her duty. 'It never occurred to me to be afraid', she told her solicitous interviewer.

'You know, before I began teaching there was a good deal of uneasiness because it was feared I wouldn't be able to control the Indian boys. But the athletes helped me. The only trouble came from some neurotic Sioux and Ojibway boys who were a long way from home and lonely and unhappy—there were a few sadists too but there was really no difficulty. The Indians had great behaviour and ceremony and were exceedingly chivalrous and decent and cooperative and . . . idealistic. There are always recalcitrants in every school, who won't work and won't accept discipline, and an Indian recalcitrant, a Sioux, perhaps tends to be more recalcitrant than the average. A boy, like Joseph Loud Bear, who was the worst . . .'

'Was he a Sioux?'

'Oh he was certainly a Sioux—very much a Sioux. But I had so little trouble it was hardly worth mentioning. My biggest bugbears were mending typewriters and minding the evening study hours.'[9]

2

In *West*, the Moore character gives a rather grimmer version of this period, saying it was a man's job, which was why she stuck it for four years, and implying that it interfered with any attempt at a cultural life, and left her little time to write or think. In fact it was during the years between Bryn Mawr and the move to New York in 1918 that a great part of her oeuvre was composed. In her entire career, on Molesworth's calculation, she published 190 poems; from 1910 to 1917, 51. In addition there are at least 74 unpublished poems in the Rosenbach archive in Philadelphia, of which around half date from the Carlisle period.

It amounts to this: that if we wanted to hold in our minds a single image of the poet Marianne Moore, it should not be the grand old lady of the New York scene so much as the earnest young woman cycling daily to the old Federal Barracks in Carlisle, her head full of George Moore, George Bernard Shaw, and Edward Gordon Craig, a woman desperately isolated but aware of her isolation and aware of what she would do if only she was not obliged by her brother to stick at the teaching. And while she is handling these pioneering generations of homesick Ojibway, or recalcitrant Sioux, all the time she is conducting a passionate conversation with one author or another—Yeats, Moore, Shaw, Tagore. These internal dialogues spill out into her poetry, so much of this, in this period, is written in the second person. This one, 'To a Strategist', was originally called 'To Disraeli on Conservatism':

> You brilliant Jew
> You bright particular chameleon, you
>   Regild a shabby fence.

They understood
Your stripes and particoloured mind, who could
　　Begrudge you prominence

And call you cold!
But when has prejudice been glad to hold
　　A lizard in its hand—

A subtle thing?
To sense fed on a fine imagining
　　Sound sense is contraband.[10]

The poetic form is seventeenth century in flavour, but the
imagery and the feel are the thing that is already original
Moore—startling at first to find a Jew so starkly addressed and
immediately compared to a lizard, a comparison which one
might expect to be insulting but which seems to be a compliment, even if conservatism is not itself being recommended.
Here, in another chameleon poem, called originally—and this
is by no means Moore's longest title in this period—'You Are
Like the Realistic Product of an Idealistic Search for Gold at
the Foot of the Rainbow':

Hid by the august foliage and fruit of the grapevine
twine
　　your anatomy
　　　　round the pruned and polished stem,
　　　　　　chameleon.
　　　　　　Fire laid upon
　　　　　an emerald as long as
　　　　the Dark King's massy
one,
could not snap the spectrum up for food as you have
done.[11]

This by the way is one of the poems Moore reprinted, then suppressed, and then, as late as 1959, reprinted again (with the title 'To a Chameleon') in the volume *O to Be a Dragon*. In the same volume she seems to have felt the need for a little padding, since she resurrects two of her student efforts from Bryn Mawr, calling one 'I May, I Might, I Must':

> If you will tell me why the fen
> appears impassable, I then
> will tell you why I think that I
> can get across it if I try.[12]

This is something for inscribing in a Victorian photograph album, and is a poor piece of versification. The other is 'A Jellyfish':

> Visible, invisible,
>   a fluctuating charm
> an amber-tinctured amethyst
>   inhabits it, your arm
> approaches and it opens
>   and it closes; you had meant
> to catch it and it quivers;
>   you abandon your intent.[13]

This is more promising (both of these poems date from 1909), as long as you can sympathize with someone wanting to catch a jellyfish by hand in the first place. Reading it, however, 'with a perfect contempt for it', we find its rhythms too trivially neat. One wonders how many people, reading the *Complete Poems*, think that Moore must have been going off, as a poet, when she wrote these; in fact she was only going off, as an editor of her own work, when she republished them in this way.

But the chameleon poem I quoted is on a different level, and it is one of those early lessons in syllabics which delight in contrasting very long with extremely short lines. The first and last lines are of thirteen syllables, the second and penultimate have one syllable apiece, which must have felt like a heady experiment when she first made it. But in revised form she breaks the thirteen-syllable line in two, and spoils the symmetry. Originally, the poem was a variant on Herbert's 'Easter Wings', although set out horizontally (which is the way Herbert's poem sometimes was and might have been in the edition Moore used).

One wonders whether the early title of 'To a Chameleon' was the first, or whether there has been some suppression of subject, just as the poem to Disraeli was first announced as 'To Disraeli on Conservatism', and only later 'To a Strategist'. In the same way 'To Browning' becomes 'Injudicious Gardening', while 'To Bernard Shaw: A Prize Bird' becomes a much quieter 'To a Prize Bird', with the Shaw connection banished to a footnote.

> You suit me well; for you can make me laugh,
> nor are you blinded by the chaff
>   that every wind sends spinning from the rick.
>
> You know to think, and what you think you speak
> with much of Samson's pride and bleak
>   finality; and none dare bid you stop.
>
> Pride suits you well, so strut, colossal bird.
> No barnyard makes you look absurd;
>   your brazen claws are staunch against defeat.[14]

Who would have guessed that this was a portrait of Shaw had the fact not been disclosed so confidently on first publication? But I suppose it does as well as a portrait of a type, or indeed as a portrait of an animal, which is what I always thought Moore's poems were until advised otherwise. Moore has this knack of looking confident at any given moment: it is what has happened before the given moments that betrays the lack of confidence. Here is the beginning of 'Picking and Choosing' as it appeared in the first collection:

> Literature is a phase of life: if
> one is afraid of it; the situation is
>   irremediable; if
> one approaches it familiarly,
> what one says of it is worthless.
>   Words are constructive
> when they are true; the opaque allusion—
> the simulated flight

> upward—accomplishes nothing.
>   why cloud the fact
> that Shaw is selfconscious in the
> field of sentiment but is
> otherwise rewarding? That James is all that
> has been
> said of him but is not profound?

By *Observations* (1924), the first volume of her poems over which Moore had editorial control, this confident judgement (James is not profound, and nobody thinks he is) has been changed to:

> That James is all that
>   has been
> said of him, if *feeling* is
>   profound?

and in the *Complete Poems*:

> that James
> is all that has been said of him.[15]

The revision has pushed the judgement in the direction of meaninglessness.

I mention this not to denigrate her total achievement, but rather to argue that admiration should focus on the admirable, and that, when a line seems to be meaningless or untrue, it is not a bad idea to entertain the possibility that it is indeed meaningless or untrue. 'Complexity is not a crime,' says Moore 'but carry it to the point of murkiness | and nothing is plain.' Well, some of the poetry is plain murky, to the point when it comes as a relief to read Moore's definition, in her review of Wallace Stevens's *Ideas of Order*: 'Poetry is an unintelligible unmistakable vernacular like the language of the animals—a system of communication whereby a fox with a turkey too heavy for it to carry, reappears shortly with another fox to share the booty.'[16]

We expect Moore to be accurate, and I do not think it is pedantic to pause over 'England | with its baby rivers and little towns, each with its abbey or its cathedral' and say—but if they have cathedrals they must be cities. We expect her to tell the truth. But in her *Paris Review* interview she says she likes end-stopped lines. She could have fooled me. She says she never 'plans' a stanza. She couldn't have written 'Virginia Britannia' if this were true. Asked about her extensive use of quotation she says:

I was just trying to be honourable and not to steal things. I've always felt that if a thing has been said in the very best way, how can you say it better? If I wanted to say something and somebody had said it ideally, then I'd take it but give the person credit for it. That's all there is to that.[17]

That's *not* all there is to that because her quotations are often modifications of her sources, and by her own admission elsewhere there are times when what looks like a quotation turns out not to be. Here is what she said in a letter to Schofield Thayer: 'As for quotations, sometimes I think a triviality gains a little weight by quotation marks; for the most part, however, my quotations have authority.'

We do well, then, not always to believe the utterances of Marianne Moore, or at least to entertain the idea that she often spoke for effect: words were a kind of finery which she loved to put on. Facts were adored for their glamour rather than their factuality. Meaning often had to be patient, waiting till after the fireworks to be fed. And the poet revealed herself in her displays rather than in her nakedness. No one saw her naked. No one was invited to.

3

I have said that she did not always lead a sheltered life, but she certainly never (after Bryn Mawr) left home, and the home she never left was a force field of astonishing strength and durability. Mrs Moore was as interested in writing her son's sermons as she was in her daughter's poems. Perhaps more so. Warner Moore, as we have seen, made several attempts in the direction of marriage. He had some impulse to escape. But when he finally made his own choice of wife Mrs Moore does not appear to have felt that she was in any way vanquished. Early on, she tried to demand that his child should be taken from its mother, Constance, to be educated by Marianne and herself. She did not succeed, but she does seem to have succeeded in obliging Warner to be dishonest with his wife when he came to see his mother and sister.

The way that I have just expressed that implies that my sympathies are with Constance. So they are. She had married into a family that spoke in a complicated code of nicknames and gender games. When they were not calling each other Rat or Mole, Marianne was depicting herself as Warner's brother, or Mrs Moore was referring to Marianne as Warner's Aunt Fangs. It is touching that Warner, after his marriage, thought that the nicknames should end, and he wrote to his mother suggesting that from now on she might feel happier calling him Warner, as if he recognized that he had grown up.

We may be sure that Marianne watched Warner's rebellion and drew her own conclusions from it. She rebelled as a writer, against the poetic conventions of the day. She rebelled as a suffragette. She was suspected by the Inspector of the Indian School of fomenting dissent, as a socialist, against conditions there—and the Indian School itself was a great-hearted gesture of protest against Washington and the Indian Bureau. She rebelled—she considered herself a pure Celt with the Irish, writing 'Sojourn in the Whale' after the Easter Rising, in which she prophesies the triumph of Irish nationalism and, in the same analogy, the cause of women. Ireland, she says,

> you have lived on every kind of shortage.
>   You have been compelled by hags to spin
>   gold thread from straw and have heard men say:
> 'There is a feminine temperament in direct contrast to
>   ours
> which makes her do these things. Circumscribed by a
>   heritage of blindness and native
>   incompetence, she will become wise and will be
> forced to give in.
> Compelled by experience, she will turn back;
> water seeks its own level':
>   and you have smiled, 'Water in motion is far
>   from level.' You have seen it, when obstacles
>   happened to bar
> the path, rise automatically.[18]

She is no stranger to rebellion, but she never seems to have rebelled against her mother. Rather she seems to have thought that, if a rebellion was in the offing, it would be better to have mother on her side.

It is clear that Bryher and H.D., when they saw her in New York, found this resolute staying at home to constitute some kind of spiritual defeat—although what would have constituted victory is not made clear, and this is one of the many weaknesses of *West*, viewed either as a novel or (what it really is) a journal. Bryher never makes it entirely clear why it should be so important for the Moore figure to come with the two women to Europe. One supposes that there was an erotic agenda, at least at the level of wishful thinking. Bryher never criticizes Mrs Moore, and she never expressly identifies Mrs Moore as the problem. But what she does do is have the Marianne figure, whenever she is becoming evasive, talk in the first-person plural:

'But remember New York is my Europe at the moment,' Anne continued. 'Even the way the lights burst out on a winter night is still an amazement to us. We have not been here ten months. . . . Here we have no neighbours but a few friends. And the cinema posters. Occasionally we visit a play. And in themselves the streets are romantic films. The shot bright silks in the windows. The furs one sees. Soft grey and black stripes like a tent. The Museum. Sometimes a circus.'

Anne leaned back with her red hair uncovered and eyelashes as fair as flax from which the gold is drained. 'There is at the Zoo a spotted lynx in a cage with markings on its fur as delicate as those frost traces . . .'

'Stop it. You ought to be ashamed of yourself. Sitting here like a pterodactyl on a rock afraid to move. I suppose you feel if you fell off into the sea you'd enjoy swimming among the anemones. And you don't quite approve of the freedom of the air. . . . You don't deserve a mind if you're so scornful of it. Cut the masochism out and come with us to England.'[19]

To which after some evasion the reply is: 'Our eagerness to be with you is keen. But we have not yet explored the possibilities of New York.' Bryher asks her readers why women should be reactionary.

Why did Anne carry it on, this Victorian tradition? Was it because America was in the throes of a somewhat similar period that she preferred a spirit already stamped with history. Yet it clashed with her hair, that curious bright forest colour, with her body that had the austere outline of a young scribe's form, and with the bright mosaic of her mind. Her shrinking from life was a masculine rather than a feminine gesture. It was the boy's denial of himself for some misunderstood ideal.

There follows a passage which makes one wonder how Moore ever continued her warm relationship with Bryher:

To create meant to live. Anne had denied life so long she was afraid now to leave her barriers behind. Duty served her for emotional outlet. She had shrivelled into an outline on a rock. . . . hard lines from which the colour had been stripped.[20]

It was all very well for Bryher. Her problem was simply that her father, Sir John Ellerman, thought that it was dangerous for his rich young daughter to gad about the world alone. Bryher solved this in 1921 by proposing to Robert McAlmon, a young writer with ambitions to go to Paris to visit Joyce. Her proposal was that she would share part of her allowance with McAlmon, and they would from time to time pay joint visits to her family, and that was that. McAlmon was bisexual, and innocent enough not to see that he would end up humiliated by this arrangement when Bryher tired of him. He accepted and the couple married on St Valentine's Day before sailing to Europe. Moore knew enough about the arrangement to know that it was a marriage of convenience—she apparently discussed it as such in a letter to Amy Lowell. But quite what Marianne *knew* or wanted to know about H.D. or Bryher, and the reasons why it suited them both to be married, is a matter for conjecture. She didn't find Bryher's marriage very romantic, as she told her friend, the homosexual novelist Glenway Wescott.

4

When they arrived in Europe, H.D., Bryer, and McAlmon, apparently without telling her, put together a collection of Moore's poems and published it with the Egoist Press. This was her first appearance in book, or rather pamphlet, form. Meanwhile Moore had been provoked into thought about the subject of marriage, and two years later Wescott's boyfriend, Monroe Wheeler, published Moore's poem on this subject as number three of the magazine *Manikin*, together with an appreciation of Moore's poetry by Wescott himself. 'Marriage' begins in that cool manner for which Moore was already well known among a small circle of connoisseurs:

> This institution,
> perhaps one should say enterprise
> out of respect for which
> one says one need not change one's mind
> about a thing one has believed in,
> requiring public promises

of one's intention
to fulfil a private obligation:
I wonder what Adam and Eve
think of it by this time,
this fire-gilt steel
alive with goldenness;
how bright it shows—
'of circular tradition and impostures,
commiting many spoils,'
requiring all one's criminal ingenuity
to avoid![21]

These lines could never have been written by a devout
Catholic daughter of a domineering Catholic mother, because
to Catholics marriage is a sacrament, whereas to Protestants
there are only two sacraments—baptism and communion. But
even so, even from a devout Presbyterian, the mockery comes
as a bit of a surprise, and we remember that every line by
Moore went first past her mother's censorship and was later
offered to her minister brother, who considered each of her
poems as a spiritual event.

It must surely be that neither Moore nor her mother saw
the mockery as in any way directed against the Church, and it
seems likely that they would both have understood a part of
the sarcasm to be directed at women like Bryher and H.D.,
who entered into matrimony and at the same time preached
freedom. One remembers too that Mrs Moore had fled her
marriage, and had seen to it that she was never drawn back
into it either by her husband or by any obligation to his
family. She had taught rather than go to them for money.
Elizabeth Bishop, whose mother also went mad, wrote much
later in a letter to Anne Stevenson: 'That generation took
insanity very differently than we do now, you know. . . . After
a couple of years, unless you cured yourself, all hope was
abandoned.'[22] We do not know what Mrs Moore had been

through, and I certainly do not want to suggest that she was hypocritical as a Christian, in the matter of her marriage. But one can at least see that there might have been something welcome, something understandable too, in her daughter's decision to use all her 'criminal ingenuity' to avoid marriage, if that was the form her rebellion was now taking.

> Below the incandescent stars
> below the incandescent fruit,
> the strange experience of beauty;
> its existence is too much;
> it tears one to pieces
> and each fresh wave of consciousness
> is poison.
> 'See her, see her in this common world,'
> the central flaw
> in that first crystal-fine experiment,
> this amalgamation which can never be more
> than an interesting impossibility . . .[23]

Is marriage no more than an interesting impossibility? She backs away from interpretation later, appending the note which calls this poem 'statements that took my fancy which I tried to arrange plausibly', but what took her fancy includes an allusion to Godwin in 'a very trivial object indeed', which the notes expand to 'Marriage is a law, and the worst of all laws . . . a very trivial object indeed.' And we go back to the spirit of Bryn Mawr with the lines:

> She says, 'Men are monopolists
> of "stars, garters, buttons
> and other shining baubles"—
> unfit to be the guardians
> of another person's happiness.'[24]

Which is sourced to Miss M. Carey Thomas:

> Men practically reserve for themselves stately funerals, splendid monuments, memorial statues, membership in academies, medals, titles, honorary degrees, stars, garters, ribbons, buttons and other shining baubles, so valueless in themselves and yet so infinitely desirable because they are symbols of recognition by their fellow-craftsman of difficult work well done.[25]

And among the titles that men had, by some mechanism, contrived to reserve to themselves was, by and large, the title of poet. If *West* is to be believed, even Moore, in her mid-thirties, did not believe that it would be as a poet that she made her name. She thought her poems might be appended to some prose work. She also thought, and told her would-be liberators as she saw them off, that she would come into her own as a writer at the age of 45. And in this you could well say she was right. She published her first full collection, *Observations,* in 1924, then nothing for the next seven years. But then, as I said, came 'The Steeple-Jack', 'The Jerboa', 'Virginia Britannia', 'The Pangolin', and so forth, the poems which we take as most typical today.

It is easy sometimes to miss the touches in the major poems that show that the young radical spirit has not been suppressed. But she means us to pause and think what she calls the Negro, in 'Virginia Britannia', 'inadvertent ally and best enemy of tyranny'. And the insistent returnings to Indian themes in the same poem are a strategic reminder that, as she puts it, 'no imperialist, | not one of us, in taking what we | pleased—in colonizing as the | saying is—has been a synonym for mercy'. Just as the steeple-jack's sign will turn out, in that poem, to be an emblem for hope, so 'Virginia Britannia' resolves into a child's intimation of glory. But we are only going to be allowed that resolution if we understand that there were losers as well as winners in the fashioning of that glory. 'The redskin with the deer- | fur crown, famous for his cruelty, is not all brawn | and animality.'[26] The understatement is supposed to be weighty. The young Moore and the older Moore are alike in this—they are great respectors of other peoples. And while it may be true to say that this respect for others has its origins in religion, still we cannot help noticing how many people belong to the same congregation and somehow manage to miss out on that respect.

She was a modernist, and I always find it touching to think of her gravitating to New York and going straight to Steiglitz's gallery, where she sees Steichen's photograph of her hero (but she can hardly have been to the theatre at the time) Edward Gordon Craig. She tells Stieglitz that she had not known there was anything like it. Stieglitz replies: 'Well, there *is* nothing like it.' Somehow she made sure that the same could be said of her.

7. The Many Arts of Elizabeth Bishop

I

'Feminists!' growled Elizabeth Bishop, and vaguely scandalized her 1977 Harvard class.[1] But in the same year, the year of the publication of *Geography III*, she also wrote a letter in which she claimed to have been a feminist since the age of 6, and she was not being contradictory. It was in the late Seventies that, for instance, some creative writing classes introduced segregation of the sexes, so that the women could express their thoughts more freely. But what Bishop meant by feminism in her own case was to be taken on equal terms with any man— not to be (as she would have felt) downgraded into the category of woman poet, not to write about 'women's experience' but to take universal experience as her legitimate range, not to be used, politically, as a member of some kind of sisterhood. When she was young, she refused to be published in a group anthology when she understood that they needed a woman to make up the numbers. Throughout her life she refused to be part of all-women anthologies, and toward the end of it (she died in 1979) she might well have resented a pressure to solidarize. She was a poet's poet (John Ashbery called her a writer's writer's writer) but she was not a lesbian's lesbian.

She cherished a long-standing aversion to a certain generation of women writers, what she called the 'our beautiful old silver' school of female writing: Virginia Woolf, Katherine Anne Porter, Elizabeth Bowen, Rebecca West. She thought they were always boasting about how 'nice' they were: 'They have to make quite sure that the reader is not going to misplace them socially, first—and that nervousness interferes with what they think they'd like to say.'

On the other hand she did read Woolf, and she did admire her. In a conversation with George Starbuck, also in 1977, she warmly recommended Woolf's *Three Guineas*, calling it Woolf's first feminist book and saying that Woolf was rather badly treated when she wrote it.[2] Actually *Three Guineas* is the sequel to *A Room of One's Own*, written in 1938, in letter form, supposedly in answer to a man's question: 'How in your opinion are we to prevent war?' The answer may strike us as strange, since it involves a disquisition on the history of women's colleges in Cambridge. Quentin Bell calls *Three Guineas* 'the product of a very odd mind'. He says her friends were silent about it, or if not silent, critical, and that Keynes was angry and contemptuous.[3]

But Woolf was right to point out that 'How in your opinion are we to prevent war?' is a question that has a puzzling implication when put to a woman, in a world in which women are excluded from higher education, and therefore from the kinds of decisions which contribute to either the prevention or promulgation of war. One supposes that Woolf's friends, in 1938, felt that this was the wrong time to raise the feminist issue, that the history of women at Cambridge was beside the point. But one remembers that Bishop, at the beginning of the Second World War, has a similar feeling to Woolf's: she felt that the war was a product of male aggression, a male ritual squabble. This is the sentiment behind the early section of the poem 'Roosters':

> Cries galore
> come from the water-closet door,
> from the dropping-plastered henhouse floor,
>
> where in the blue blur
> their rustling wives admire,
> the roosters brace their cruel feet and glare

with stupid eyes
while from their beaks there rise
the uncontrolled, traditional cries.

Deep from protruding chests
in green-gold medals dressed,
planned to command and terrorize the rest,

the many wives
who lead hens' lives
of being courted and despised;

deep from raw throats
a senseless order floats
all over town. A rooster gloats . . .[4]

and so on. Reading it aloud decades later, at the request of
friends, Bishop suddenly realized it sounded like a feminist
tract, and she tells George Starbuck it wasn't originally
intended to sound that way at all. He replies, alluding to radical feminists of the day, 'I'm afraid it's their banner now.
You'll never get it away from them.' Later Bishop admits that
the first part of 'Roosters' is a feminist tract in a way, although
she hadn't thought of it that way.[5]

   She hadn't thought of it that way because the quite distinct
second part of the poem, beginning with the lines 'St. Peter's
sin | was worse than that of Magdalen', draws the whole poem
in the direction of a religious meditation: the rooster symbol-
izes Peter's denial of Christ, but even that denial—Bishop
points out—was eventually forgiven. So the rooster (this is the
prayer contained in the poem) may come for us to symbolize
forgiveness.

   The bird had first suggested itself as a symbol of war
because Picasso had used it that way in _Guernica_. Her mind
had been on war—the poem was completed in 1940—rather
than on male agression as such. 'St. Peter's sin' was a sin of the
spirit, and it must be that the author of the poem identifies

with Peter as a sinner. She must see herself as capable of the denial of Christ and she must meditate on Peter's tears of repentance. This is a poem, like Edith Sitwell's 'Still Falls the Rain' and Marianne Moore 'In Distrust of Merits', in which the poet sees the war that is taking place as a consequence of her own sinful condition.

This religious feeling of responsibility—quite foreign to Virginia Woolf—is expressed by Marianne Moore in the final lines of her meditation on the war in full swing (published in *The Nation* in May 1943):

> Hate-hardened heart, O heart of iron,
>   iron is iron till it is rust.
> There never was a war that was
>   not inward I must
> fight till I have conquered in myself what
> causes the war, but I would not believe it.
>   I inwardly did nothing.
>   O Iscariotlike crime!
>   Beauty is everlasting
>   and dust is for a time.[6]

Sitwell's poem, inspired by the air raids, is explicitly Christian in meaning, but gives a dramatic place for the struggle with belief. She introduces the two famous lines from the last soliloquy of Marlowe's Faustus:

> Then—O Ile leap up to my God: who pulls me doune—
> See, see where Christ's blood streames in the
>   firmament.[7]

Moore's poem, by contrast, stems from firm belief—it is based on her mother's views about the war: it was her mother who thought she must 'fight till I have conquered in myself what | causes war'.

Bishop's poem is one of religious sensibility, but not necessarily belief. As far as one can tell, religious belief was by then,
for Bishop, a thing of the fairly distant past, but religious
sensibility stayed with her in her poetry, partly because
among her models were Herbert and Crashaw. The model for
the stanza form of 'Roosters' is a Crashaw poem, although a
secular rather than a sacred one ('Wishes: To his supposed
Mistress'). Readers of David Kalstone's book, *Becoming a Poet*,
will remember that in the notebook which Bishop took along
for her first meeting with Moore in 1934, the notebook into
which she had copied out 'The Jerboa' from a magazine,
counting the syllables and marking the rhymes, she wrote out
a list of topics of conversation, whose first column reads:

> Modern Bestiary
> Hopkins
> Crane? Stevens
> H & H poetry
> 17th century
>   connection with prose
>   Herbert
>   Crashaw
> how would she read its rhythms[8]

The presence of Hopkins on the list reminds us that a year
before the meeting with Moore, Bishop, then a student at
Vassar, had been engaged on a 'Hymn to the Virgin', a wild
sacred parody of Hopkins's sprung rhythm:

> Pull back the curtains, quick now that we've caught the
>   mood of
> Adoration's shamefaced exposé and brazen knee-
>   bending.
> Let's see, and quick about it, God's-beard, Christ's
>   crown, baby-brood of

Strawberry ice-cream colored cherubim, tin-winged,
    ascending
Chub-toes a'dangle earthwards . . .[9]

And so on. Preposterous ('Ah! wouldst not, wax-faced, wooden-bodied one, have us to worship us—wise?'), intoxicated with Hopkins's eccentricities, and yet at the same time— I think—moved to mirth, even in this 'Hymn to the Virgin'. One can forget, if one is too used to associating Bishop with great sorrow, borne over the years, that there was also, at Walnut Hill and Vassar, the girl with the fund of jokes and stories, who translated Aristophanes in her senior year, wrote school plays in which she played the villain, who went with their friends to a poetry reading by Edna St Vincent Millay— a solemn occasion for which Millay wore a long artistic robe and clutched at a curtain, while Bishop and her friends sat doubled up with laughter; the Bishop whose occasional rude rhymes stuck in the memories of her college contemporaries, who set her friends tasks like 'Use the word menstruation in a sentence' and supplied her own example: Mariners 'feeding their pilot biscuits to the gulls: *menstrurations* all over the beach'.

There is no great distance between the student admiring Hopkins and the aspiring poet bent double with laughter at his effects, borrowing sprung rhythm to take it for a run around the block, trying it out, putting it through its paces, jamming the gears. And the baroque subject of the parody—a moth-eaten, flyblown, gimcrack idol of the Virgin—is as it happens the kind of thing she would later become very familiar with in South America. The tattiness of it, the 'Long-hardened candle-grease about Thy feet', seems to have been observed by the mature poet.

An imperfect object, cheaply made, and the focus of intense feeling. Decades later, in her obituary tribute to a woman writer she really *did* admire, Flannery O'Connor,

Bishop recalled a present she had once sent O'Connor from Brazil:

> a cross in a bottle, like a ship in a bottle, crudely carved with all the instruments of the passion, the ladder, pliers, dice, etc., in wood, paper, and tinfoil, with a little rooster at the top of the cross. I thought it was the kind of innocent religious grotesquery she might like . . .

The response was gratifying. O'Connor wrote back:

> If I were mobile and limber and rich I would come to Brazil at once after one look at this bottle. Did you observe that the rooster has an eyebrow? I particularly like him and the altar cloth a little dirty from the fingers of whoever cut it out . . . I am altogether taken with it. It's what I'm born to appreciate.[10]

And there is something inborn in Bishop's appreciation of such objects. It was not learned elsewhere, as far as I can see. It came to her naturally, along with a memory which, she believed, went back to the days of her learning to walk. Here is the description of the doll in the short story 'Gwendolyn':

> She had a large wardrobe, which my Aunt Mary had made, packed in a toy steamer trunk of green tin embossed with all the proper boards, locks, and nail-heads. The clothes were wonderful garments, beautifully sewn, looking old-fashioned even to me. There were long drawers trimmed with tiny lace, and a corset cover, and a corset with little bones. These were exciting, but best of all was the skating costume. There was a red velvet coat and a turban and muff of some sort of moth-eaten brown fur, and, to make it almost unbearably thrilling, there was a pair of laced white glacé-kid boots, which had scalloped

tops and a pair of too small, dull-edged, but very shiny
skates loosely attached to their soles by my Aunt Mary
with stitches of coarse white thread.

The looseness of the skates did not bother me. It went
very well with the doll's personality, which in turn was
well suited to the role of companion to an invalid. She
had lain in her drawer so long that the elastic in her
joints had weakened; when you held her up, her head
fell gently to one side, and her outstretched hand would
rest on yours for a moment and then slip wearily off.[11]

Just as the sick child loves the doll for its imperfections, so the
writer gets worked up into a crescendo of excitement over the
expressiveness of the weakened elastic.

People sometimes wrote that Bishop's poetry would be
unthinkable without the example of Marianne Moore. I don't
quite understand what they mean. It's not the influence I
would deny, only the unthinkability. There are aspects of the
later Auden that are unthinkable without the influence of
Moore. But considering that Bishop's career was nurtured by
Moore, and that the early poetry was submitted to her for
vetting, that Moore had a powerful, definite personality and
that Moore's mother was even more powerful and definite,
what is remarkable about Bishop's first volume of poems is,
rather, its independence of spirit.

That vetting process lasted from 1934 to the well-docu-
mented incident in 1940 when Moore and her mother sat up
late into the night rewriting 'Roosters', ruining the Crashaw
stanzas, purging the language of what they considered
obscenities while inadvertently introducing double entendres
by substituting the word cock for rooster. This was when
Bishop put her foot down, and insisted that she could and
would use the word water-closet in her poem. And so the
vetting ceased. Bishop never submitted poems to them again.[9]

But it would be wrong to take the 'Roosters' episode as

emblematic of the relationship between Moore and Bishop. Moore knew something about her own limitations, as well as something about Bishop's. In 1938 Bishop submitted her story 'In Prison' for a competition by the *Partisan Review*, and failed to tell Moore first. Moore wrote: 'It was very independent of you to submit your prize story without letting me see it. If it is returned with a printed slip, that will be why.' But when the story won the contest, Moore was first impressed and then moved to offer the following interesting advice:

> I can't help wishing you would sometime in some way, risk some unprotected profundity of experience; or since no one admits profundity of experience, some character-istic private defiance of the significantly detestable. Continuously fascinated as I am by the creativeness and uniqueness of these assemblings of yours—which are really poems—I feel responsibility against anything that might threaten you; yet fear to admit such anxiety, lest I influence you away from an essential necessity or partic-ular strength. The golden eggs can't be dealt with theo-retically, by presumptuous mass salvation formulae. But I do feel that tentativeness and interiorizing are your danger as well as your strength.[13]

One could hardly call this tone of voice dirigiste. Moore obvi-ously understood the difference between directing and influ-encing.

And Bishop had approached Moore, as we have seen, not as a blank slate begging to be scrawled on but as a rather well-read young woman whose teacher found her, generally speak-ing, quite capable of attending to her own education. She is said to have known Wallace Stevens's *Harmoniun* by heart. That would be a large amount of Stevens. Crashaw, as we have seen, was already a hero, and Herbert—from whom Moore herself had borrowed—had a special significance for Bishop.

Later, writing to Moore from Key West, she causes her friend some amusement by saying: 'The Negroes have such soft voices and such beautifully tactful manners—I suppose it is farfetched, but their attitude keeps reminding me of the *tone* of George Herbert: "Take the gentle path," etc.' When she is tempted by psychoanalysis, prompted by the publication of a book by Karen Horney on self-analysis, she says: 'I had infinitely rather approach such things from the Christian viewpoint myself—but the trouble is I've never been able to find the books, except Herbert.'[14]

This notion that Herbert might be used as a guide to self-analysis reflects Bishop's taste for the baroque and the emblematic in literature. She claimed to have modelled her poem 'The Weed' on Herbert's 'Love Unknown', which tells a long story in which the poet offers his lord and master his heart, placed in the middle of a bowl of fruit, only to have his heart rejected as being foul and hard and dull. The story proceeds like a dream and ends on an interpretation. Bishop's 'The Weed' imitates the sombre, dreamy procedures of its model, and describes how an emblematic weed (never interpreted) grows through the heart (of the poet). In the last lines, which sound just like Herbert, the weed speaks:

'I grow,' it said,
'but to divide your heart again.'

Division being for Bishop what affliction was for Herbert.

'17th century | connection with prose | Herbert | Crashaw'— the topics she had jotted down to discuss with Moore. It is illuminating, I think, to read in Brett Millier's biography that she took extensive notes from a book called *The Baroque Style in Prose* by M. W. Croll, and that she associated this style with Hopkins. She thought that Hopkins and the Baroque sermonists attempted to portray 'not a thought, but a mind thinking', to 'dramatise the mind in action rather than in repose'. Meaning the word mind in its broadest sense—the feeling mind, feeling its way to thought.

The lines from 'The Weed'—

> A few drops fell upon my face
> and in my eyes, so I could see . . .
> that each drop contained a light,
> a small, illuminated scene; . . .[15]

—are all that remains of a beautiful passage from Bishop's notebooks of 1934–5 (quoted by Kalstone):

> The window this evening was covered with hundreds of long, shining, drops of rain, laid on the glass which was covered with steam on the inside. I tried to look out, but could not. Instead I realized that I could look into the drops, like so many crystal balls. Each bore traces of a relative or friend: several weeping faces slid away from mine; water plants and fish floated within other drops; watery jewels, leaves and insects magnified, and strangest of all, horrible enough to make me step quickly away, was one large drop containing a lonely, magnificent human eye, wrapped in its own tear.[16]

This kind of prose poem is a form for which Bishop had an affinity—a form favoured by the Surrealists (it is a pity Bishop did not translate more of Max Jacob's essay in the genre). 'The Weed' is a grafting of Surrealism onto the baroque. 'The Monument' is another of these mysterious emblem-poems, but, while a prose poem such as 'The Hanging of the Mouse' has an exact analogy in the proto-surrealism of Grandville, Bishop was never the fanatical or doctrinaire Surrealist. Her poetic temperament was too eclectic for that, and she was not, like the typical Surrealist, an attention-seeker.

Praising Lowell's poems much later, Bishop wrote of 'that strange kind of modesty that I think one feels in almost [everything] contemporary one really likes—Kafka, say, or Marianne, or even Eliot, and Klee and Kokoschka and Schwitters. . . . Modesty, care, *space*, a sort of helplessness but determination at the same time.'[17] To this admittedly somewhat various list one might add Joseph Cornell, who enjoyed a long correspondence with Marianne Moore, inspired at least two collages by Bishop herself, and she translated a poem about Cornell by Octavio Paz. And then there is Alexander Calder, who was a friend of Bishop's Brazilian lover, Lota de Macedo Soares; one of Calder's mobiles is depicted in a painting Bishop did of the house she shared with Lota in Petrópolis.

2

It is clear from William Benton's introduction to *Exchanging Hats: Paintings*, which reproduces forty of Bishop's watercolours and other artworks, that many of her paintings are missing or may be expected to turn up out of the blue. Bishop's paintings and collages were undertaken in a strictly non-professional spirit, but they are the works of an intelligent amateur of painting, and it is not wishful to compare the spirit in which they are done with the sensibility that produced the poems. *Interior with Extension Cord* shows the awkward and inadvisable way in which an electrical cable has been stapled up one bedroom wall, diagonally across the ceiling and down the other side in order to provide light at a narrow table, an improvised workplace. One could easily imagine a poem featuring the same objects we view from (one guesses) the bed: the cheval mirror, the Van Gogh print in the rather overpowering frame, the view through the door straight out onto a meadow or mountain, the ink bottle, and is it a glue pot? Somehow the extension cord would work all these together into some significance: 'modesty, care, *space*, a sort of helplessness but determination at the same time.'

The watercolour of a chandelier and its shadow across the ceiling, surely another view from the bed, in one of those New York hotels in which Bishop spent many miserable months—the catalogue says the picture 'seems untypically arty'—has surely something to do with the impulse that wrote 'Sleeping on the Ceiling':

> It is so peaceful on the ceiling!
> It is the Place de la Concorde.
> The little crystal chandelier
> is off, the fountain is in the dark.
> Not a soul is in the park.[18]

In the poem, Bishop imagines an inverted world, in which the chandelier becomes a fountain in the middle of a quiet square. In order to leave this area, one has to 'go under the wallpaper | to meet the insect-gladiator': the square with its fountain is safe and quiet, while the world outside is full of fearful challenges. In the picture, the chandelier is on, and casts a multiple shadow, which is no doubt what caught the poet's fancy.

The stoves in many of the paintings are much as we imagine the stove in 'Sestina' to have been. It was called Little Marvel. In a pen and ink sketch, two stoves are called 'Ideal' and 'Fancy'. *E. Bishop's Patented Slot-Machine* is a depiction in watercolour of another Cornell-like device, an amusement arcade machine with a handle for the visitor to turn. Labels in the picture show how the handle activates an electric coil which sends a spark to a crystal ball, which hangs in the air between what appears to be a ship and its invented reflection. Perhaps Alice Methfessel, Bishop's friend and the owner of many of her surviving artworks, knows what the joke or private significance of this was. *Anjinhos* ('Angels') is one of the Cornell-type boxes, provoked by a young girl's drowning in Rio de Janeiro and featuring assorted beach flotsam, two butterflies, and a background of printed paper angel heads—more of the 'innocent religious grotesquery'.

Bishop never made any attempt to sell her paintings, and only two were exhibited during her lifetime (in 1971, at the Arts Club of Chicago, in an exhibition of paintings by writers). To judge by the inscriptions on those that have survived, it would seem that generally speaking these objects were made as gifts for friends: that was as far as the ambition went, and that seems fine. The graphic style pays homage to primitive painting, and among the anthology of quotations at the end of *Exchanging Hats* there is this from 'The USA School of Writing'—(a memoir written in 1966). Bishop is talking about the hopeless authors with whom she had to deal when working for a shady writing school.

> There seemed to be one thing common to all their 'primitive' writing, as I suppose it might be called, in contrast to primitive painting: its slipshodiness and haste. Where primitive painters will spend months or years, if necessary, putting in every blade of grass and building up brick walls in low relief, the primitive writer seems in a hurry to get it over with. Another thing was the almost complete lack of detail. The primitive painter loves detail and lingers over it and emphasizes it at the expense of the picture as a whole. But if the writers put them in, the details are often impossibly or wildly inappropriate, sometimes revealing a great deal about the writer without furthering the matter in hand at all. Perhaps it demonstrates the professional writer's frequent complaint that painting is more fun than writing.[19]

There seems to be a great deal of the essential Bishop in these observations: her writing has a knack for detail which the paintings sometimes share. *Tombstones for Sale*, the cover illustration on the *Collected Prose*, in which the tombstones leaning against a shed are indeed inscribed 'For Sale', is a good example. Some people have reacted against this sort of thing in Bishop's art as a whole. Thom Gunn, writing about the earlier poems, found they were

> like playthings, fresh-painted, decorative, charming, original, and yet tiny. She specialized, Alice-like, in altering the scale of things. 'Cirque d'Hiver' was *about* a toy— a mechanical horse with a dancer on its back. 'The Man-Moth' and 'Sleeping on the Ceiling' were only two of her childlike fantasies. . . . No wonder she admired Paul Klee, whose work I once remember seeing unkindly characterised by John Richardson as, after all, rather *twee*.[20]

Gunn afterward revised his judgement upward: it certainly seems wrong to dismiss her poem 'The Man-Moth' as childlike, although it is true that it has its origins in whimsy. The Man-Moth is a newspaper misprint for the word mammoth. In order to accommodate this imaginary being, the poet invents a lunar cityscape. In this world, inhabited only, it seems, by Man and the Man-Moth (who spends most of his time underground), the Man-Moth is fearful because 'He thinks the moon is a small hole at the top of the sky, | proving the sky quite useless for protection', and he must investigate this hole (even though he dreads the climb, and believes that if he reaches the hole he will be forced through it against the light) because 'what the Man-Moth fears most he must do'. So far from being 'tiny', 'The Man-Moth' has a scale that reaches from the individual to the planet, to the terrifying source of fatal light: it is a touchstone of pure poetic invention. Like the prose poem from the notebook mentioned earlier, it ends in a tear: and indeed it must have its origin in that same 1930s notebook, which contains a line about the third rail:

> The *third rail* is almost worth some sort of prose poem.
> Running along silently, as insincere as poison—

This in 'The Man-Moth' becomes:

>   Each night he must
> be carried through artificial tunnels and dream
>   recurrent dreams.
> Just as the ties recur beneath his train, these underlie
> his rushing brain. He does not dare look out of the
>   window,
> for the third rail, the unbroken draught of poison,
> runs there beside him. He regards it as a disease
> he has inherited the susceptibility to. He has to keep
> his hands in his pockets, as others must wear
>   mufflers.[21]

The third rail, the electric rail, is therefore the temptation to commit suicide.

Bishop herself knew very well the fear of having inherited some self-destructive susceptibility. She began drinking at about 21, and she suffered from a crippling shame at her alcoholism. Looking back at her childhood, she engaged in a recurrent speculation about what went wrong for her, at what moment. This speculation led to one great story, 'In the Village' (about the moment her mother was taken away to be hospitalized for ever), which Robert Lowell condensed into a poem, 'The Scream'. In England we got to know the poem well (it is in *For the Union Dead*) long before we saw Bishop's story, which had not been collected, and certain lines strike us as pure Lowell, although they are actually pure Bishop:

At the fitting
the dressmaker crawled on the floor,
eating pins, like Nebuchadnezzar
on his knees eating grass.[22]

In the States, Bishop decided to revive this story by placing it between the two sections of *Questions of Travel* (1965) in the same way as Lowell had printed '91 Revere Street' in the American edition of *Life Studies* (1959). That mixture of prose and poetry in a volume has been successfully imitated since, but because of the complex publishing history not everyone knows that Lowell's prose memoirs (as well as the poem 'The Scream') owe a literary debt to Bishop.

Lowell was a good borrower—'Skunk Hour' could hardly be a handsomer tribute to 'The Armadillo'—whereas Bishop was less successful when she tried to borrow from Lowell's *Life Studies* for her never-finished poem 'A Drunkard'. A part of this is published by David Kalstone, and another part in Brett Miller's biography. It describes the Salem fire of 1914, when Bishop was 3, staying with her mother at Marblehead across the water. The child watches the fire from her crib, suffers an intense thirst, and cannot get her mother's attention. The next day, she walks along the beach and finds a woman's black stocking. Her mother tells her to put it down. Bishop felt that since that day, that reprimand, she had 'suffered from abnormal thirst'. It is another attempt to point at a fatal moment, just like 'In the Village', but she never managed to make the moment—the fire, the thirst, the reprimand—convincingly fatal. But that fatalism can be found elsewhere in the poetry, lurking for instance in one of the 'Songs for a Colored Singer':

Lullaby.
Let nations rage,
let nations fall.

> The shadow of the crib makes an enormous cage
> upon the wall.[23]

She seems really to have believed in that cage, that shadow of
the crib, that fate, and to have counted her periods of happiness as a kind of remission.

8. *Lady Lazarus*

Marianne Moore, Elizabeth Bishop, Sylvia Plath—Bryn Mawr class of 1909, Vassar class of 1934, Smith class of 1955—educated women of three generations who achieved pre-eminence as poets. That sounds like a circumlocution. It *is* a circumlocution, but I feel I would betray the spirit of Moore and Bishop by calling them women poets. Moore was a feminist, a suffragette, a Woman Who Did.[1] Although it appears that marriage was never one of her ambitions, as it happened she made the sacrifice or renunciation common among the women of her time who had a vocation. She was drawn to the avant-garde, to modernism in the making, and if her creations are strikingly impersonal (so that even a poem purportedly about her father turns out to be a fiction), that impersonality is not untypical of modernism. Utterly original, she was at once recognizable as a fellow spirit and equal among the likes of Pound, Eliot, Stevens, and Williams.

With Bishop we encounter an emancipated woman for whom men were only intermittently 'in the picture'. In her youth she formed friendships with strikingly intelligent non-marrying women and their mothers: Margaret Miller and her mother, Louise Crane and hers, Marianne Moore and hers. She had modest independent means, and therefore was not subject to either of the conflicts between marriage and writing or between writing and a career—her desperate conflicts lay elsewhere. Plath, when she came to read Bishop, did so with great admiration: her 'fine originality, always surprising, never rigid, flowing, juicier than Marianne Moore, who is her godmother'.[2] Godmother is a good term for that relationship.

But who would Bishop's peers have been? They would have been anyone of her generation, regardless of gender. Robert Lowell was the poet she measured herself against, whose triumphs sometimes inspired in her a sort of generous envy and sorrow.

With Plath we encounter a character entirely different, a 'poetess' who sees herself as the latest in a line of poetesses, and who sees her rivals in art as women. It is hard to imagine Moore or Bishop writing anything remotely like this:

> Arrogant, I think I have written lines which qualify me to be The Poetess of America (as Ted will The Poet of England and her dominions). Who rivals? Well, in history Sappho, Elizabeth Barrett Browning, Christina Rossetti, Amy Lowell, Emily Dickinson, Edna St. Vincent Millay—all dead. Now: Edith Sitwell and Marianne Moore, the ageing giantesses, and poetic godmother Phyllis McGinley is out—light verse: she's sold herself. Rather: May Swenson, Isabella Gardner, and most close, Adrienne Cecile Rich—who will soon be eclipsed by these eight poems: I am eager, chafing, sure of my gift, wanting only to train and teach it—I'll count the magazines and the money I break open by these eight poems from now on. We'll see . . .[3]

She was in her mid-twenties when she wrote this, and the eight poems which she had just completed were nowhere near her best, or her most celebrated, work. But as her reputation grew she retained the self-description: on 12 October 1962, the same day she composed 'Daddy', she wrote in a letter to her mother:

> I miss *brains*, hate this cow life, am dying to surround myself with intelligent, good people. I am a famous poetess here—mentioned this week in *The Listener* as one of

the half-dozen women who will last—including
Marianne Moore and the Brontës!

Later the same month, in a letter to her brother and his wife:

> The critic of the *Observer* is giving me an afternoon at his
> home to hear me read all my new poems! He is *the* opin-
> ion-maker in poetry over here, A. Alvarez, and says I'm
> the first woman poet he's taken seriously since Emily
> Dickinson! Needless to say, I'm delighted.[4]

Less than four months later Alvarez wrote her epitaph in
the *Observer*, beginning: 'Last Monday, Sylvia Plath, the
American poetess and wife of Ted Hughes, died suddenly in
London.' Alvarez thought of Plath, he says, 'as the most gifted
woman poet of her time'.

It was a heartfelt tribute, and not an inappropriate one. If
he had written such a thing about Bishop, it would have
ruined her day, but he had told Plath as much to her face, and
it made hers. Neither Moore nor Bishop seems to have traced
her ancestry back through a line of women poets. Bishop only
began taking an interest in Dickinson in the 1950s, when
Thomas H. Johnson's edition appeared, and even then, after
she had decided that Dickinson was 'about the best we have',
she could add, in a letter to Lowell, 'she does set one's teeth
on edge a lot of the time, don't you think?'[5] Moore admired
Dickinson but was never remotely influenced by her. Moore's
influence, which she had to escape, was Swinburne. Ezra
Pound had shared the same early infatuation.

Plath's ambition to be a poetess, seen from one angle, looks
of a piece with the general conventionality of her upbringing
and early attitudes. In contrast to Bryn Mawr, where feminism
was part of the fabric, Smith was presided over by men, and
aimed to produce the kind of woman who would be a credit
to her husband.

At Smith one used one's education as a training for typing up one's husband's Ph.D. thesis—that was the standard fate of the alumnae. There is nothing odd about the obsession with marriage revealed by Plath's college journals. That was in line with the prevailing ideology of the institution, and was the theme of Adlai Stevenson's commencement address at Plath's graduation in 1955. The highest vocation of women, this divorcé said, was to achieve a creative marriage, to be, as Nancy Hunter Steiner remembered it:

> thoughtful, discriminating wives and mothers who would use what we had learned in government and history and sociology courses to influence our husbands and children in the direction of rationality. Men, he claimed, are under tremendous pressure to adopt the narrow view: we would help them resist it and we would raise children who were reasonable independent, and courageous.[6]

Clearly not everyone in the class of '55 was of the same opinion. Here is Polly Longsworth:

> I think we were in a condition of mind where we could hear Stevenson's message—we'd been brought up on it—but not believe it. Smith had told us differently for four years. It was only later, when his words began to prove true, that most of us got mad.[7]

But Nancy Hunter Steiner remembers that

> The speech was eloquent and impressive and we loved it even if it seemed to hurl us back to the satellite role we had escaped for four years—second-class citizens in a man's world where our only possible achievement was a vicarious one.[8]

A part of the surprise with Plath is to move backward from an initial reading of *Ariel* to the discovery of this markedly conventional background. With Bishop, you feel that everything is of a piece—the poet at college was remembered for having done interesting, faintly rebellious things, like discovering that although cars were restricted there was no rule against going for rides in a horse and buggy, or like keeping a jar of Roquefort beside her bed and dosing herself with cheese last thing at night in order to render her dreams more vivid. With Plath one discovers that, when there was a rebellion at Smith against the campus warm weather uniform of Bermuda shorts, button-down collars, and loafers, and some girls pioneered a look that consisted of bare feet and tattered jeans, not only was Plath on the side of Bermuda shorts—she tried hard to bring the rebels before the Honor Board 'for infringement of rules'. With Plath people seemed to have remembered details such as the matching white and gold luggage with which she arrived at Cambridge; and for some reason what sticks in my mind is the 'lovely pink knitted suit dress' which her mother brought along for her daughter's wedding, 'intuitively never having worn' and which Plath decided would do very well for her.

I know that we are told that both the letters to her mother and the journals are edited in different ways by interested parties to bring out certain characteristics at the expense of others. But no amount of editing can have been responsible for this striking dividedness—Plath's conventional attitudes and shallow ambitions on the one hand, and the other self with its burning, mysterious purpose. When Plath talks of herself as a woman poet, as a poetess, this may seem un-hip even for its day. But it is possible to look at that un-hip self-definition, and see it as a source of her success.

To return to the point made at the start of Chapter 6, that something has held women back when it came to the writing of poetry, and that the problem might well have been something to do with the antiquity and prestige of the art; it might easily be that, like it or not, there was something masculine in the archetype of poet, with which it was difficult for a woman to come to terms. Dickinson found another archetype: she became a sibyl and the price she paid for that was that she lived in a bottle. Moore armed herself as a rebel, and she found, as so many women have done, that eccentricity can be a good friend for a while, although in the end it exacts its price. The eccentric, in the end, invites you not to take her too seriously.

We can never tell whether Moore, a personality apparently perfectly protected, a connoisseur of every sort of armour, achieved what she did only at the cost of the suppression of what might be taken as womanly. We know that Bishop was extremely cautious with the deployment of her private life and tenderest emotions in her poetry. Bishop wrote some love lyrics, most notably that beautiful 'The Shampoo' (which went round the magazines for two years before finding a publisher). One could guess, though, that she would have liked to develop more in this direction.

Plath had the right—of course she had the right—to abjure the male archetype, to try to revive the meaning of the word poetess. It was bound to be disruptive. There is analogy between poets and priests here. A woman priest is not simply a woman exercising equal rights to do the same job as a man. Her doing that job profoundly changes the nature of that job, in the way that a woman becoming an engine driver does not. Women becoming priests upsets the symbolism of the whole religion or sect. In the Christian context, that is why it is so impossible to use the word priestess, since it comes with such a rich freight of pagan significance. It is odd that the word should retain its power to shock: 'I dropped in at the butchers and there was our new priestess'—one would immediately suspect she was consulting the innards of a chicken. When Bishop and her college friends sat doubled up with laughter at

Edna St Vincent Millay's reading, with Millay wearing her long robe and clutching a curtain, what the girls were laughing at was a poetess, a woman imagining that a poetess must be something like a priestess.

And that takes us straight to Plath's terrifying last poem, 'Edge':

> The woman is perfected.
> Her dead
>
> Body wears the smile of accomplishment,
> The illusion of a Greek necessity
>
> Flows in the scrolls of her toga,
> Her bare
>
> Feet seem to be saying:
> We have come so far, it is over.
> Each dead child coiled, a white serpent,
> One at each little
>
> Pitcher of milk, now empty.
> She has folded
>
> Them back into her body as petals
> Of a rose close when the garden
>
> Stiffens and odors bleed
> From the sweet, deep throats of the night flower.
>
> The moon has nothing to be sad about,
> Staring from her hood of bone.
>
> She is used to this sort of thing.
> Her blacks crackle and drag.[9]

The woman in the robe, in the scrolls of her toga, has achieved, at last, her ambition: death for her, death for her children.[10] And since this is a scene which has about it the illusion of Greek necessity, of *anangke*, we think of tragedy and we think of Medea, who kills her two children. *Medea* is a tragedy about a divorce: Jason had married Medea after she helped him gain the Golden Fleece; but he left her for Glauce, the daughter of the king of Corinth; Medea is a witch, and when she is faced with exile she tricks Jason into allowing her two children to go to Glauce with presents, saying she wishes Glauce to look after the children. Glauce accepts the presents and agrees to look after the children, but when she puts on the crown and robe that Medea has sent her she becomes engulfed in flames and dies; when her father finds her and embraces her, he dies as well; then Medea, to complete her revenge, kills her two children with a sword.

That is the story according to Euripides (whom the Corinthians are said to have bribed with fifteen talents of silver to tell it in this way). In Plath's version Medea seems to have poisoned their milk (Medea was known for her skill as a poisoner), and you may feel, as I do, that the expression 'each little pitcher of milk' actually refers to the woman's breasts. The woman has poisoned her children with her own milk, and now there is no more of it, but the children are folded back into the woman's body, she has taken them back from Jason. And then the 'sweet, deep throats of the night flower' from which odours bleed remind us of a possibility of slitting one's throat as well.

The petals of the rose closing is a piece of poetic invention: some flowers close at night but most roses don't. What the feet seem to be saying, 'We have come so far', may or may not contain an echo of Bishop's 'Cirque d'Hiver': 'we stare and say, "Well, we have come this far." '

Three generations are involved (Moon/mother, the Priestess, and her children) if you will accept Plath's 'The Moon and the Yew Tree' as a gloss on 'Edge':

> The yew tree points up. It has a Gothic shape.
> The eyes lift after it and find the moon.
> The moon is my mother. She is not sweet like Mary.

> Her blue garments unloose small bats and owls.
> How I would like to believe in tenderness—
> The face of the effigy, gentled by candles,
> Bending, on me in particular, its mild eyes.[11]

But she can't believe in the gentleness of the Virgin Mary, the image of the sweet attentive mother, attentive to her in particular. She can't believe, in the next stanza, in the blue saints in the church. There is only the moon, her indifferent mother—bald and wild, 'white as a knuckle and terribly upset'. And the yew tree whose message is blackness and silence—presumably the ever-withdrawing husband/father of so many poems.

The message to the mother from 'Edge'—'The moon has nothing to be sad about. . . . She is used to this sort of thing'—would seem to be something Plath could easily decipher: why be sorry, you've seen all this before, you knew what distress I was in, you did nothing to help me. The message to the husband depends on whether you believe 'Edge' to be a suicide note, or something he might come to read when she was still alive. When printed in *Ariel* the poem was placed second to last, presumably in order to reduce the sense that, with this poem, Plath was signing off. The *Collected Poems* has it chronologically last, after the utterly different 'Balloons' (written on the same day). There is no way of settling the question of Plath's intentions during the last days of her life. If she had not died but had published the poem (as she was doing with other poems of that time, including ones that were distressing to Hughes), then it would have carried an implied threat: maybe I should settle this by dying, and take the children with me. As it turned out, the poem says to us all, I contemplated this solution, and it seemed beautiful to me, it would have left me fulfilled, 'perfected', smiling.

It is a lyric moment of utter pitilessness—pitiless towards her estranged husband, her mother, her children—and pitiless too, it had better be said, towards herself. Medea does die in the Euripides version. Plath did not kill her children. Instead, she left milk and bread beside their cots. The window was open, the door sealed against the gas. One can only call the poem 'Edge' the product of a deranged mind if one is constantly claiming that the mind can be deranged in other ways but remain capable of exerting the kind of artistic control we see here displayed.

Plath was angry, very angry, but anger does not of itself produce lyric poetry, and one can see, from time to time during the *Ariel* period—by which I mean not the last days with their legendary productivity but the three years or so over which the total contents of the volume were produced— what happened when rage got in the way, as in 'Words heard, by accident, over the phone':

> O mud, mud, how fluid!—
> Thick as foreign coffee, and with a sluggy pulse.
> Speak, speak! Who is it?
> It is the bowel-pulse, lover of digestibles.
> It is he who has achieved these syllables.
>
> What are these words, these words?
> They are plopping like mud.
> Oh god, how shall I ever clean the phone table?

Which line suddenly introduces a bathetic, suburban tone. The poem ends by addressing the phone itself, which has offended by being party to the adultery the poet has suspected:

> Muck funnel, muck funnel—
> You are too big. They must take you back![12]

To be fair, this poem was not included on Plath's own list for *Ariel*, nor was the flood of bad imitations of Plath caused by her bad or self-parodying poems. The bad imitators were inspired by the best of Plath, poems in which one would hesitate to change a word.

I include 'Lady Lazarus' among these, and it is interesting in connection with 'Lady Lazarus' to see how far back the idea for this poem goes, at least to Cambridge in 1956, in a passage where she records her plan to visit a psychiatrist that week 'just to meet him, to know he's there'. The passage, with its recollection of her nervous breakdown and suicide attempt in 1953, continues:

And, ironically, I feel I need him. I need a father. I need a mother. I need some older, wiser being to cry to. I talk to God, but the sky is empty, and Orion walks by and doesn't speak. I feel like Lazarus: that story has such a fascination. Being dead, I rose up again, and even resort to the mere sensation value of being suicidal, of getting so close, of coming out of the grave with the scars and the marrying mark on my cheek which (is it my imagination?) grows more prominent: paling like a death-spot in the red, windblown skin, browning darkly in photographs, against my grave winter pallor.[13]

This comes from what is labelled an excerpt from a letter to her Cambridge friend, Richard Sassoon—the journals contain these drafts of letters, imaginary or intended for real is not clear. The date is 19 February 1956. The dating of 'Lady Lazarus' is 23–9 October 1962. I mention this only to give emphasis to the length of gestation. The myth of Plath's brief, fierce month or so of inspired utterance followed by—with its illusion of a Greek necessity—her suicide is a particular hindrance to understanding her writing, which is after all the produce of a very early vocation as a writer, relentlessly pursued.

If I say I wouldn't want a word changed in 'Lady Lazarus', that implies that I wouldn't want the Nazi/Jewish imagery dropped, that I do not think it an illicit appropriation. Well, that is my position, in the case of this poem and with 'Daddy'. I follow Jacqueline Rose in this.[14] Plath was highly conscious of her German/Austrian heritage. She was born in 1932, and was therefore perfectly able to sense the significance of the Second World War. Her father was a first-generation Prussian immigrant. Her mother was a second-generation Austrian, who, Anne Stevenson tells us, spoke German at home until grade school, when 'patriotic Americans were frequently vicious to German-speaking immigrants during the First World War'.

Fear of persecution for being a German, whether her own fear or her mother's, would certainly be part of her heritage. And if she thought of her father as a persecuting figure (rightly or wrongly is not the issue), and she knew her father to be a Prussian, then it is by no means far fetched for her to have wondered whether she might not be a Jew (either from her mother's side or through simply not knowing quite what a Jew was, but knowing they were being persecuted). Or if 'Daddy' enacts an argument with her father, an old argument the point of which is that she has not been able to end it, it is part of the nature of this argument that she should insult his ghost in a way that is supposed to provoke him into having a go at her, thereby proving her point.

Plath's imitators and admirers may have given these procedures a bad name.

> Hitler entered Paris the way my
> sister entered the room at night,
> sat astride me, squeezed me with her knees,
> held her thumbnails to the skin of my wrists and
> peed on me, knowing Mother would
> never believe my story.

Which seems to imply that Hitler merely peed on Paris. Or:

THE DEPARTURE
(to my father)

Did you weep like the Shah when you left? Did you
    forget
the way you had had me tied to the chair, as
he forgot the ones strapped to the grille
in his name? You knew us no more than he knew
    them,
his lowest subjects, his servants, and we were
silent before you like that, bowing
backwards, not speaking, not eating unless we were
told to eat, the glass jammed to our
teeth and tilted like a brass funnel in the
soundproof cellos of Teheran . . .[15]

But it is a long way from this impertinent harangue back to
the argument of 'Daddy'. Rose quotes from Plath's journals a
passage dated 28 December 1950, written at the time of the
composition of the short story 'The Shadow'.

My present theme seems to be the awareness of a complicated guilt system whereby Germans in a Jewish and
Catholic community are made to feel, in scapegoat fash-
ion, the pain, psychically, the Jews are made to feel in
Germany, by the Germans without religion. The child
can't understand the wider framework. How does her
father come into this? How is she guilty for her father's
deportation to a detention camp?[16]

The story differs slightly from the outline, but the point
remains that the child does not know what is going on, what
her parents are arguing about. She is taunted with having a
German father, something she hotly denies, only to be
informed by her mother that her father is indeed a German
citizen, and that he has been 'asked' to go and live in a

detention centre. This is unfair. But God has permitted it to happen.

The 'Shadow' of Plath's title is a character in a radio programme whose regular opening line was: 'Who knows what evil lurks in the hearts of men? The Shadow knows, heh, heh, heh, heh.' Despite her mother's protectiveness, the child is beginning to learn about evil, about the Japanese prison camps, about the war. But the partial understanding is the clue to the drama.

'Daddy' was intended by Plath to be, like 'The Shadow', a poem of partial understanding, a short story in the form of a poem. We have a problem in reading it like that, because the energy of the emotion is so strong we feel it must come direct from the author herself, who must be talking about her historic father and (in an aside about the vampire who said he was you) her actual husband. That is the objection raised by Seamus Heaney in *The Government of the Tongue*:

> A poem like 'Daddy,' however brilliant a *tour de force* it can be acknowledged to be, and however its violence and vindictiveness can be understood or excused in the light of the poet's parental and marital relations, remains, nevertheless, so entangled in biographical circumstances and rampages so permissively in the history of other people's sorrows that it simply overdraws our rights to its sympathy.[17]

This is courteously put, as ever, but if you accept that Plath was drawing on the history of her own people's sorrows (that is to say, German immigrants in America), a great part of the objection disappears. And, by the way, although there is no justification for rampaging permissively, a great deal of art is made from the history of other people's sorrows.

Plath saw her task as one of discovery: How should a *woman* write poetry? In one of her letters to her mother, just before her marriage, she says:

I know that within a year I shall publish a book of 33 poems which will hit the critics violently on some way or another. My voice is taking shape, coming strong. Ted says he never read poems by a woman like mine; they are strong and full and rich—not quailing and whining like Teasdale or simple lyrics like Millay; they are working, sweating, heaving poems born out of the way words should be said.

And in the same letter, speaking apparently of her newly acquired certainty of self (acquired by listening to Beethoven with Ted Hughes) she says: 'I know this with a sure strong knowing to the tips of my toes, and having been on the other side of life like Lazarus, I know that my whole being shall be one song of affirmation and love all my life long.'[18] This prophecy proved false. One turns to the poems she includes with the letter—'Firesong', 'Strumpet Song', and 'Complaint of the Crazed Queen'. They sound like this:

> Sweet salts warped stem
> of weeds we tackle towards way's rank ending;
> scorched by red sun
> we heft globed flint, racked in veins' barbed
>   bindings . . .[19]

Or in the contemporary 'Ode for Ted':

> Loam-humps, he says, moles shunt
> up from delved worm-haunt;
> blue fur, moles have; hefting chalk-hulled flint
> he with rock splits open
> knobbed quartz; flayed colors ripen
> rich, brown, sudden in sunglint.[20]

They sound, in other words, as if written by someone who has just fallen in love with Ted Hughes. Which is fair enough, for a while. The question when Plath begins to sound like Plath will divide people. I hear lines in *The Colossus*, rather than whole poems. In the first part of 'Two Views of a Cadaver Room':

> In their jars the snail-nosed babies moon and glow.
> He hands her the cut-out heart like a cracked
>   heirloom.[21]

Or in that long-popular poem 'Metaphors', the one that begins 'I'm a riddle in nine syllables', and its contemporary—although it was not collected until 1981—'Electra on Azalea Path', perhaps it is the subject, the daughter's visit to the father's grave, rather than the tone of voice that identifies the authorship:

> I am the ghost of an infamous suicide,
> My own blue razor rusting in my throat.
> O pardon the one who knocks for pardon at
> Your gate, father—your hound-bitch, daughter, friend.
> It was my love that did us both to death.[22]

Or in 'The Manor Garden' when 'The pears fatten like little buddhas'.

But tone of voice, like handwriting, or like the graphic style that tells you the name of the artist immediately, whatever purpose it has been put to—that tone of voice for me comes, not at some high-pitched shriek or in some angry gesture, but in a poem dated some time in 1960 when the poet seems to have lost faith in her work hitherto. It is called 'Stillborn'—and continues a strong memory of the cadaver room already mentioned.

> These poems do not live: it's a sad diagnosis.
> They grew their toes and fingers well enough,

Their little foreheads bulged with concentration.
If they missed out on walking about like people
It wasn't for any lack of mother-love.

O I cannot understand what happened to them!
They are proper in shape and number and every part.
They sit so nicely in the pickling fluid!
They smile and smile and smile and smile at me.
And still the lungs won't fill and the heart won't start.

They are not pigs, they are not even fish,
Though they have a piggy and a fishy air—
It would be better if they were alive, and that's what
    they were.
But they are dead, and their mother near dead, with
    distraction,
And they stupidly stare, and do not speak of her.[23]

Marianne Moore's published letters do not include the
'queerly ambiguous, spiteful letter', as Plath puts it, in which
Moore responded for a request for a reference. 'Don't be so
grisly', said Moore, and 'You are too unrelenting'.[24]
Certainly 'Stillborn' is an unrelenting poem—fifteen lines of
development for a single metaphor—and that a metaphor
taken from common speech. It must have been galling to
Plath that both Auden and Moore at different periods, when
shown her work, disliked it, while both of them liked and
encouraged Ted Hughes's. But Moore was the reader when
Knopf took on *The Colossus*, from which she said that the
seven-part 'Poem for a Birthday' should be cut (as being too
like Roethke).

Grisly and unrelenting, yes, but I was looking out for that
particular tone of voice, the tone she acquires when she is not
yelling (and most of the time she is not yelling). 'These poems
do not live: it's a sad diagnosis.' 'The tulips are too excitable,
it is winter here | Look how white everything is, how snowed-
in.' 'This is the light of the mind, cold and planetary. | The

trees of the mind are black. The light is blue.' This is the quiet, quizzical Plath, the Plath of the 'Bee Meeting' and 'The Arrival of the Bee Box' poems.

The earliest English readers of Plath knew little about her, except perhaps that she was American and that she was sad, had died young. We thought of her, perhaps, as the latest Faber poet. I don't think we really found her shocking—that makes us perhaps sound naive, or uncaring, but I don't think the meaning or significance of 'Daddy' or 'Lady Lazarus' had really sunk in. The poems were thrilling, incantatory, taboo-breaking. Yet they were poems, not yet manifestos.

In the early Seventies, Elizabeth Bishop came back to the States after a long absence and the suicide of her friend, Lota de Macedo Soares. She found she was going to have to do something to perk up her poetry readings. She wrote: 'It seems impossible, just to get up and read after what's been going on lately—I shd. have a small combo at least.'[25] What had been going on lately was Anne Sexton, reading to an accompaniment of a rock-and-roll band named after her best-known poem, 'Her Kind'. Germaine Greer, without mentioning the combo, quotes a description of Sexton's act:

> Anne Sexton liked to arrive about ten minutes late for her own performance: let the crowd work up a little anticipation. She would saunter to the podium, light a cigarette, kick off her shoes, and in a throaty voice say, 'I'm gonna read a poem that tells you what kind of poet I am, what kind of woman I am, so if you don't like it you can leave.' Then she would launch into her signature poem:
>
> > I have gone out, a possessed witch,
> > haunting the black air, braver at night;
> > dreaming evil, I have done my hitch

over the plain houses, light by light:
lonely thing, twelve-fingered, out of mind.
A woman like that is not a woman, quite.
I have been her kind.

I have found the warm caves in the woods,
filled them with skillets, carvings, shelves,
closets, silks, innumerable goods;
fixed the suppers for the worms and the elves:
whining, rearranging the disaligned.
A woman that is misunderstood.
I have been her kind.

I have ridden in your cart, driver,
waved your nude arms at villagers going by,
learning the last bright routes, survivor
where your flames still bite my thigh
and my ribs crack where your wheels wind.
A woman like that is not ashamed to die.
I have been her kind.[26]

The invention of the woman poet as evil or threatening archetype, witch, harridan, maenad, Medea, the doomed woman,
was not Sylvia Plath's single-handed achievement, but *Ariel* is
one of those books whose effect could not have been
predicted, may not even have been wished. Goethe never
wanted young men to commit suicide after reading *The
Sorrows of Young Werther*. As long as Plath thought of herself as
Lazarus, she might desire a life of affirmation and love. But
Lazarus was a man. When she thought of herself as Lady
Lazarus, the serial suicide, the phoenix-like, man-eating
priestess poetess, she subscribed to a fatal vocation. At the
beginning of Chapter 6 I cited an opinion of Germaine Greer,
that it was when women stopped adoring poetry they began
to be able to write it. Here's another, that 'Even when the
poetry is good, perhaps especially when the poetry of self-
annihilation is good, the destruction of the woman is too

high a price to pay.'[27] Perhaps that striking posthumous fame which Bishop found in the Eighties, perhaps it came as a sort of corrective to the posthumous fame of Plath in the Seventies: the woman, the poet, must suffer no less, but her sufferings are there to be endured.

9. *Men, Women, and Beasts*

Among the still somewhat shocking early poems of D. H. Lawrence is a group of lyrics about his mother's final sickness and death, in which the poet deliberately presents himself as his mother's lover. He carries his mother downstairs, and later finds her hairs on his jacket. He contemplates her on her sickbed:

> My love looks like a girl tonight,
> > But she is old.
> The plaits that lie along her pillow
> > Are not gold,
> But threaded with filigree silver
> > and uncanny cold.[1]

A few lines on, we discover that she is indeed dead, 'And her dead mouth sings | By its shape, like thrushes in clear evenings.' He calls his dead mother 'My love', 'the darling', 'like a young maiden', 'like a bride', and indeed the poem itself is called 'The Bride'. And its author is quite clearly the groom.

Next to it in the volume called *Amores*, Lawrence's second collection, published in 1916, we find 'The Virgin Mother':

> My little love, my darling,
> You were a doorway to me:
> You let me out of the confines
> Into this strange countrie
> Where people are crowded like thistles,
> You are shapely and comely to see.

And under this stanza, in the manuscript, an exasperated hand has written 'You love it, you say!!!!!' and in the margin, 'I hate it', and by the next stanza 'I hate it' again. In the third stanza Lawrence develops the theme of his indebtedness:

> You sweet love, my mother
> Twice you have blooded me,
> Once with your blood at birth-time
> Once with your misery.
> And twice you have washed me clean,
> Twice-wonderful things to see.

Beside this verse the horrified scholiast has written 'Good God!!!!!' and by the last stanza again 'I hate it'. Here is how the poem was originally going to conclude:

> And so, my love, Oh mother
> I shall always be true to thee.
> Twice I am born, my mother
> As Christ said it should be,
> And who can bear me a third time?
> —None love—I am true to thee.

After which Frieda Lawrence, who was responsible for these marginalia, has written:

Yes, worse luck—what a poem to write! yes, you are free, poor devil, from the heart's homelife free, lonely you shall be, you have chosen it, you choose freely, now go your way.—Misery, a sad, old woman's misery you have chosen, you poor man, and you cling to it with all your power. I have tried, I have fought, I have nearly killed myself in the battle to get you into connection with myself and other people, sadly I proved to my self that *I*

can love, but *never* you.—Now I will leave you for some
days and I will see if being alone will help you to see me
as I am, I will heal again by myself, you cannot help me,
you are a sad thing, I know your secret and your despair,
I have seen you are ashamed—I have made you better,
that is my reward—[2]

Lawrence's major poetry grew out of rows like this. It is true
that Lawrence was a writer—a poet, a novelist—well before he
met Frieda. It is true also that all her objections to that poem
did not stop Lawrence from publishing 'The Virgin Mother',
did not stop him from giving it an ending which is even more
mawkish than the first:

> Is the last word now uttered?
> Is the farewell said?
> Spare me the strength to leave you
> Now you are dead.
> I must go, but my soul lies helpless
> Beside your bed.[3]

It is true finally that many of Lawrence's contemporaries
thought Frieda's pretensions to have anything to do with the
development of Lawrence's genius quite ridiculous. But
contemporaries can be just as wrong as posterity, on occasion.
The struggle with Frieda, from Lawrence's point of view, was
of the essence, and we have already heard an authentic
Laurentian note in her bitter comment on the poem: 'I have
tried, I have fought, I have nearly killed myself in the battle to
get you into connection with myself and other people'. The
struggle is not, as the modern cliché has it to get in touch with
one's *own* feelings. The struggle is with the Other, the struggle
of man with Woman.

We are told that when Frieda came up behind Lawrence
and hit him over the head with an earthenware plate,

Lawrence did not complain about being hit, only about being hit from behind. He hit Frieda in their rows and she hit him. He felt free to hate her for a while, just as she was free to despise and mock him. This was all part of the process of becoming connected. What Lawrence loathed in a person, what spelled death to him, was narcissistic self-enclosure. That is what he saw in the homosexuals he met in Cambridge and Bloomsbury, and what gave him the horrors so he had nightmares about it.

Odd then, you might say, that Lawrence should turn so enthusiastically to Walt Whitman, the apostle of comradely man-to-man love; and not just to Whitman as a poet but to Whitman as a political, spiritual mentor. But it turns out that this was not some kind of inconsistency in Lawrence. It was part of the same development, the same enquiry into his own and human nature. When he was not chasing Frieda around the kitchen table in a white rage, he might also be found in the passionate pursuit of blood brotherhood—toiling in the fields alongside his friend, the self-educated Cornish farmer William Henry Hocking.

Quite how the relationship with Hocking should be defined is a question which the Cambridge biography discusses at length and convincingly. There is no evidence of a consummated sexual relationship with Hocking, and if he had discussed such desires with him (as it seems he did—for Hocking warned his younger brother about Lawrence), it would have been for him, says Kinkead-Weekes, 'an adder in the marsh'. Lawrence's answer to himself in the face of this adder would have been that 'once that dark anal fount of corruption had been openly confronted, the thought could lie down peacefully in the mind's sunshine, its taboo neutralised, but also no longer powerful through the fascination of the forbidden'.[4]

'There is all the difference in the world,' Lawrence wrote in a letter from 1917, between *understanding* the extreme and awful workings of sex, or even fulfilling them, responsibly; and abnormal sex. Abnormal sex comes from the fulfilling of violent or extreme desires, *against the will.* It is not the desires which are wrong, nor the fulfilment *per se*, but the fixed will in ourselves, which asserts that these things *should not be*, that only a holy love should be.—You see it is impious for us to assert so flatly what *should* be, in face of what *is.* It is our responsibility to know how to accept and live through that which *is.* It is labouring under the burden of self-repudiation and shame which makes abnormality. And repudiation and shame come from the false doctrines we hold. Desire is from the unknown which is the Creator and the Destroyer, beyond us, that which precedes us and brings us into being. Therefore Desire is holy, belonging to the mystic unknown, no matter *what* the desire. Abnormality and insanity comes from the split in the self, the repudiation and the condemning of the desire, and the furtive fulfilment at the same time. This makes madness.[5]

And in the next paragraph Lawrence says: 'Art itself doesn't interest me, only the spirit content.' Frieda's attack in the margins of his notebook, her sense of herself wrestling Lawrence away from his sickly eroticizing of his mother's death, her desire to force him into contact with her, Frieda— this is all entirely apropos in the case of Lawrence. Frieda's literary judgement is not at issue. It is her spiritual judgement which counts.

And when Lawrence turns to Whitman it is not for literary but for spiritual reasons, and it is not to sit at his feet as a disciple—it is to wrestle with Whitman. 'In Whitman' he says in the essay 'Democracy', 'at all times, the true and the false are so near, so interchangeable, that we are almost inevitably left with divided feelings'.[6] And in the essay on Whitman in

Studies in Classic American Literature, in which the poet is placed at the *end* of the American Tradition, among what Lawrence calls 'post-mortem effects' are listed: 'A certain ghoulish insistency. A certain horrible pottage of human parts. A certain stridency and portentousness. A luridness about his beatitudes.' It hardly sounds like the start of a eulogy, and in the next instance Lawrence's fury has seized upon a line of Whitman's:

I AM HE THAT ACHES WITH AMOROUS LOVE

And he rolls it round his mouth and spits it out. And then he picks it up again and puts it back in his mouth and rolls it around some more and spits it out again:

> Think of having that under your
> skin. All that!
> I AM HE THAT ACHES WITH AMOROUS LOVE

Walter, leave off. You are not HE. You are just a limited Walter. And your ache does not include all Amorous Love, by any means. If you ache you only ache with a small bit of amorous love, and there's so much more stays outside of your ache, that you might be a bit milder about it.

> O AM HE THAT ACHES WITH AMOROUS LOVE.
> CHUFF! CHUFF! CHUFF!
> CHU-CHU-CHU-CHU-chuff!
> Reminds one of a steam engine.
> A locomotive. . . .[7]

And he hasn't finished yet, by any means.

Auden, in his Lawrence essay, defends this grand manner in Whitman:

Whitman quite consciously set out to be the Epic Bard of America and created a poetic *persona* for the purpose. He keeps using the first person singular and even his own name, but these stand for a *persona*, not an actual human being, even when he appears to be talking about the most intimate experiences. When he sounds ridiculous, it is usually because the image of an individual obtrudes itself comically upon what is meant to be a statement about collective experience. *I am large. I contain multitudes* is absurd if one thinks of Whitman himself or any individual; of a corporate person like General Motors it makes perfectly good sense.

Auden goes on to say that, while Whitman appears to have been very unlike his persona, Lawrence 'wrote for publication in exactly the same way as he spoke in private' and 'it is doubtful if a writer ever existed who had less of a *persona* than Lawrence'.[8]

What Auden says of Whitman's persona applies particularly to the 'Calamus' poems, the section of *Leaves of Grass* which speaks most of comradely love, but which contrives to leave doubt in the mind about what is meant of any of its key terms. When we read, say, the erotic poems of Cavafy, we are in no doubt at all what is being talked about—a love life necessarily furtive but which constitutes the most highly valued experience of the poet. When we read Whitman, who appears to be proclaiming some message at the top of his voice, a message which is intended to transform the whole of society, we find ourselves in a quandary about what the message actually is. There is a Higher Furtiveness in Whitman, as the poet himself recognized. He told Edward Carpenter: 'There is something in my nature *furtive* like an old hen! You see a hen wandering up and down a hedgerow, looking apparently quite unconcerned, but presently she finds a concealed spot, and furtively lays an egg, and comes away as though nothing had happened!'[9]

Everything Whitman says about man-to-man love has a quality of deniability, precisely because, as Auden says, the 'I' of the poems is not an actual human being. By an extraordinary feat of communication, Whitman managed to conjure up a homoerotic vision for those who wanted to hear about it, and indeed for those who were ready to be outraged; meanwhile those who wanted manliness, nudism, and elevated thoughts found manliness, nudism, and elevated thoughts.

Above all Lawrence did not turn to Whitman for his elevated thoughts. Whitman, he wrote,

> was the first heroic seer to seize the soul by the scruff of her neck and plant her down among the potsherds.
> 'There!' he said to the soul. 'Stay there!'
> Stay there. Stay in the flesh. Stay in the limbs and lips and in the belly. Stay in the breast and womb. Stay there, O, Soul, where you belong.
>
> Stay in the dark limbs of negroes. Stay in the body of the prostitute. Stay in the sick flesh of the syphilitic. Stay in the marsh where the calamus grows. Stay there, Soul, where you belong.

Thought is rooted in feeling, feeling is a function of the body, desire is a mystery, and all desires are holy. Lawrence does not see Whitman as a corporate being. He will not allow him his persona. He would have him write as a distinct individual, distinctiveness being a Lawrentian moral quality, and where Whitman is hesitant and cryptic Lawrence would have him explicit, committed, and queer.

Exasperation was the name of Lawrence's Muse. A part of the exasperation in the published version of the Whitman essay becomes more understandable when you see what Lawrence had to suppress. The first version of the essay, which Lawrence anticipated would have to be either dropped or

revised, confronts Whitman's queerness in a way the
published version does not. The published version talks about

> This awful Whitman. This post mortem poet. The poet
> with the private soul leaking out of him all the time. All
> his privacy leaking out in a sort of dribble, oozing into
> the universe.

The unpublished version, which is summarized and excerpted
by Kinkead-Weekes, pays tribute to Whitman's exploration of
the secrets of the 'lower self', but Lawrence finds that it
amounts to a 'monstrous, a shattering half-truth, a devastating, thrilling half-lie'. Whitman cannot 'merge himself altogether into woman' (*a*) because such merging is impossible,
and (*b*) because he is too proud: to 'yield himself to complete
absorption and inglutination by the woman' would be 'a
débâcle far too ignominious for a great man like Whitman'.
   But behind the celebration of comradely love in the
Calamus poems lies an ancient mystery: that of the
'"passional" circuit between the lower ganglia of man with
man'. Beyond the lower and sacral ganglia—beyond the inter-
course of man with woman—beyond all this, says Lawrence in
his weird way,

> beyond all this is the coccygeal centre. There the deepest
> and most unknowable sensual reality breathes and
> sparkles darkly, in unspeakable power. Here, at the root
> of the spine, is the last clue to the lower body and being,
> as in the cerebellum is the last supper clue. . . . Here is
> our last and extremist reality. And the port, of egress and
> ingress, is the fundament, as the vagina is port to the
> other centre.
>   So that, in the last mystery of established polarity, . . .
> the last perfect balance is between two men, in whom
> the deepest sensual centres, and also the extreme upper

centres, vibrate in one circuit, and know their electric establishment and readjustment as does the circuit between man and woman. There is the same immediate connection, the same perfection in fulfilled consciousness and being.[10]

He is talking about sodomy, but not the nasty kind of sodomy that went on in Cambridge, or the pederastic sodomy of ancient Greece, in which the adult possesses and imposes himself upon the youth, but rather Lawrence is talking about a darkly sparkling democratic sodomy, a sodomy of the open road.

Once Lawrence had identified this mystery, he could, to all intents and purposes, forget all about it. It no longer troubled him or gave him nightmares. Auden thought that Lawrence was the only English poet to have been beneficially influenced by Whitman. There is a reason for this: there was never any danger of Lawrence mistaking his own personality for that of Whitman, no danger of his merging—he hated merging—himself with Whitman. Merging was death, because merging was the loss of self. Merging was Whitman's fatal tendency:

Whitman came along, and saw the slave, and said to himself: 'That negro slave is a man like myself. We share the same identity. And he is bleeding with wounds. Oh, oh, is it not myself who am also bleeding with wounds?'

This was not *sympathy*. It was merging and self-sacrifice. 'Bear ye one another's burdens'; 'Love thy neighbour as thyself'; 'Whatsoever ye do unto him, ye do unto me.'

If Whitman had truly *sympathised*, he would have said: 'That negro slave suffers from slavery. He wants to free himself. His soul wants to free him. He has wounds, but they are the price of freedom. The soul has a long

journey from slavery to freedom. If I can help him I will:
I will not take over his wounds and his slavery to myself.
But I will help him fight the power that enslaves him
when he wants to be free, if he wants my help, since I see
in his face that he needs to be free. But even when he is
free, his soul has many journeys down the open road,
before it is a free soul.'

The writer who makes such distinctions is not going to allow
Whitman to impose upon him. Lawrence begins in exasperation, and he will only allow himself to admire when he sees
how and where Whitman fails.

Compare that little poem by Ezra Pound, 'A Pact'.

> I make a pact with you, Walt Whitman—
> I have detested you long enough.
> I come to you as a grown child
> Who has had a pig-headed father;
> I am old enough now to make friends.
> It was you that broke the new wood,
> Now is a time for carving.
> We have one sap and one root—
> Let there be commerce between us.[11]

That was first collected in *Lustra*, in 1916. Lawrence, surely,
would have hated that last line. 'Let there be commerce
between us'—as if one turned to Whitman for commerce. And
what, come to think of it, could Whitman gain from
commerce with Pound? 'We have one sap and one root'—this
is a kind of identification that Lawrence would never make.
Furthermore, Pound seems to be valuing Whitman for a
poetic achievement on which he, Pound, can now build, or
from which he can now profit. But Lawrence is not interested
in poetic achievement in that way at all:

The essential function of art is moral. Not aesthetic, not decorative, not pastime and recreation. But moral. The essential function of art is moral.

But a passionate, implicit morality, not didactic. A morality which changes the blood, rather than the mind. Changes the blood first. The mind follows later, in the wake.[12]

And we have already heard Lawrence say that art itself doesn't interest him, a remark which, like Wilfred Owen's 'Above all I am not concerned with poetry', is designed to provoke the interest it affects to shrug off.

If we turn to what Eliot and Pound wrote about *vers libre* at around the time that Lawrence was wrestling with Whitman, we experience an inevitable pang of disappointment, since by that time both Eliot and Pound were, in different ways, washing their hands of it. '*Vers libre* does not exist,' says Eliot. '*Vers libre* has not even the excuse of a polemic; it is a battle-cry of freedom, and there is no freedom in art.'[13] And Pound more than once commends Eliot's saying that 'no *vers* is *libre* for the man who wants to do a good job'. Not such an inspiring way of putting things, when you come to think of it. Do you want to write a poem? Do you want to be a poet? Or do you want to be a jobbing poet?

It is as if we had come upon Pound and Eliot when a subject had gone stale on them, and they were sitting nodding by the fire and wondering whether to turn in. But when we turn to Lawrence, in the same years, we seem to enter a different period. The terms in which Eliot speaks are irrelevant. If 'there is no freedom in art' that doesn't matter, since Lawrence isn't interested in art. But he is interested in freedom, and he posits a kind of poetry

of that which is at hand: the immediate present. In the immediate present there is no perfection, no consummation, nothing finished. The strands are all flying, quivering, intermingling into the web, the waters are shaking the moon. There is no round, consummate moon on the face of running water, nor on the face of the unfinished tide. There are no gems of the living plasm. The living plasma vibrates unspeakably, it inhales the future, it exhales the past, it is the quick of both, yet it is neither. . . . The perfect rose is only a running flame, emerging and flowing off, and never in any sense at rest, static, finished. Herein lies its transcendent loveliness. . . . We look at the very white quick of nascent creation. A water-lily heaves herself from the flood, looks round, gleams, and is gone.[14]

There would be no point in trying to stop this rhapsodic flow and ask Lawrence what he thinks of Eliot's observation, that, in what passes for free verse, there is scansion, that behind much contemporary poetry lies 'the constant suggestion and skilful evasion of iambic pentameter', or to offer for his consideration Pound's view that 'the desire for vers libre is due to the sense of quantity reasserting itself after years of starvation'[15]—the sense of quantity as in Latin quantitative measures. Lawrence has no dialogue with such measures. He has nothing against traditional form, nothing against metre, nothing against rhyme. But he is talking about something completely different: not *vers libre*, as pioneered in France or Belgium in the 1880s, but that freedom claimed by Whitman in the 1850s. The freedom of the soul's encounters on the Open Road. Free verse, he says,

is, or should be, direct utterance from the instant, whole man. It is the soul and the mind and the body surging at once, nothing left out. They speak all together. There is some confusion, some discord. But the confusion and the discord only belong to the reality, as noise belongs to the plunge of water.[16]

Eliot said that *vers libre* did not exist. If it existed it would have
a positive definition, but it can only be defined by negatives:
no pattern, rhyme, or metre. Lawrence in one swoop gives
exclusively to free verse what (in my definition) is the scope
of the lyric itself—the present moment, the lyric moment. But
this act of definition is nothing more nor less than the asser-
tions of his rights as a poet.

Certain poets create in us an instant wariness. Pound,
having hated Whitman, came to see him as the best of his
tradition, 'but he never pretended to have reached the goal.
He knew himself, and proclaimed himself "a start in the right
direction." He never said, "American poetry is to stay where I
left it"; he said it was to go on from where he started it.'[17]
Pound is thinking: Where do I stand in relation to this, and
what can I do next? He is thinking about building up a tradition of American poetry. Lawrence couldn't care less about
that. Lawrence fears Whitman at the same time as he respects
him profoundly, and he reflects that

> We should not fear him if he sang only of the 'old
> unhappy far-off things', or of the 'wings of the morning'.
> It is because his heart beats with the urgent, insurgent
> Now, which is even upon us all, that we dread him. He is
> so near the quick.[18]

And Lawrence himself is among those authors we dread. We
dread turning back to him, in case he turns out to be other
than we remember; in case, turning back to him, we
encounter our former selves. We don't want to be ambushed
by disillusionment. Auden wrote:

> Lawrence, Blake and Homer Lane, once healers in our
>   English land;
> These are dead as iron for ever; these can never hold
>   our hand.

Lawrence was brought down by smut-hounds, Blake
    went dotty as he sang,
Homer Lane was killed in action by the Twickenham
    Baptist gang.[19]

Auden was lucky. The Lawrence he admired in his early days
was the Lawrence of his 'think' books, such as *Fantasia of the
Unconscious*. The poetry, he tells us, 'offended my notions of
what poetry should be'.

> When a poet who holds views about the nature of poetry
> which we believe to be false writes a poem we like, we are
> apt to think: 'This time he has forgotten his theory and
> is writing according to ours.' But what fascinates me
> about the poems of Lawrence's which I like is that I must
> admit he could never have written them had he held the
> kind of views about poetry of which I approve.[20]

A part of Lawrence's wrongness, Auden thought, derived
from his identification of art with life, his belief that a poem
could grow the way a flower grows. Lawrence fails to distinguish between natural growth and human construction. He
does not see how the natural gesture of the ballet dancer
derives from years of vigorous training—if it is to look
natural.

But I think Lawrence can be defended from this charge, and
defended much in the spirit of Auden's essay. Auden says that

> Very few statements which poets make about poetry,
> even when they appear to be quite lucid, are under-
> standable except in their polemic context. To understand
> them, we need to know what they are directed against,
> what the poet who made them considered the principal
> enemies of genuine poetry.[21]

In the case of Lawrence, whether or not the actual enemy was Eliot or Pound or someone else, the enemy was certainly the kind of arguments they were putting forward about *vers libre*. To continue a passage I quoted earlier, Lawrence says that

> It is no use inventing fancy laws for free verse, no use drawing a melodic line which all the feet must toe. Free verse toes no melodic line, no matter what drill-sergeant. Whitman pruned away his clichés—perhaps his clichés of rhythm as well as of phrase. And this is about all we can do, deliberately, with free verse. We can get rid of the stereotyped movements and the old hackneyed associations of sound or sense. We can break down those artificial conduits and canals through which we do so love to force our utterance.[22]

Lawrence goes on from here to evoke the notion of spontaneity, but it is quite clear in the context that spontaneity is a goal. Free verse is not like automatic writing (whatever that is supposed to be). In place of what Auden would call Making, Lawrence proposes—Editing; all we can do is prune away the clichés of rhyme and phrase; all we can do is edit out the stereotypes.

This may be an incomplete description of the composition of free verse, but it hardly counts as a wrong theory. In Lawrence's hands free verse is a form of mimesis. There are a million forms of mimesis, as you know. If I sit down to listen to something called, say 'A Spring Symphony', I shall expect to be affected in some way that I can associate with spring. But I do not demand that the instruments imitate birdsong. The object of Lawrence's mimesis in his free verse is the motion of thought, the impulse of the spirit. The poems do not *contain* an argument; they sound like an argument going on:

You tell me I am wrong
Who are you, who is anybody to tell me I am wrong?
I am not wrong.[23]

They do not present finished perceptions so much as perceptions as they evolve. No value seems to be set on concision.
Lawrence addresses the turkeycock:

> Your wattles are the colour of steel-slag which has been
>   red-hot.
> And is going cold,
> Cooling to a powdery, pale-oxidized sky-blue.
>
> Why do you have wattles, and a naked wattled head?
> Why do you arch your naked-set eye with a more-than-
>   comprehensible arrogance?
>
> The vulture is bald, so is the condor, obscenely,
> But only you have thrown this amazing mantilla of
>   oxidized sky-blue
> And hot red over you.[24]

Another poet might have hit upon that image of cooling steel-
slag and thought: this is so accurate that once I have said it
the turkey is there before the reader. I should simply say it and
move on. But Lawrence is not describing a turkeycock—he is
dramatizing the contemplation of a turkeycock. He returns to
the wattle, returns to his image, and his reward for returning
is the wild comparison of the wattle with the mantilla. And
yet he hasn't finished with that wattle yet, not by any means.

It is true as Auden says that most of Lawrence's finest
poems are in *Birds, Beasts and Flowers*. But Auden seems harsh
in his judgement that Lawrence 'detested nearly all human
beings if he had to be in close contact with them; his ideas of
what a human relationship, between man and man or man
and woman, ought to be are pure daydreams because they are

not based upon any experience of actual relationships which might be improved or corrected'.[25] That is to overlook the relationship with Frieda. Auden airbrushes Frieda out of the picture a few lines earlier than this judgement, saying that he finds Lawrence's love poems embarrassing 'because of their lack of reticence; they make me feel like a Peeping Tom'. Bertrand Russell, on reading the volume *Look! We Have Come Through!*, remarked that he was glad for them but didn't see why he should look. H.D. told Lawrence that the poems 'won't do at all; they are not *eternal*, not sublimated: too much body and emotions'.[26]

But if you believe with Keats that 'the genius of Poetry must work out its own salvation in a man' and that it is better to leap headlong into the sea than to stay on the green shore, and pipe a silly pipe, and take tea and comfortable advice, then *Look! We Have Come Through!*—the book that forms the link between the Georgian Lawrence and the Classic Lawrence of *Birds, Beasts and Flowers*—is worth paying attention to. Those who saw Frieda and Lawrence when they were having a row might well have thought the book's title a little optimistic, a touch 'previous'. But it was a bold and unusual project to chart the course of such a stormy relationship in a mixture of traditional forms and the newly acquired Whitmanesque mode. One has to look far back, to Meredith's *Modern Love* of 1862, to find anything like a precedent. Successors come more easily to mind, among them sequences of poems by Robert Lowell and Ted Hughes.

Lawrence set out to describe his coming of age as a man. Here is the 'Argument' with which he prefaces the series:

> After much struggling and loss in love and in the world
> of man, the protagonist throws in his lot with a woman
> who is already married. Together they go into another
> country, she perforce leaving her children behind. The

conflict of love and hate goes on between the man and the woman, and between these two and the world around them, till it reaches some sort of conclusion, they transcend into some condition of blessedness.[27]

The summary is interesting because it includes a fact about Frieda which was indeed crucially important in the rows they had: Frieda had left her children behind and was at first forbidden to see them, and then humiliated to discover that they had turned against her; it was Frieda's torment over her children that drove Lawrence wild with rage. But very little of this actually gets into the poems. Lawrence is not as ruthless with Frieda's private life as he was capable of being with others'. On the other hand the 'argument' only touches indirectly on a subject that the poems do indeed deal with— Lawrence's grieving, and finally ceasing to grieve, over his mother. It was this grieving that sent Frieda up the wall, as we heard in the marginalia with which I began.

Lawrence was fully aware of the cost to Frieda, to her children, and to Ernest Weekley, Frieda's husband, of what he and Frieda had decided to do: not just their falling in love but their abjuring of some halfway house arrangement, whereby Frieda would pretend to have given Lawrence up in return for being allowed to live with her children. Lawrence's honesty had come at a high price. And he had learned what it was to be hated. His Christianity had once been strong, and so was his sense of living in sin. This is one of those cases where biography does indeed help to unlock the poetry.

Read by itself, the poem called 'Meeting Among the Mountains' might puzzle. The biography helps to make its meaning clear. Lawrence is in the Alps, contemplating a wayside crucifix. A peasant comes along the road in a bullock cart. Something about the peasant disturbs Lawrence. He feels he is being hated. What the poem does not divulge is that the peasant reminds him of Weekley. Lawrence suffers an emotional hallucination: Weekley goes by in the bullock cart, filled with Christian hatred for the wrong Lawrence has done him:

> Then among the averted pansies, beneath the high
> White peaks of snow, at the foot of the sunken Christ
> I stand in a chill of anguish, trying to say
> The joy I bought was not too highly priced.

> But he has gone, motionless, hating me,
> Living as the mountains do, because they are strong,
> With a pale, dead Christ on the crucifix of his heart,
> And breathing the frozen memory of his wrong.

> Still in his nostrils the frozen breath of despair,
> And heart like a cross that bears dead agony
> Of naked love, clenched in his fists the shame
> And in his belly the smouldering hate of me.

> And I, as I stand in the cold, averted flowers,
> Feel the shame-wounds in his hands pierce through my
>   own,
> And breathe despair that turns my lungs to stone
> And know the dead Christ weighing on my bone.[28]

It is hard to pick up a book with a thousand poems and read one's way straight through, and it is hard to read Lawrence using the *Complete Poems*. Ideally one should start with a copy of *Birds, Beasts and Flowers* (but be aware that the paperback reprint by Black Sparrow Press omits all the tortoise poems): this is where 'Snake' is to be found, and the two poems about bats, and the fig poems which found their way as a monologue by Alan Bates into the film *Women in Love*, and the incomparable flower poems, and 'Bibbles', which Auden correctly called the best poem ever written about a dog. (From the description given by David Ellis in the last volume of the Cambridge biography of the row Lawrence had with the original Bibbles, one may conclude that Auden was right to say that Lawrence was 'no person to be entrusted with the care of a dog'.)[29]

Next one should turn to an edition which unfortunately does not yet exist: a single-volume paperback containing all of *Look! We Have Come Through!* in the correct order, and with just a few notes of a biographical kind. Thereafter there is much to discover among the earlier and later volumes, including the important late poems 'The Ship of Death' and 'Bavarian Gentians'. But one should not turn Lawrence into a task, a *devoir*, an *impegno*. Lawrence is the least difficult of modern poets from the point of view of simple comprehension. But he was a famously difficult man to get on with, and when you find him difficult in that sense you should put him down, leave him to cool off, turn to whatever is more congenial.

The authors of the Cambridge biography did not have this luxury; they had to stick by him, daily, through thick and thin. And they are, all of them, exemplary. Lawrence used to be a cause, served by bad-tempered fanatics. In these three volumes he is treated equably—Othello's plea, 'Nothing extenuate', seems to have been their policy—with the result that, in the end, because he trusts the biographers, the reader may end up feeling more sympathetic to Lawrence than he expected. John Worthen is particularly good on the background—the nuances of class, what was poverty, what was a respectable income. In Ellis's final volume Lawrence goes back to his native Midlands just after the general strike of 1926, by which time the miners were defeated, impoverished, and radicalized. Lawrence already hated socialism, let alone bolshevism, but Ellis makes it clear that, shocked though he was by what he found back home, Lawrence was not, in the years of his declining health, any longer a political animal. His ideas, such as they were, would not translate into action. A belief in natural or sacred authority would not translate into violent authoritarianism. He was not spared from an early death by becoming a fascist.

Death, though, had been one of his themes. His view of life was predicated on a view of death. One should make a good death. One should even look forward to the mystery of death. That is the theme of both 'The Ship of Death' and 'Bavarian Gentians'. But, as Ellis's story progresses, life and poetry diverge. Lawrence was dying of pulmonary tuberculosis, but had a horror of admitting out loud that it was anything worse than a condition of the bronchial tubes, or a recurrent malaria, or the grippe, or an asthma caused by the activity of the vagal nerve and provoked by eating the wrong sort of food. He tried stiff porridges and yoghourt and fruit, interlaced for a short while with small doses of arsenic and phosphorus.

Meanwhile in his poetry he was welcoming the dark, and, though there is in the mythology an implication that Persephone will return from the dead, that spring will follow winter, there is no implication in 'Bavarian Gentians' that the wedding guest will return from the dark. The poetry embraced death. The dying man saw with horror his own dead body on the table opposite his bed. When Frieda was out of the room for a moment, he grasped Maria Huxley's wrists and said, 'Maria, Maria, don't let me die.' Those were his last words, according to one version. According to another, his last words to Frieda were 'Wind my watch'.

Wind my watch, don't let me die; they seem to be the same last words.

10. *Auden on Shakespeare's Sonnets*

Although Auden's engagement with Shakespeare produced the most wonderful and surprising results, both in prose and in verse, it is not to be supposed that, during his lifetime, he was always listened to on the subject with sympathy or even respect. Throughout his adult life, Auden enjoyed celebrity as a poet, but that celebrity did not automatically entitle him to assume the august mantle of critic and teacher. Here he is, glimpsed through the memoir of Charles H. Miller, at Ann Arbor, Michigan, in 1941:

> When he got to Shakespeare, he drew blackboard diagrams to show that Othello was stupid and that Iago was the most honest character in the play. I wasn't the only student to be put off, or let down, by his seeming flippancy towards Shakespeare; few of us had known so unorthodox a teacher, and none of us had known such a *presence* with such methods.

And here is the same witness, five years later, in New York:

> At the New School lecture on Shakespeare, Amalia and I sat down front, as we had in Angell Hall at Ann Arbor. We smiled knowingly when Wystan made conscious efforts to be 'original' about Shakespeare's plays, and we weren't surprised when a few elderly academics got up and walked out in protest at Wystan's lack of humility before the Bard.[1]

Charlie and Amalia, newly married college friends, smiling knowingly at each other with Wystan up there on the platform—good old Wystan—and the elderly academics walking out: it is a charming and believable scene. People normally write in memoirs about the experiences that made a real impact on them in life. Here, more valuably, we have a description of somebody making absolutely no impact whatever.

Charlie Miller knew Auden very well: he shared a house with him on campus, cooked for him, told him his nightmares, showed him his journals, liked, admired him even, kept a useful record of his conversation, thought of his English 135 class that year in Michigan as 'an individual monument'. But he seems never to have taken Auden seriously as a critic of Shakespeare, either in his youth or at the time he was writing his book.

And you can see why. You can see how an offence had been committed against the decorums. The students listened attentively, but suspected they were being taken for a ride. How could Iago be shown, by diagrams, to be the most honest character in the play? Well, we no longer have the diagrams, but we do seem to have the remainder of the argument on Auden's essay on *Othello*, 'The Joker in the Pack'. Everything that Iago says to Othello, Auden argues,

> is designed to bring to Othello's consciousness what he has already guessed is there. Accordingly, he has no need to tell lies. Even his speech, 'I lay with Cassio lately,' can be a truthful account of something which actually happened: from what we know of Cassio, he might very well have such a dream as Iago reports.[2]

In fact, Iago does tell some definite lies, but rather fewer than you'd expect. He is economical with the untruth.

Auden loved expressing himself aphoristically, and often an

aphorism is a statement which is only true if handled with a certain sympathy. Auden said: 'Every woman wants to play Hamlet, just as every man wants to play Lady Bracknell.' The comic effect comes from the disparity in the level of ambition between woman and man: cross-dressing suggests to the one the opportunity to satisfy the highest cravings of the spirit, to the other nothing grander than the opportunity to camp it up.

One evening in Michigan, Auden talked to Charlie Miller about Shakespeare. He said:

> When a director seeks an actor to play the role of Hamlet, he may as well go out in the street and take the first person who comes along. Because the role doesn't require an actor. One has only to recite Hamlet's speeches, which are instruction and arguments to himself on how to act the roles he decides to play.[3]

Of course the role does in fact require an actor, someone with the stamina, the voice, the fencing skill, and so forth. But if Auden is taken as meaning that the actor will find no great mystery in how to play the part, so long as he pays attention to the internal directions—that is, to the pointers given by the author within the speeches themselves—this is profoundly true, not only of Hamlet but of Shakespeare in general.

Quite how many worthwhile performances of Shakespeare Auden would have seen, I do not know. Probably not many. In 1939 he expressed the belief that *The Merry Wives of Windsor* and *All's Well that Ends Well* were subjects with which Shakespeare could do nothing. 'Genius', he wrote,

> is rarely as artistically successful as talent. Had his range and power of expression been less, [Shakespeare] would have been a better writer for the theater. In *Troilus and Cressida* and *Measure for Measure*, for example, what he is

interested in expressing, the vastness of human corruption, is a lyrical not a dramatic theme, and is more than the plots and characters can bear.[4]

With the exception of *The Merry Wives of Windsor*, all these plays used to be categorized as problematic. *Measure for Measure*, for instance, was much disliked, and considered a dramatic failure, and it was only in the latter part of the twentieth-century that directors such as Peter Brook and Jonathan Miller had success with it. Auden's dismissal of such pieces is conventional rather than odd.

What *is* odd is the habit of mind in Auden that considers, say, the character of Falstaff, finds him out of place in *Henry IV*, imagines Falstaff out of the play and in the audience watching the play without him, commends Queen Elizabeth's perceptiveness in wanting to see Falstaff in a comedy, and finds that Falstaff only really becomes a fully achieved character in Verdi's opera. Or finds Iago's motivation more fully explicated in Boito's libretto than in Shakespeare's play. As if Falstaff and Iago are pre-existent essences. Falstaff has to wait around for Verdi in order to find his essence truly expressed.

Auden's playfulness might have been better appreciated by his students if the word ludic had enjoyed an earlier vogue, and someone could have whispered in their ear: this isn't irreverence—this is ludicity. But of course an essay like 'The Joker in the Pack' goes well beyond the ludic. As it develops its notion of Iago as practical joker, and then, by a surprise manoeuvre, presents the sinister practical joker as a scientific enquirer, the piece converts itself into a moral essay of plain earnestness: an attack on society's acceptance of our right to knowledge at whatever cost, from the gossip column to the cobalt bomb.

A horror of public gossip, a dislike for the glib intrusion on another's private life, seems to have crept over Auden in his later years, and it provides the theme for both the opening and the conclusion of his essay on Shakespeare's sonnets, which forms the introduction to the Signet Classics edition, where he attacks the 'blurring of the borderline between the desire for truth and idle curiosity', arguing that

> A great deal of what today passes for scholarly research is an activity not different from that of reading somebody's private correspondence when he is out of the room, and it doesn't really make it morally any better if he is out of the room because he is in his grave.[5]

Auden had come to believe that Shakespeare's sonnets had been procured by the 'Onelie begetter', that this was the meaning of Thorpe's dedication, and that they had been published without Shakespeare's permission.

> How the sonnets came to be published—whether Shakespeare gave copies to some friend who betrayed him, or whether some enemy stole them—we shall probably never know. Of one thing I am certain: Shakespeare must have been horrified when they were published.[6]

In other words, Auden believed the sonnets to be an intimate record of the poet's involvement with a young man and a woman, and that both of these affairs were, in different ways, extremely intense. But what Auden did not wish to say was that Shakespeare's love for the young man was homosexual. He did not want to use the word—or indeed the word heterosexual—about the kind of love he felt was involved.

In a passage which has since become notorious, Auden tries to avoid two interpretational fallacies:

> Confronted with the extremely odd story they [the sonnets] tell, with the fact that, in so many of them, Shakespeare addresses a young man in terms of passionate

devotion, the sound and sensible citizen, alarmed at the thought that our Top-Bard could have any experience with which he is unfamiliar, has either been shocked and wished that Shakespeare had never written them, or in defiance of common sense, tried to persuade himself that Shakespeare was merely expressing in somewhat hyperbolic terms, such as an Elizabethen poet might be expected to use, what any normal man feels for a friend of his own sex. The homosexual reader, on the other hand, determined to secure our Top-Bard as a patron saint of the Homintern, has been uncritically enthusiastic about the first one hundred and twenty-six of the sonnets, and preferred to ignore those to the Dark Lady in which the relationship is unequivocally sexual, and the fact that Shakespeare was a married man and a father.[7]

The expression Homintern, formed by analogy with Comintern, was one which Auden had been wanting to get into print for decades. It was supposed to refer to an international conspiracy of buggers, to any one of whom being a member of the Homintern would be like being one of the elect. Co-opting Shakespeare would be good for the prestige of the club, but Auden was reluctant to admit him to full membership.

In *Such is My Love*, a study of the sonnets published in 1985, Joseph Pequigney criticized Auden's 'eccentric and unpersuasive performance' in his essay, and contrasted the public disavowal with a remark Auden made during an evening at the Stravinskys in 1964. Auden, according to Robert Craft, had said, 'It won't do just yet to admit that the top bard was in the homintern'. Actually that is not the whole of what Auden said, but I shall come back to that. Pequigney argues that this statement, if accurate,

is startling, and less for what it says than for gainsaying the stand taken in the Signet introduction, which was written at about the same time. If Auden did not believe what he wrote there and prudently falsified his opinion—and we can never be certain which of the two views he held—we have not necessarily the only instance of a discrepancy between what the expositor wrote and what he privately thought, but it is the only instance I know of where the discrepancy can be documented as being at least feasible.[8]

This notion of Auden's two-facedness, somewhat tentatively formulated by Pequigney, has been expressed more sharply since. Bruce R. Smith, in *Homosexual Desire in Shakespeare's England*, complains:

In a preface that has been read by tens of thousands of undergraduates W. H. Auden . . . insists on the sonnets' mystical and idealistic view of the young man and derides attempts to claim Shakespeare for the Homintern. Yet Auden himself is reported to have confessed to a gathering at Igor Stravinsky's apartment, in the very year he wrote the preface, that 'it won't do just yet to admit that the top Bard was in the homintern.' If the report is true, Auden's hypocrisy has had particularly unfortunate results . . .[9]

Because Auden had since been cited as an authority on the matter. Next comes Marjorie Garber, in a book called *Vice Versa* (1995), who regurgitates Pequigney and Bruce Smith, concluding that

To say publicly that Shakespeare was, or might have been, homosexual—had, or might have had, male lovers—was dangerous in 1964. The 'top Bard' had to be above rebuke, which meant that he had to be heterosexual.[10]

Most recently we have Katherine Duncan-Jones, in the introduction to her New Arden edition of the Sonnets:

> Though anyone with a knowledge of Auden's biography might expect him to celebrate and endorse the homo-erotic character of 1–126, he was absolutely determined not to do so, at least publicly. In his 1964 Signet edition Auden claimed—as G.Wilson Knight had done, that the primary experience explored in *Sonnets* was 'mystical', and he was extremely scathing about putative readers of homosexual inclinations who might be 'determined to secure our Top-Bard as a patron saint of the Homintern'. Yet his public adoption of this position seems to have been a characteristic instance of Auden's cowardice, for later in 1964 he confessed to friends that a public account of Shakespeare (evidently equated by Auden with the speaker in *Sonnets*) as homosexual 'won't do just yet'. Perhaps Auden was referring to the changes in legislation then under discussion: Parliament finally decriminalized homosexual acts between consenting adults in July, 1967.

And Duncan-Jones concludes:

> Consequent changes of attitude have been slow to take effect. Not until the American Joseph Pequigney's *Such Is My Love* in 1985 was a homoerotic reading of Shakespeare's Sonnets positively and systematically championed.[11]

You see how the charges have been firmed up with each repetition of the indictment, so that what began as a 'startling discrepancy' has hardened into a characteristic instance of cowardice. Auden may not have dared yet to be frank about Shakespeare's sexuality, Duncan-Jones surprisingly suggests, because the law on homosexual acts had not yet been reformed in Britain. But Auden was in the States, and anyway talking about a long-dead man. It is amazing that Garber should think it 'dangerous' to call Shakespeare a homosexual in 1964. Auden's sexual tastes were well known to those who employed him. What possible danger could there be?

And if Auden was characteristically a coward in these matters, why would he have voluntarily published, in 1961, his preface to Cavafy's poems, in which he states quite simply:

> Cavafy was a homosexual, and his erotic poems make no attempt to conceal the fact. Poems made by human beings are no more exempt from moral judgment than acts done by human beings, but the moral criterion is not the same. One duty of a poem, among others, is to bear witness to the truth. A moral witness is one who gives true testimony to the best of his ability in order that the court (or the reader) shall be in a better position to judge the case justly; an immoral witness is one who tells half-truths or downright lies: but it is not the witness's business to pass verdict.

And Auden goes on, in a way I take to be characteristic:

> As a witness, Cavafy is exceptionally honest. He neither bowdlerises nor glamorises nor giggles. The erotic world he depicts is one of casual pickups and short-lived affairs. Love, there, is rarely more than physical passion, and when tenderer emotions do exist, they are almost always one-sided. At the same time, he refuses to pretend that his moments of sensual pleasure are unhappy or spoilt by guilt. One can feel guilty about one's relation to other persons—one has treated them badly or made them unhappy—but nobody, whatever his moral convictions, can honestly regret a moment of physical pleasure as such.[12]

I don't think the author of that last remark had hang-ups, public or private, about Shakespeare's sexuality.

And anyway, what *did* Auden say, that night at the Stravinskys's? He said, according to Craft, that 'it won't do just yet to admit that the top Bard was in the homintern or, for that matter, that Beethoven was queer'. But nobody thinks that Beethoven was queer. Was Auden trying to provoke Stravinsky with the thought that all top-flight artists were in the homintern? Possibly that was the drift of his joke, since he also that evening said that Rilke was 'the greatest Lesbian poet since Sappho'.

Could Auden conceivably have been drunk? Well, he did burst into song from time to time. He sang, very melodiously, bits of Rossini's *Petite Messe Solonelle,* and he did consume a jug of Gibson's before the meal (a Gibson's being a very strong Martini with a pickled onion in the bottom—and Auden was quite particular about the onion), a bottle of champagne during, and a whole bottle of Cherry Heering afterwards, prompting Craft to wonder whether he was under the impression it was Chianti. Vera Stravinsky said of Auden after this performance: 'He must have multiple stomachs like a cow, the gin going to the omasum, while the wine stops in the reticulum, and the kerosene stays in the rumen.' Stravinsky was impressed by Auden's liver power but said that 'livers learn, of course, and Wystan's would naturally be the most intelligent in town'.

I am aware that to point out that Auden might have been high as a kite when he was holding forth at the Stravinskys's of an evening will do little to redeem him in the eyes of the critical tradition I have traced. For his chief sin is not what he said in the evening but what he had written in the sober morning. Auden was disobliging. The poet from whom one might have expected a 'celebration' and 'endorsement', a 'positive' and 'systematic' championing of the homoerotic Shakespeare had let the side down. Of all people, Auden should have known better.

It should be said of these critics that, with the exception of Pequigney, who comes across as an orthodox and devoted Freudian, they inhabit a theoretical world which was quite unknown to Auden, since it really only came into being after his death. They use the weapons of this theory when it suits them, but they also have a habit of paying verbal homage to a whole lot they don't believe in, and which they ignore as convenient.

I think that Auden would have been interested in Foucault's *The History of Sexuality*, which appeared in French three years after his death, and which made the fruitful proposal that the modern conception of homosexuality was a nineteenth-century invention. Sodomy had previously been conceived juridically as a series of forbidden acts which anyone might commit. The sodomite had been, says Foucault, a temporary aberration, whereas

The nineteenth-century homosexual became a personage, a past, a case history, and a childhood, in addition to being a type of life, a life form, and a morphology, with an indiscreet anatomy and possibly a mysterious physiology. Nothing that went into his total composition was unaffected by his sexuality. It was everywhere present in him: at the root of all his actions because it was their insidious and indefinitely active principle; written immodestly on his face and body because it was a secret that gave itself away. It was consubstantial with him, less as a habitual sin than as a singular nature. We must not forget that the psychological, psychiatric, medical category of homosexuality was constituted from the moment it was categorised—Westphal's famous article of 1870 on 'contrary sexual sensations' can stand as its date of birth—less by a type of sexual relations than by a certain quality of sensibility, a certain way of inverting the masculine and the feminine in oneself.[13]

This 'interior androgyny', this 'hermaphrodism of the soul', was a new conception in 1870, and if it was a new conception it must follow that, even if there were men and women in Renaissance England who were in some medical, physiological, or morphological way identical with the modern homosexual, their understanding of themselves would be entirely different from that of—to take a striking recent incident—the 16-year-old boy who sued his school on the grounds that, he being gay, the school should have done more to protect him from bullying on that count. Auden himself, born in 1907, could never at the age of 16 have come to such a conclusion about his fixed sensibility (let alone his rights), but he did perhaps belong to the first generation of children who could—given the right library, which of course Auden's father did indeed possess—have researched these recent theories of sexuality for themselves. He could have read Havelock Ellis's *Sexual Inversion* (1897) but he died too young to read a work such as Alan Bray's *Homosexuality in Renaissance England* (1982), which begins with a polite but wholesale rejection of Ellis, whose

> deliberately sober prose barely disguises a captivating and persuasive picture of the place homosexuality occupied in the Renaissance, and has thus acquired an extraordinary currency since the days of the sexual radicals at the turn of the century, of which [whom] Ellis was one. Its core is a catalogue of poets and painters, philosophers and statesmen of the Renaissance: Michelangelo, Leonardo, Christopher Marlowe, Francis Bacon, these together with a glittering array of monarchs and a host of lesser artists are the stuff of which this picture is made. The dark constraints of the monkish Middle Ages were past; sexual and artistic freedom went hand in hand . . . Its slender foundation is an uncritically simple reading of the literature of the time; and it significantly takes no

account of the considerable evidence for the deep horror with which homosexuality was widely regarded. It was brilliant propaganda, but it was not sober history.[14]

This kind of brilliant propaganda, which Auden would have read in his teens at the same time as he was making his first acquaintance with the works of Freud, includes such literary works as the foundation stone of queer sonnet theory, Oscar Wilde's 'The Portrait of Mr W. H.', which Auden in later life described as 'shy-making'—that is, deeply embarrassing. Of course, among the books we find most embarrassing in later life are those which meant most to us at a certain point in our vulnerable youth, and whose glaring faults we now suddenly perceive. Auden may well once have had a high opinion of Wilde's short story. He later agreed with one of its propositions, as we shall see.

I wonder what Auden would have thought of Alan Bray's argument that to talk of any individual in the Renaissance as having been 'a homosexual' is 'an anachronism and ruinously misleading'. Auden refers to both Marlowe and Richard Barnfield as homosexuals, but I think he would have been interested, rather than put out, to be told, as Bray tells us, that Barnfield's commonplace book, not intended for publication, is 'both robustly pornographic and entirely heterosexual'.[15]

And how do you suppose Auden would have responded to Eve Kosofsky Sedgwick's essay in *Between Men* (the book, we are told by its jacket, that 'turned queer theory from a latent to a manifest discipline'), which refers to the fair youth sonnets as heterosexual. At one point Sedgwick imagines the objection: 'If all this is heterosexual, the commonsensical reader may ask, then what on earth does it take to be homosexual?' And she provides the answer:

One thing it takes is a cultural context that defines the homosexual as against the heterosexual. My point is obviously not to deny or to de-emphasize the love between men in the Sonnets, the intense and often genitally oriented language that describes that love, even the possibility that the love described may have been genitally acted out ... I am saying that within the world sketched in these sonnets, there is not an equal opposition or choice posited between two such institutions as homosexuality (under whatever name) and heterosexuality. The Sonnets present a male–male love that, like the love of the Greeks, is set firmly within a structure of institutionalised social relations that are carried out via women: marriage, name, family, loyalty to progenitors and posterity, all depend on the youth's making a particular use of women that is not, in the abstract, seen as opposing, denying, or detracting from his bond to the speaker.[16]

This is written very much in the same spirit as Foucault and Bray, and I think Auden would have seen this as a good description of the state of affairs depicted in the Sonnets.

A great thing to remember about these recent readings of the Sonnets is that you cannot mix and match—you cannot take a point from one and marry it to a point from the other. Pequigney cannot be made to work with spare parts from Duncan-Jones or Sedgwick. The spare parts won't fit. For instance, Sedgwick believes that the finer points of the sexual discourse of the period have been lost for ever: we cannot be certain about implications and equivocations. Pequigney, the maximalist, believes that by broadening our attention to bawdy language (that is, by admitting that the same bawdy term might be used in a homosexual as well as heterosexual context), and by paying attention to the insights of Freud, you can find out what went on between the poet and the young man (including anal sex).

Sonnet 33 ('Full many a glorious morning have I seen'), in

which the morning sun shines first, before it 'Anon [permits] the basest clouds to ride | With ugly rack on his celestial face', is evidence for Pequigney that the young man, after spending an hour in Shakespeare's company, went off and permitted some base fellow to 'ride upon his face'—that is, he went off and gave someone a blow job. This reading is not repeated in the New Arden edition. Not surprisingly. For Duncan-Jones thinks that the Sonnets are dedicated, with Shakespeare's authorization, and in expectation of a reward which she estimates at something between £5 and £10, to the Earl of Pembroke, who is or was the object of Shakespeare's love. It surely follows that, however tough they are on the earl, the sentiments expressed must be publishable. How could Shakespeare expect Pembroke to be pleased at being publicly accused of being the passive partner in oral sex with a commoner? This would surely have ranked as a most disgraceful allegation, enough to put both Shakespeare and his publisher Thorpe in grave danger. Oddly enough, if Pequigney's reading had merit, Auden, who believed Shakespeare would have been horrified at the publication of his poems, could just about have accepted it. But Duncan-Jones, who commends Pequigney as positive and systematic, cannot possibly do so.

Still, the New Arden edition does leave one wondering what Pembroke would have thought about Sonnet 20 ('A woman's face with nature's own hand painted'). This is the sonnet which establishes the androgynous beauty of the young man, and which seems to make explicit the extent of the poet's interest in him. The conceit is that he was first intended to be a woman, but then nature fell in love with him and gave him a penis, thereby frustrating any sexual ambition on the part of the poet. Here are the last lines:

And for a woman wert thou first created,
Till nature as she wrought thee fell a-doting,

> And by addition me of thee defeated,
> By adding one thing to my purpose nothing:
>> But since she pricked thee out for women's
>> pleasure,
>> Mine be thy love, and thy love's use their treasure.

Nature, by the way, is here seen, in the primary sense, as a gardener, who takes the young man, as a seedling, and 'pricks [him] out'—that is to say, with a wooden prick or dibbler, she plants him out (sense 22 in the *OED*).

It seems to be universally agreed that there is a double entendre: 'since she pricked thee out' meaning 'since she kitted thee out with a prick, for the pleasure of women'. The last line of the sonnet seems to mean: give me your love, but let women enjoy sexual relations with you. This is the kind of division of the spoils that Eve Sedgwick adumbrated in the passage quoted earlier—a male–male love in a world whose 'institutionalised social relations are carried out via women'. I tend to believe that, if the Sonnets have a story to tell, it is the story of the unrealistic nature of this proposal to divide the spoils.

I think most people feel that Sonnet 20 is odd, and striking, and takes some explaining. Auden, who talks about the Vision of Eros, makes quite clear what his critics forget, that 'the medium of the Vision is . . . undoubtedly erotic. Nobody who was unconscious of an erotic interest on his part would use the frank, if not brutal, sexual image which Shakespeare employs in speaking of his friend's exclusive interest in women.' And he quotes the final couplet of the sonnet.

The New Arden edition tells us that 'the naivety of the sonnet is too simple to be believed ("because we are both men we can have no sexual congress")'; also that the language is too 'slippery and self-subverting' to be trusted. When nature adds 'one thing to my purpose nothing', the added feature, the penis, is in the primary sense 'of no value to the loving poet' but, since the word 'nothing' can allude to the female genitalia, there would be a paradox that 'the one thing that nature added is, for my purposes, equivalent to a woman's sexual parts'. So Shakespeare is saying publicly to the Earl of Pembroke, albeit in a slippery way, Nature has given you a penis which, for my purposes, is, or could be, a vagina.

I may be obtuse but I don't get it.

The mention by Eve Sedgwick of the Greeks reminds me of a distinction made by Kenneth Dover in his study, *Greek Homosexuality*. According to Dover, there is no sense in the sources available that there was anything wrong for the Greeks in an older man being attracted to a beautiful youth, nothing wrong that is in feeling an explicitly sexual attraction. What was wrong, in the view of Socrates, was the yielding to the feeling. And if we return for a moment to Foucault's distinction between homosexuality before and after 1870, one supposes that it could at least be that in Shakespeare's day, when an older man found himself attracted to a beautiful youth, he might feel nothing wrong in the attraction itself, however much he might fear the consequences of yielding to physical temptation. Whereas, after 1870 or thereabouts, the desire alone might set off an alarm-bell. A man might feel: oh my god, I'm an invert, a Uranian, an Urning—or whatever.

Whether or not we believe the sonnets to have been authorized by Shakespeare for publication, or filched from him by treachery, the fact was that they were publishable, were indeed published, and no traceable scandal ensued. One may hypothesize that they were read in shocked disbelief—as they were in the eighteenth and nineteenth centuries—and that the Earl of Pembroke threw his copy across the room. But that is as far as rational hypothesis can take us. Unless a commentator feels that he or she has cracked a code in them, making them comprehensible in a way not available to Shakespeare's contemporaries (and of course there have been commentators who have thought exactly that), then exegesis must be influenced by the thought: these are publishable sentiments for the period.

Auden read the Sonnets at an early age, according to Richard Davenport-Hines, in order to make sense of his feelings for a fellow undergraduate, Bill McElwee, perhaps sometime around 1926. McElwee was very fond of Auden, but not in the way Auden hoped. Later, in Berlin, Auden had an affair with a Hamburg sailor called Gerhart Meyer, whose name resounds in the poem '1929':

> So I remember all of those whose death
> Is necessary condition of the season's putting forth,
> Who, sorry in this time, look only back
> To Christmas intimacy, a winter dialogue
> Fading in silence, leaving them in tears.
> And recent particulars come to mind:
> The death by cancer of a once hated master,
> A friend's analysis of his own failure,
> Listened to at intervals throughout the winter
> At different hours in different rooms.
> But always with success of others for comparison,
> The happiness, for instance, of my friend Kurt Groote,
> Absence of fear in Gerhart Meyer
> From the sea, the truly strong man.[17]

Gerhart Meyer was a hustler who, within a short while of getting to know Auden, proposed that they take a trip together to Hamburg. For the journey, Auden packed Donne, the Sonnets, and *Lear.* Meyer had the capacity for making Auden intensely jealous, whether with girls on the train or with a lover or client in Hamburg. Abandoned by Meyer, Auden found himself awake most of the night. He writes in his journal:

> First I posture before the glass, trying to persuade myself, but in vain, that I am up to his physical level. Then I read

the Sonnets to prove my superiority in sensibility. Every time I hear the taxi I go to the window, but it's only a whore returning. At three the porter comes and takes away my key locking the door. By five I am convinced Gerhart has run off with my money.[18]

Quarrels ensue. Gerhart is always going off with whores and is demanding of presents. Within ten days, the following exchange is enough to disillusion Auden. He says: 'I should like to take you to the mountains with me.' Gerhart replies: 'I don't like mountains. I only like towns where there are shops.' Auden thinks: 'This is the revolt of the symbol. The disobedience of the daydream. From that moment I love him less . . .'.

And indeed from that moment Gerhart disappears from Auden's journal. But the way he is written off contains, as David Luke, who found the journal among Auden's possessions at Christ Church after his death, points out, the germs of the idea which Auden was later to formulate about the sonnets, three and a half decades later. Auden wrote on the last day of the affair:

When someone begins to lose the glamour they had for us on our first meeting, we tell ourselves that we have been deceived, that our phantasy cast a halo over them which they are unworthy to bear. It is always possible however that the reverse is the case: that our disappointment is due to a failure of our own sensibility which lacks the strength to maintain itself at the acuteness with which it began. People may really be what we first thought them, and what we subsequently think of as the disappointing reality, the person obscured by the staleness of our senses.[19]

When Auden's critics deride him for treating Shakespeare's experience in the Sonnets as mystical, they sometimes give the impression that this is to undermine the reality of the experience. But that is to misunderstand Auden. As David Luke comments:

> The theory of love here proposed in passing by the 22-year-old Auden, a theory which remained with him during those thirty-five years and indeed for the rest of his life, rests on an essentialist view of the human person, deriving ultimately from Plato, which is now out of fashion. The lover, it suggests, perceives the beloved as he or she 'really' is; the eyes of love are not blind but visionary, they behold a deeper, 'more real' reality, but only while the passion of love is sustained. When that fades, the vision fades with it into the light of common day.[20]

The echo of Wordsworth here is not accidental, for Auden thought that 'natural mystical experiences' are described in certain of Wordsworth's poems, in Plato's *Symposium*, in Dante's *La Vita Nuova,* and in Shakespeare's Sonnets. Auden does not tack Shakespeare's name onto this list in order to rescue his respectability. He does so in order to underline the mystery of the experience described. Echoing his earlier views, he says that

> Whatever the contents of the [mystical] experience, the subject is absolutely convinced that it is a revelation of reality. When it is over, he does not say, as one says when one awakes from a dream: 'Now I am awake and conscious again of the real world.' He says, rather: 'For a while the veil was lifted and a reality revealed which in my "normal" state is hidden from me.'[21]

What is striking about Auden's attitude to the primary experience of love as expressed in the Sonnets is not its inconsistency with, so much as its rootedness in his experience, not his hypocrisy so much as the longevity of his ideas. For instance, the notion that things go wrong with Gerhart Meyer when the symbol revolts, when the daydream becomes disobedient, retains its associative force for Auden in the conversation recorded by Howard Griffin in the late forties or early fifties. It is here, incidentally, that we learn that Auden thought it likely, as Oscar Wilde had proposed, that the young man of the Sonnets was an actor. 'To Shakespeare,' he says, 'W. H. stands for change . . . Of course, in those days boys assumed women's parts often to great effect for, since they were able to do so for only a few years, this volatility added a kind of pathos to the performance and compelled a healthy detachment on the part of the audience.' It is the fleeting nature of beauty, Auden says, that makes it moving to others, and 'One should take it as a momentary thing. To become preoccupied with it means a neurosis.'

Again and again, the conversation touches on the parallel between the relationship between Shakespeare and the young men, and that between Socrates and Alcibiades. Auden says: 'According to Socrates physical beauty may cause in some men a memory of divine beauty. In poets and artists the sight even of earthly beauty may bring about a noble madness.' The situation between Alcibiades and Socrates 'embodies the endless war between external and inward beauty. You remember at the conclusion of the *Symposium* Alcibiades compares Socrates to the statuettes of Silenus sold in shops, which open to reveal images of gods inside.' A litle later, when he returns to the theme, Griffin interjects that 'Socrates did not try to control Alcibiades, to mold him. Alcibiades wished to be his pupil but Socrates saw in his friend an inability to master himself.' Auden replies:

Yes, this situation with W. H. seems to be the one thing Shakespeare cannot be objective about. The plays as distinct from the sonnets neatly illustrate the difference between *speaking* and *speaking out*. That people have found it needful to use the tautology 'speaking out' shows that speech instead of affording a medium of communication has become, largely, a device of strategy and evasion. Much conversation has fallen to the plane of sales talk or the newspaper paragraph. On the rare times when people try to find words for what they feel, we say they *speak out*. In the Sonnets—particularly such ones as CX or CXXIX—Shakespeare speaks out, whereas in the plays he just speaks—beautifully, divinely of course. In *Macbeth* or *Hamlet* he is creating a world of language but in the *Sonnets* he desperately tries to do that which is forbibben: to create a human being. With the ardor of a Paracelsus, who incidentally was a contemporary, he mixes words as if they were chemicals that might bring forth a homunculus. Evidently he has selected someone at a stage of possibility. He wants to make an image so the person will not be a dream but rather someone he knows as he knows his own interest. He wishes the other to have a free will yet his free will is to be the same as Shakespeare's. Of course great anxiety and bad behaviour result when the poet's will is crossed as it is bound to be. This type of relationship needs a lot of testing to see if the magic is working. Sonnets like the CXXXVII show us that in this case the magic did not work.[22]

The symbol has revolted, the daydream has disobeyed. And this, as Auden knew, was something that must always eventually happen.

11. Blake Auden and James Auden

You will remember that Auden, when an undergraduate at Oxford, took a look at the literary scene in general and decided that it offered an empty stage. 'Evidently they are waiting for Someone', he said with, Stephen Spender tells us, 'the air of anticipating that he would soon take the centre of it'. Auden's fantasy, however, was to be at the centre, not to be the sole figure. Christopher Isherwood was to be the novelist. Robert Medley was to be the painter. Cecil Day-Lewis was in there in some poetic capacity, as were Louis MacNeice and Spender. Spender told Auden he wondered whether he, Spender, ought to write prose. But Auden put his foot down. 'You must write nothing but poetry, we do not want to lose you for poetry.' 'But do you really think I'm any good?' gulped Spender. 'Of course,' Auden frigidly replied. 'But why?' 'Because you are so infinitely capable of being humiliated. Art is born of humiliation.'[1]

In the end, Spender did write some prose, including *World within World*, the autobiography from which I am quoting, and a rare book called *European Witness*, which I strongly recommend. He kept an important journal, and also tried his hand at fiction, as did Day-Lewis. The real division of the spoils was between Auden and Isherwood, the pre-eminent poet and the pre-eminent novelist. Isherwood kept away from poetry, apart from a few very early verses, and some translations. Auden kept away from anything remotely like the novel. The two men collaborated on drama—it was territory which they could divide up amicably. Isherwood wrote filmscripts while Auden wrote fine texts for documentaries, two of which have held their own as poems. Isherwood later worked on a Frankenstein movie, for which Jonathan Keates later suggested the subtitle *Mr Norris Changes Brains*. Auden got opera. Isherwood took Hollywood. Neither stepped on the other's turf.

Prose, though, prose could not be easily divided up, or left, as we have heard, to Spender as his own. Prose is too important, too unsatisfactory a concept, too interesting in its ramifications. How could Auden have been given Poetry, Isherwood the Novel, and Spender—Prose. It doesn't add up. It doesn't *divide* up. And besides—*Auden* needed prose.

He needed it in various ways, one of which was to make a living, for, as he claimed in the introduction to *The Dyer's Hand*, he wrote all his lectures, introductions, and reviews because he needed the money. He hoped some love went into their writing. But when he looked over his criticism again he decided to reduce it to a set of notes. There was something, in his opinion, false about systematic criticism. When Alan Ansen had said to him in 1946, 'I should think you might almost be ready to issue a volume of collected prose,' Auden said, 'I don't think so. Criticism should be casual conversation.'

And indeed his table talk is and was very much like the opening sections of *The Dyer's Hand*:

The most painful of all experiences to a poet is to find that a poem of his which he knows to be a forgery has pleased the public and got into the anthologies. For all he knows or cares, the poem may be quite good, but that is not the point; *he* should not have written it.

No poet or novelist wishes he were the only one who ever lived, but most of them wish they were the only one alive, and quite a number fondly believe their wish has been granted.

Some books are undeservedly forgotten; none are undeservedly remembered.

One cannot review a bad book without showing off.[2]

These come from the page, whereas this comes from conversation:

Yeats spent the first half of his life writing minor poetry,
and the second half writing major poetry about what it
had been like to be a minor poet.

And this:

Eliot wrote nothing *but* late poetry [*smiling*] after
Gerontion, anyway.

The word *smiling* is put in by Ansen to mark Auden's realiza-
tion that what he had said wasn't really true.

For a long time Auden's periodical criticism remained
uncollected, until Auden himself had probably forgotten
much of what he had written and where it was to be found.
The Dyer's Hand, first published in 1962, was put together
under Auden's direction by an assistant whose job it was to go
to the libraries and copy out the pieces in question.
Presumably Auden then carried out his paring down of the
essays. *Forewords and Afterwords* (1973), the prose book
published ten years later, was selected and overseen by Edward
Mendelson, who became Auden's executor and who
published in 1977 *The English Auden*, which collected for the
first time the journalism of the Thirties. Until that publication, it would have been only a very attentive reader, and one
with a long memory, who could have formed an opinion of
Auden's work overall. And I should add that the recent, definitive collectiion of *Prose 1926–1938* is only the beginning of the
gathering of the fugitive pieces. Although we are in a much

better position now than we recently were to see Auden whole, we will not truly be able to do so until we can see the Prose whole.

The reason for this is not that we expect it to outshine the poetry, or to supplement its perceived deficiencies. The reason is that in Auden's work prose and poetry interpenetrate to a far greater extent than in the work of any other English-language poet of this century. There are vectors in Auden's work—the Blake vector, the late Henry James vector—which can be traced in prose and poetry alike:

> The sword sung on the barren heath,
> The sickle in the fruitful field:
> The sword he sung a song of death,
> But could not make the sickle yield.
>
> Amoeba in the running water
> Lives afresh in son and daughter.
> 'The sword above the valley'
> Said the Worm to the Penny.
>
> Abstinence sows sand all over
> The ruddy limbs and flaming hair,
> But desire gratified
> Plants fruits of life and beauty there.
>
> Those who will not reason
> Perish in the act:
> Those who will not act
> Perish for that reason.

Without Contraries is no progression. Attraction and Repulsion, Reason and Energy, Love and Hate, are necessary to Human existence.

He who undertakes anything, thinking he is doing it out of a sense of duty, is deceiving himself and will ruin everything he touches.

Those who restrain desire, do so because theirs is weak enough to be restrained; and the restrainer or reason usurps its place and governs the unwilling.

The Prolific and the Devourer: the Artist and the Politician. Let them realise that they are enemies, i.e., that each has a vision of the world which must remain incomprehensible to the other. But let them also realise that they are both necessary and complementary, and further, that there are good and bad politicians, good and bad artists, and that the good must learn to recognise and to respect the good.

to the Devourer, it seems as if the producer was in his chains: but it is not so, he only takes portions of existence and fancies that the whole.

But the Prolific would cease to be Prolific unless the Devourer, as a sea, received the excess of his delights. . . .

These two classes of men are always upon earth, and they should be enemies; whoever tries to reconcile them seeks to destroy existence.

That was Blake, Auden, Blake, Auden, Blake, Auden, Blake, Auden, Blake. I edited out Blake's ampersands.[4]

Blake sat at Auden's left when he wrote, urging concision, definite views, plain language. He was not the Blake of the long line, of the interminable prophetic books, but the fiery Blake of *The Marriage of Heaven and Hell*, the Blake of the notebooks.

Henry James sat on Auden's right, suggesting fascinating syntaxes and ways of prolonging a sentence, giving a nuance to a nuance. This is the late Henry James, making his appearance as early as the early 1940s. 'A mannered style,' Auden wrote later, 'that of Góngora or Henry James, for example, is like eccentric clothing: very few writers can carry it off, but one is enchanted by the rare exception that can.'[5] And again, in the essay on James's *The American Scene*, Auden says:

James had been evolving a style of metaphorical description of the emotions which is all his own, a kind of
modern Gongorism, and in *The American Scene* this
imagery, no longer inhibited by the restraining hand of
character or the impatient tug of plot, came to its fullest
and finest bloom.

Indeed, perhaps the best way to approach this book is
as a prose poem of the first order, . . . relishing it sentence
by sentence, for it is no more a guidebook than the 'Ode
to a Nightingale' is an ornithological essay.[6]

And he recommends the reader who finds James's late manner
hard to get on with to read the last paragraph of the chapter
on Richmond, describing the statue of General Lee—a purple
patch, he calls it, adding that there are many others which
match it. It reads:

The equestrian statue of the Southern hero, made to
order in far-away uninterested Paris [and how like Auden
that phrase sounds], is the work of a master and has artistic interest—a refinement of style, in fact, under the
impression of which we seem to see it, in its situation, as
some precious pearl of ocean washed up on a rude bare
strand. The very high florid pedestal is of the last French
elegance, and the great soldier, sitting on his horse with
a kind of melancholy nobleness, raises his handsome
head as he looks off into desolate space. He does well, we
feel, to sit as high as he may, and to appear, in his lone
survival, to see as far, and to overlook as many things; for
the irony of fate, crowning the picture, is surely stamped
in all sharpness on the scene about him. The place is the
mere vague centre of two or three crossways, without
form and void, with a circle half sketched by three or
four groups of small, new, mean houses. It is somehow
empty in spite of being ugly, and yet expressive in spite

of being empty. 'Desolate,' one has called the air; and the effect is, strangely, of some smug 'up-to-date' specimen or pattern of desolation. So long as one stands there the high figure, which ends for all the world by suggesting to the admirer a quite conscious, subjective, even a quite sublime, effort to ignore, to sit, as it were, superior and indifferent, enjoys the fact of company and therefore, in a manner, of sympathy—so that the vast association of the futile for a moment drops away from it. But to turn one's back, one feels, is to leave it alone again, communing, in its altitude, which represents thus some prodigious exemplary perched position, some everlasting high stool of penitence, with the very heaven of futility. So at least I felt brought round again to meeting my first surprise, to solving the riddle of the historic poverty of Richmond. It is the poverty that *is*, exactly, historic: once take it for that and it puts on vividness. The condition attested is the condition—or, as may be, one of the later, fainter, weaker stages—of having worshipped false gods. As I looked back, before leaving it, at Lee's stranded, bereft image, which time and fortune have so cheated of half the significance, and so, I think, of half the dignity, of great memorials, I recognised something more than the melancholy of a lost cause. The whole infelicity speaks of a cause that could never have been gained.[7]

So Auden heard this music, this Gongorism, and was enchanted. And he needed this prose for his own prose, and this poetry for his own poetry. He was not alone in his love of the late James, but he was not, on the other hand, one of a mob, and that sense, perhaps, of personal discovery, that sense that the late James was lying around neglected, made his appropriations possible.

To those who were anyway disillusioned with Auden, this Jamesian influence was unwelcome. But Auden needed influences. He always needed influences. When he ran out of influences, he entered a depression and very soon died. So we should think twice before bemoaning the James vector, or wishing it away. Here is the opening passage of 'At the Grave of Henry James', the poem Auden wrote in the spring of 1941, which began life as a 28-stanza blockbuster, by 1945 had been reduced to 24, and finally got boiled down to ten stanzas only:

> The snow, less intransigent than their marble,
> Has left the defence of whiteness to these tombs,
>   And all the pools at my feet
> Accommodate blue now, echo such clouds as occur
> To the sky, and whatever bird or mourner the passing
>   Moment remarks they repeat

> While rocks, named after singular spaces
> Within which images wandered once that caused
>   All to tremble and offend,
> Stand here in an innocent stillness, each marking the
>   spot
> Where one more series of errors lost its uniqueness
>   And novelty came to an end.

> To whose real advantage were such transactions
> When words of reflection were exchanged for trees?
>   What living occasion can
> Be just to the absent? O noon but reflects on itself,
> And the small taciturn stone that is the only witness
>   To a great and talkative man

> Has no more judgment than my ignorant shadow
> Of odious comparisons or distant clocks
>   Which challenge and interfere
> With the heart's instantaneous reading of time, time
>   that is
> A warm enigma no longer in you for whom I
>   Surrender my private cheer

Startling the awkward footsteps of my apprehension,
The flushed assault of your recognition is
   The *donnée* of this doubtful hour:
O stern proconsul of intractable provinces,
O poet of the difficult, dear addicted artist,
      Assent to my soil and flower.[8]

Edward Mendelson calls this poem 'dismayingly loqua-
cious'—a judgement with which Auden eventually concurred,
as we have seen. And it is true that in the original version—
and to a lesser extent in its final truncated form—Auden turns
James into a saint, who is asked to pray for him. Mendelson
says: 'James could safely be called upon to pray when he was
dead, however seldom he prayed in life.'[9]

Mendelson points out an interesting circumstance of this
poem's first publication. It came out first in *Horizon*, later in
the *Partisan Review*, where it would have been read as part of a
critical battle 'to canonise American literature as a precursor of
English and European modernism'. The key figure in this
movement was an acquaintance of Auden's, F. O. Matthiessen,
whose *American Renaissance* came out later in the same year.
Auden's enthusiasm for James and Melville was genuine and
unaffected, but still one might suppose that there was a particular pleasure in paying tribute to the culture in which he was
making his home (the grave of Henry James, incidentally,
being the family plot in Cambridge, Massachusetts). On the
poem's first English publication, the *New Statesman*
commented that James and Auden had one thing in common:
'they both changed nationality for the same reason—the
neutrality of the United States.'[10]

A cutting remark, one of the first of many, for Auden's decision to move to the United States was, as you know, held
against him. In fact although he applied for American citizen-
ship in 1940, he did not receive it until 1946. The adaptation of
an American prose style for poetic purposes might well have

contained an element of needling defiance of the English reader of the time—especially for the kind of reader who wanted his Auden sharp and political, wanted more of the Popular Front style rhetoric which the poet had deliberately decided to put behind him.

Auden was a rhetorician. He knew himself to be a rhetorician of the highest powers, and, when he saw the power he had, he recoiled from it in deep horror. And as he recoiled, he filled his followers with dismay, since *they* could not see the furies that he saw. They saw the beauty of the rhetoric of *Spain*, that astonishingly simple device of repetition and change between 'yesterday', 'today', and 'tomorrow', sustained over 104 lines with such a profusion of imagery. Auden saw only the lines of which Maynard Keynes wrote that 'in this he is speaking for many chivalrous hearts'.

> Today the deliberate increase in the chances of death;
> The conscious acceptance of guilt in the necessary
>   murder—[11]

the lines which provoked Orwell's first, scurrilous attack in the *Adelphi* (December 1938):

> Our civilisation produces in increasing numbers two types, the gangster and the pansy. They never meet, but each is necessary to the other. Somebody in eastern Europe 'liquidates' a Trotskyist; somebody in Bloomsbury writes a justification of it. And it is, of course, precisely because of the utter softness and security of life in England that the yearning for bloodshed—bloodshed in the far distance—is so common among our intelligentsia. Mr. Auden can write about 'the acceptance of guilt for the necessary murder' perhaps because he has never committed a murder, perhaps never had one of his friends murdered, possibly never seen a murdered man's

corpse. The presence of this utterly irresponsible intelli-
gentsia, who 'took up' Roman Catholicism ten years ago,
'take up' Communism today and will 'take up' the
English variant of fascism a few years hence, is a special
feature of the English situation. The importance is that
with their money, influence and literary facility they are
able to dominate large sections of the press.[12]

It is interesting that Nicholas Jenkins, who researched what
little is known about Auden's six weeks in Spain during the
Civil War, comes to the conclusion that 'Spain', the poem,
takes sides in the internecine political battles that were taking
place on the Aragon Front. He quotes Cyril Connolly's formulation of the two opposing positions: 'The Communists and
Socialists say: "First win the war, then attend to the revolution." The younger Anarchists and the P.O.U.M. say: "The war
and the revolution are indivisible, and we must go on with
both of them simultaneously".'[13] Jenkins thinks that
'Tomorrow . . . | All the fun under Liberty's masterful shadow
. . . | Tomorrow . . . | The eager election of chairmen | by the
sudden forest of hands. But today the struggle,'—such defer-
rals allude to the Communist or Socialist line as against that
of Orwell's POUM. If that is true, it helps explain the particular dislike that Orwell took to a poem which he also affected
to believe was 'one of the few decent things to have been written about the Spanish war'.

It depends, though, what Auden meant by the struggle, and
I do not necessarily think that he would have considered the
war and the revolution to be divisible, or that the revolution
should be deferred. After all, the lines 'Today the expending of
powers | on the flat ephemeral pamphlet and the boring meet-
ing' define political work as part of the present struggle.
Furthermore, Orwell does not, in the notorious passage in
Inside the Whale, object to Auden on the grounds that Jenkins's
theory would lead us to expect. He quotes two stanzas:

Tomorrow for the young the poets exploding like bombs,
The walks by the lake, the weeks of perfect communion;
  Tomorrow the bicycle races
Through the suburbs on summer evenings. But today the
  struggle.

Today the deliberate increase in the chances of death,
The conscious acceptance of guilt in the necessary
  murder;
  Today the expending of powers
On the flat ephemeral pamphlet and the boring meeting.

Now Orwell travesties the second stanza. He says that it

> is intended as a sort of thumbnail sketch of a day in the
> life of a 'good party man'. In the morning a couple of
> political murders, a ten-minutes' interlude to stifle 'bour-
> geois' remorse, and then a hurried luncheon and a busy
> evening chalking walls and distributing leaflets. All very
> edifying.

Of course it is Orwell who has inserted the 'good party man',
the *political* murders, the bourgeois remorse, the luncheon
and the evening chalking walls. All this by way of inducing
outrage, softening the reader up for what follows:

> But notice the phrase 'necessary murder'. It could only
> have been written by one to whom murder is at most a
> *word*. Personally I would not speak so lightly of murder. It
> so happens that I have seen the bodies of numbers of
> murdered men—I don't mean killed in battle, I mean
> murdered. Therefore I have some conception of what
> murder means—the terror, the hatred, the howling rela-
> tives, the post-mortems, the blood, the smells. To me,
> murder is something to be avoided. So it is to any ordinary
> person. The Hitlers and Stalins find murder necessary, but

they don't advertise their callousness, and they don't speak of it as murder; it is 'liquidation,' 'elimination' or some other soothing phrase. Mr. Auden's brand of amoralism is only possible if you are the kind of person who is always somewhere else when the trigger is pulled. So much of left-wing thought is a kind of playing with fire by people who don't know that fire is hot.[14]

Auden, it seems clear to me, had used the word 'murder' as an intensifier, not in any casual sense: to kill, even in defence of the Spanish Republic, is murder, and we have to accept this. But the non-combatant pansy poet had injured the deepest vanity of Orwell, the man of action, the veteran of the colonial police, who had fought with the POUM and who knew that killing on the battlefield and murder were two quite different things. So, we may ask, after Orwell's strident assertion of his credentials, what *does* distinguish the dead on the battlefield from the bodies of the murdered? 'The terror, the hatred, the howling relatives, the post-mortems, the blood, the smells'—what essential difference is there here? One might sympathize with Orwell if he had addressed what was really upsetting him—that Auden had inadvertently accused him of being a murderer. Orwell *did* have a clear sense of the distinction to be made between the different kinds of killing going on in Spain, and he made it, not in his attack on Auden, but in the classic *Homage to Catalonia*.

Auden himself, who thought Orwell's attack 'densely unjust', wrote to Monroe K. Spears in 1963:

I was *not* excusing totalitarian crimes but only trying to say what, surely, every decent person thinks if he finds himself unable to adopt the absolute pacifist position. (1) To kill another human being is always murder and should never be called anything else. (2) In a war, the members of two rival groups try to murder their opponents. (3) *If* there is such a thing as a just war, then murder can be necessary for the sake of justice.[15]

Point (1) in this argument is evidently wrong if we accept that there is such a thing as a legal definition of murder, but the fact remains that Auden was emphasizing, rather than overlooking, the nastiness of war, rather than condoning political liquidations.

It is true that there were writers involved with Spain and the Communist Party who, so far from shying away from the murder side of things (the liquidations on the republican side), considered it a mark of their seriousness that they accepted that 'you can't make an omelette without breaking eggs'. A good example of this type of character is Hemingway, who derided John Dos Passos for coming to Spain in the Civil War and trying to find out what had happened to his friend, José Robles. The Popular Front officials, who wanted to keep him on side, were trying to protect Dos Passos from the news that Robles had been executed. Hemingway, on learning of Robles's execution, decided that he must, a priori, have been a spy. He not only told Dos Passos the news, at a festive lunch to honour the XVth International Brigade. He also told his friend that Robles had got what he deserved. Dos Passos refused to believe that Robles had been guilty of treason. Hemingway was so keen to prove himself the kind of guy who knew that you couldn't make an omelette without breaking eggs that he denounced Dos Passos, first in a public meeting in New York, later in an article called 'Treachery in Aragon', and subsequently in one called 'Fresh Air on an Inside Story' in which an absurd figure, a famous American writer, decides there is terror in Madrid.

'You can't deny there is a terror,' said this expert. 'Everywhere you can see evidences of it.'

'I thought you said you hadn't seen any evidences.'

'They are everywhere,' said the great man.

I then told him that there were half a dozen of us newspaper men who were living and writing in Madrid whose business it was, if there was a terror, to discover it and report it. That I had friends in the Seguridad that I had known from the old days and could trust, and that I knew three people had been shot for espionage that month. I had been invited to witness an execution but had been away at the front and had waited four weeks for there to be another. That people had been shot during the early days of the rebellion by the so-called 'uncontrollables' but that for months Madrid had been as safe and well policed and free from any terror as any capital in Europe. Any people shot or taken for rides were turned in at the morgue and he could check for himself as all journalists had done.[16]

This awful insiderism (which is not as far as it should be from Orwell's 'Don't talk to me about murder, I know more about murder than you do'), this 'don't be a bourgeois liberal wimp and ask why your worthless traitor friend has disappeared', this boasting of reliable friends in the secret police, all this is very far from Auden's spirit. Auden went to Spain and wrote a short descriptive article for the *New Statesman*. He worked for a while, perhaps, in radio propaganda. He visited the Aragon front. He seems to have been shocked rigid by some experiences, although no one appears to have found out what these were. He wrote 'Spain', which was sold to raise money for medical aid. After Orwell's attack on him, he tried to change the offending lines:

To-day the inevitable increase in the chances of death,
The conscious acceptance of guilt in the fact of murder . . .

But it was no good in the long run, for he began to see the ending of the poem as grotesquely immoral. So he dropped it and suppressed it. And at the same time he tried to suppress in himself the urge to create a stirring rhetoric which would move men or classes to action. It is no exaggeration to say that the horror he felt at his own powers—or his own potential— was, though in differing degree, the same kind of horror with which he observed the power of Hitler. From this horror proceeded much that his admirers observed with dismay: the self-deflation, the retreat from activism, the putting of a distance between himself and his followers, the return to religion.

Imagine someone who has grown up a great admirer of Blake. He or she leaves university, gets married, has a baby. One day the babysitter goes mad and kills the baby. A few months later, the grieving parent happens to pick up a copy of *The Marriage of Heaven and Hell*, and reads the line; 'Sooner murder an infant in its cradle than nurse unacted desires.' One would think: I used to like this, as a thought expressed with a curious extremism; now I can hardly look at the page.

And Blake himself, having once been such an oddity that he seemed beyond normal reproach, would suddenly lose the benefit of the doubt. Suddenly one would ask— if one turned to him at all—exactly what manner of meaning any one of his strange pronouncements was supposed to have, and one would be soon impatient. For instance, under the maxim I have quoted comes the next: 'Where man is not, nature is barren.' Once it might have seemed to possess a mysterious beauty—a beauty often possessed by statements that are, strictly speaking, untrue. But now one would have lost patience with that sort of untruth, and with one's former self, as one who used to delight in it.

You have to imagine Auden, at the end of the Thirties, reading his own works in rather the same spirit as our imaginary parent reading Blake. Once, in his invented world, Auden could, at a stroke of the pen, have a spy taken out and shot. Now he has passed through a world where spies are indeed taken out and shot, and where revolutionary rhetoric, such as he had once delighted in, has proved deadly. So he reads his own works, and those of his more ambiguous heroes, with wariness and impatience. He takes Lawrence's dictum: 'Anger is sometimes just, justice is never just.' It is, he says, 'admirable advice to lovers, [but] applied politically can only mean: "Beat up those who disagree with you".' He says:

> Writers who try, like D. H. Lawrence in *The Plumed Serpent*, to construct political systems of their own, invariably make fools of themselves because they construct them in terms of their own experience, and treat the modern state as if it were a tiny parish and politics as if it were an affair of personal relations, whereas modern politics is almost exclusively concerned with relations that are impersonal.[17]

'Lawrence, Blake and Homer Lane'—of the old trinity it was Blake who lasted longest with Auden, and whose manner he was closely imitating in 'The Prolific and the Devourer', the prose work he wrote, but never published, in 1939. For instance, the thought quoted earlier—'He who undertakes anything, thinking he is doing it out of a sense of duty, is deceiving himself and will ruin everything he touches'— comes in the context of a discussion of the writer's relation to politics:

> Crisis. Civilisation is in danger. Artists of the world unite.
> Ivory Tower. Escapist. Ostrich.
> Yes, the Crisis is serious enough, but we shall never

master it, if we rush blindly hither and thither in blind obedience to the frantic cries of panic.

You cannot give unless you also receive. What is it that you hope to receive from politics? excitement? experience? Be honest.

The voice of the Tempter: 'Unless you take part in the class struggle, you cannot become a major writer.'

The artist qua artist is no reformer. Slums, war, disease are part of his material, and as such he loves them. The writers who, like Hemingway and Malraux, really profited as writers from the Spanish Civil War, and were perhaps really some practical use as well, had the time of their lives there.[18]

And it is in 'The Prolific and the Devourer' that we find, placed in apposition: 'The Dictator who says "My People": the Writer who says "My Public".' And: 'If the criterion of art were its power to incite to action, Goebbels would be one of the greatest artists of all time.'[19]

> The nights, the railway arches, the bad sky,
> His horrible companions did not know it;
> But in that child, the rhetorician's lie
> Burst like a pipe: the cold had made a poet.[20]

That was Auden on Rimbaud, at the end of 1938. The child becomes a poet when the rhetorician's lie bursts. But what if the rhetorician is the poet himself? 'Crisis. Civilisation. Artists of the world unite. Ivory Tower. Escapist. Ostrich.' It has been pointed out that the wording is reminiscent of a letter composed by Nancy Cunard in 1937, requesting contributions for a book, *Authors Take Sides on Vietnam*. Auden may well have allowed his signature to be appended before he saw the text, which begins:

SPAIN

THE QUESTION.

WRITERS and POETS OF ENGLAND, SCOTLAND,
IRELAND and WALES.

It is clear to many of us throughout the whole world that
now, as certainly never before, we are determined, or
compelled, to take sides. The equivocal attitude, the
Ivory Tower, the paradoxical, the ironic detachment
will no longer do.[21]

And a little lower down, we find: 'Today, the struggle is Spain',
picked up from Auden's poem which had been published two
months earlier.

Orwell, on receiving this manifesto, wrote to *Left Review*:

Will you please stop sending me this bloody rubbish.
This is the second or third time I have had it. I am not
one of your fashionable pansies like Auden and Spender
. . . By the way, tell your pansy friend Spender that I am
preserving specimens of his war-heroics and that when
the time comes when he squirms for shame at having
written it, as the people who wrote the war-propaganda
in the Great War are squirming now, I shall rub it in good
and hard.[22]

What Orwell was sick of, Auden too was sick of. He had to
stop putting his art at the service of the cause. The Ivory Tower,
he had come to see, like the Point in mathematics, is really
only a useful mathematical concept without actual existence,
meaning complete isolation from all experience. 'The closest
approximation in real life is schizophrenia.' And how could
Auden, of all people, envisage an art in which the equivocal
attitude, the paradoxical or ironic detachment was banned—
worse still, worst of all, demand such an art of others.

12. *Auden in the End*

'Art is born of humiliation', said the young Auden to the young hopeful Spender. And we saw in Chapter 10 how he continued to believe this. He thought of the Sonnets as a private record of Shakespeare's humiliation at the hands of both the young man and the Dark Lady, for the sonnets addressed to her are 'concerned with that most humiliating of all erotic experiences, sexual infatuation'. 'Simple lust', said Auden,

> is impersonal, that is to say the pursuer regards himself as a person but the object of his pursuit as a thing, to whose personal qualities, if she has any, he is indifferent, and, if he succeeds, he expects to be able to make a safe getaway as soon as he becomes bored. Sometimes, however, he gets trapped. Instead of becoming bored, he becomes sexually obsessed, and the girl, instead of conveniently remaining an object, becomes a real person to him, but a person whom he not only does not love, but actively dislikes.[1]

And Auden adds that 'No other poet, not even Catullus, has described the anguish, self-contempt and rage produced by this unfortunate condition so well as Shakespeare in some of these Sonnets'.

As for the young man:

> the impression we get of his friend is one of a young man who was not really very nice, very conscious of his good

looks, able to switch on the charm at any moment, but
essentially frivolous, cold-hearted, and self-centred,
aware, probably, that he had some power over
Shakespeare—if he thought about it at all, no doubt he
gave it a cynical explanation—but with no conception of
the intensity of feelings he had, unwittingly, aroused.
Somebody, in fact, rather like Bassanio in *The Merchant of
Venice*.[2]

Auden thought that the Sonnets told the story 'of an agonized
struggle by Shakespeare to preserve the glory of the vision he
had been granted in a relationship, lasting at least three years,
with a person who seemed intent by his actions upon cover-
ing the vision with dirt'.

More than one reader has sensed in these lines a bitterness
deriving from Auden's own circumstances with Chester
Kallman, his lover with whom he continued to live for at least
part of the year long after their sexual relations had ceased.
Auden considered himself married to Kallman, but, since his
friend had turned elsewhere for sex, he came to make his own
sexual arrangements too. Since Auden is often depicted as the
suffering victim in this relationship, it is worth pointing out
that, if he had been attacking Kallman in his depiction of the
young man in the Sonnets, he would (*a*) have been casting
himself as Shakespeare, and (*b*) have been mounting an attack
which would have been very hard for Kallman to counter.
And how could you live happily with someone who attacks
you in print?

Auden was powerfully aware of the difficulty involved in
being on the receiving end of an intensely felt love, and you
may remember that in his definition of the Vision of Eros he
more or less excluded the possibility that the vision could be
mutual. Beatrice, had she lived, could never have, as it were, reci-
procated Dante's experience of her. As Auden put it: 'The story
of Tristan and Isolde is a myth, not an instance of what can

historically occur.' Auden also felt that the vision he was talking about could not long survive an actual sexual relationship. In a letter to David Luke, he emphasizes that '*all* the authorities agree that the vision cannot survive any prolonged sexual relations'. But he doesn't say who *all* these authorities are.

Actually the story Shakespeare's Sonnets tell, if they do tell a story, seems to me to be of relevance to Auden's life in a way he might not have acknowledged. You will remember that the conclusion of Sonnet 20 proposes that the young man should grant the poet his love, while bestowing his sexual attention on women: 'Since she prick'd thee out for women's pleasure,' says the poet, 'Mine be thy love, and thy love's use their treasure.' The poet thinks he can split love in two, but this plan gets its comeuppance when the young man goes anywhere near the Dark Lady. In his own life, Auden felt that having made his commitment he should stick to it. If Kallman had shifted his sexual attentions elsewhere, perhaps Auden could still have his love in the important sense. He was not to waver from this unhappy ambition for the next, the last, thirty years of his life.

Sometimes in his poetry he expresses a stoic resignation

> Looking up at the stars, I know quite well
> That, for all they care, I can go to hell,
> But on earth indifference is the least
> We have to dread from man or beast.
>
> How should we like it were stars to burn
> With a passion for us we could not return?
> If equal affection cannot be,
> Let the more loving one be me.
>
> Admirer as I think I am
> Of stars that do not give a damn,
> I cannot, now I see them, say
> I missed one terribly all day.

> Were all stars to disappear or die,
> I should learn to look up at an empty sky
> And feel its total dark sublime,
> Though this might take me a little time.[3]

One of those poems which was probably not much liked when it came out in 1958, but which hangs around, and reverberates, largely because of that couplet:

> If equal affection cannot be,
> Let the more loving one be me.

A thought that anyone might wish to take consolation from at some point in life.

But Auden was not always stoical or resigned in this way. His jealousy had been stirred by Kallman to such an extent that at one point—or so he believed—he came within an ace of strangling him. And that fury returned to haunt him.

> Make this night loveable,
> Moon, and with eye single
> Looking down from up there
> Bless me, One especial,
> And friends everywhere.
>
> With a cloudless brightness
> Surround our absences;
> Innocent be our sleeps,
> Watched by great still spaces,
> White hills, glittering deeps.
>
> Parted by circumstance,
> Grant each your indulgence
> That we may meet in dreams
> For talk, for dalliance,
> By warm hearths, by cool streams.

> Shine lest tonight any,
> In the dark suddenly,
> Wake alone in a bed
> To hear his own fury
> Wishing his love were dead.[4]

To be in love and wish your lover dead, to be in love and know that you have to conceal it, to be in the grip of a sexual obsession with someone you discover you dislike—all these humiliating experiences turn up in Auden's work, and it is worth noting that the humiliation did not begin with Kallman. From the earliest of Auden's published lyrics we are invited to see love as transitory:

> Nor speech is close nor fingers numb
> If love not seldom has received
> An unjust answer, was deceived.
> I, decent with the seasons, move
> Different, or with a different love . . .[5]

The lover behaves decently in the sense that he changes and accepts change. This is the behaviour of nature. Love is seasonal. And it happens that in Auden's early poetry an incantatory style can create an effect of beauty while the subject under discussion might be something the reader, if he only understood it better, might be shocked by. It was Christopher Isherwood in *Christopher and his Kind* (1976) who explained that Auden had written a beautiful poem, just to please Isherwood, about a boyfriend of Isherwood's known as Bubi:

> Before this loved one
> Was that one and that one,
> A family
> And history

And ghost's adversity,
Whose pleasing name
Was neighbourly shame.
Before this last one
Was much to be done,
Frontiers to cross
As clothes grew worse,
And coins to pass
In a cheaper house
Before this last one
Before this loved one.[6]

Perhaps it would always have been clear to the reader that there was something going on here which was not quite right—that, as the second stanza puts it, this love affair was 'no real meeting', 'a backward love'. Perhaps also those frontiers to cross as clothes grew worse and coins to pass in a cheaper house suggested that what was going on was not, as it were, entirely respectable. But whether the words 'rent-boy' or 'male prostitute' or 'promiscuous sex' came to mind among the original readers of the poem is another question. Such words seem to come from a very different vocabulary from that of the poem.

Much of Auden's early poetry was written in a kind of code, and this was a source of its bewitching power. Readers of poetry divide into two kinds: those who, confronted with what appears to be like a code insist that they must crack it, and those who are happy to listen to the spell, without enquiring too closely what it might mean:

Garlic and sapphires in the mud
Clot the bedded axletree.[7]

as Eliot so aptly put it. But what does it mean?

> The trilling wire in the blood
> Sings below inveterate scars
> Appeasing long forgotten wars.[8]

What is a trilling wire? Some people *have* to know the answer. Others don't. (I think a trilling wire is a telegram people used to send to Professor Lionel Trilling, begging for his help in elucidating passages like these.)

What Auden wrote in code—to the extent that his circle might posess a key to the code while the general public did not—would have been read within his circle with the sense of pleasure and privilege enjoyed by the initiate; perhaps too as a joke on the general public. How many readers do you think understood the dedication of *Poems* (1930) as having a sexual meaning?

> Let us honour if we can
> The vertical man,
> Though we value none
> But the horizontal one.[9]

And would they have been right to do so? Does it mean: let us try to honour the living, although it is the dead we value? (An odd message, surely.) Or honour man in his active mode, though we value only the—what? The unconscious, the contemplative man?

A poem may be at the same time transparent and undis-closing, *en code* and *en clair*:

> Dear, though the night is gone,
> The dream still haunts to-day
> That brought us to a room
> Cavernous, lofty as
> A railway terminus,
> And crowded in that gloom

Were beds, and we in one
In a far corner lay.

Our whisper woke no clocks,
We kissed and I was glad
At everything you did,
Indifferent to those
Who sat with hostile eyes
In pairs on every bed,
Arms round each other's necks,
Inert and vaguely sad.

What hidden worm of guilt
Or what malignant doubt
Am I the victim of,
That you then, unabashed,
Did what I never wished,
Confessed another love;
And I, submissive, felt
Unwanted and went out?[10]

Our pronouns have preserved a tact which allows Auden to write a poem in this way without specifying what sexes are involved. And there is generosity in this, since any reader can be the lover, the speaker of this poem. It is based on a dream of Auden's about a particular male lover. Read as a poem about two men, it yields further meanings, hitherto perhaps concealed: the hostility of the other lovers comes across as the hostility of society, while the location of the dream in a railway terminus has associations with a particular kind of transient affair. But of course the fear expressed by the whole dream—the fear of being unwanted—is universal.

The speaker in the poem, on the other hand, has dreamt the dream and is aware not only of the miserable feeling of being unwanted, but also of having created the scenario, which implies that he might in some guilty way wish the affair with the lover to end. Likewise in 'Lay your sleeping head, my love' it is the speaker, the poet, whose arm is faithless. It is the speaker who, while wishing to preserve the beautiful moment, is aware that it may pass on the stroke of midnight. And this sense of transience is not unwelcome—it is merely defied for the time being. This is the early Auden, the Auden of the Thirties, speaking. He may have suffered. He may have been humiliated, and his art may have come from this humiliation. But he could still, generally speaking, display a happy optimism in the matter of love.

This song was written for Benjamin Britten:

Underneath the abject willow,
  Lover, sulk no more:
Act from thought should quickly follow.
  What is thinking for?
Your unique and moping station
  Proves you cold;
  Stand up and fold
Your map of desolation.

Bells that toll across the meadows
  From the sombre spire,
Toll for those unloving shadows
  Love does not require.
All that lives may love; why longer
  Bow to loss
  With arms across?
Strike and you shall conquer.

Geese in flocks above you flying
  Their direction know;
Brooks beneath the thin ice flowing
  To their oceans go;
Coldest love will warm to action,
  Walk then, come,

No longer numb,
Into your satisfaction.[11]

Just over half a dozen years after composing this, Auden, in 1943, wrote to Elizabeth Mayer that 'Being Anders wie die Andern'—he meant *Anders als die Andern*, different from the others (it was the title of a film about homosexuality made in 1919)—'has its troubles. There are days when the knowledge that there will never be a place which I can call home, that there will never be a person with whom I shall be one flesh, seems more than I can bear, and if it wasn't for you, and a few—how few—like you, I don't think I could.'[12] Auden was not usually given to self-pity, and one is pulled up by the assertion that there would never be a place he could call home. He had lived, it is true, a peripatetic life—as a teacher and writer—but nothing so fractured as to mark him out from the rest of humanity in this respect.

And yet it may be that Auden seriously believed that he was somehow condemned to be homeless. Even when he bought his house in Austria in 1957 and began to write the series of poems about it that were gathered in *About the House*, the series was called *Thanksgiving for a Habitat*, as if the use of the word 'home' might be somewhat pushing it. And in the dozen poems in the series, the word seldom crops up:

Territory, status

and love, sing all the birds, are what matter:
    what I dared not hope or fight for
is, in my fifties, mine, a toft-and-croft
    where I needn't, ever, be at home *to*

those I am not at home *with*, not a cradle,
    a magic Eden without clocks,
and not a windowless grave, but a place
    I may go both in and out of.[13]

The second use of the word home is in the final poem, addressed to Kallman, which is about the living room. It simply says that 'every home should be a fortress, | equipped with all the very latest engines, | for keeping Nature at bay'.[14] He is referring to the fact that the living room had small windows, which he liked to keep tight shut.

To define one's home so baldly as 'a place | I may go both in and out of' seems extremely odd until we turn to John Fuller's commentary, which gives us the reference to George Macdonald's *Lilith*. It comes from the advice a raven gives to Mr Vane:

'The only way to come to know where you are is to begin to make yourself at home.'
'How am I to begin that when everything is so strange?'
'By doing something.'
'What?'
'Anything; and the sooner you begin the better! For until you are at home, you will find it as difficult to get out as it is to get in . . . Home, as you know, is the only place where you may go out and in. There are places you can go into and places you can go out of; but the one place, if you do but find it, where you may go out and in both, is home.'[15]

The commentary suggests that 'what the quotation does not say, but which Auden may have had in mind (significantly in the context of a poem about certain death and illusory Edens) is that the one place you only come out of is the womb, and the one place you only go into is the tomb'.[16] Auden's riddling use of an anyway riddling Macdonald is an indication that there was some significance in his suppression of the subject 'home'.

One may ask why Auden should be under the illusion—or burdened with the belief—that he had not had a home before moving to Austria. He had never been under any illusion about having roots—his roots, if he had had them, would have been in Birmingham. His mythical North of England (which began at Crewe station) to which he often referred and returned in prose and verse, was well understood to be a place of his own invention. Nothing would have been simpler than to hop on a train to Carlisle, if hopping on that train would have met the need for home. But there was a forward impulse in Auden's life that involved renunciation. He had renounced in his poetry a certain kind of rhetoric. He had renounced political engagement. He had really renounced England, and that was not forgiven him.

I think also that this forward impulse of renunciation is reflected in the feeling he would have, after finishing a poem, that he would never be able to write another line again—as if by the end of each poem all his talent had been evacuated. And then there was a feeling, once when he was preparing a collected poems in New York, that he would put them all together in a book because he never wanted to write like that again. He would be shot of them.

When Auden *did* go back, the upshot was often unhappy. This was true both of the trip to England he made at the end of the war, and of his attempt to move back to Oxford in the last year of his life. It is true also that when he was elected Professor of Poetry at Oxford, he was terrified of giving his inaugural lecture. According to Davenport-Hines, it was partly the animosity that his election to this chair had aroused which gave him the dark-night-of-the-soul experience out of which he wrote 'There Will Be No Peace'.

> Though mild clear weather
> Smile again on the shire of your esteem
> And its colours come back, the storm has changed you:
>   You will not forget, ever,
> The darkness blotting out hope, the gale
>   Prophesying your downfall.

You must live with your knowledge.
Way back, beyond, outside of you are others,
In moonless absences you never heard of,
    Who have certainly heard of you,
Beings of unknown number and gender:
    And they do not like you.

    What have you done to them?
Nothing? Nothing is not an answer:
You will come to believe—how can you help it?—
    That you did, you did do something;
You will find yourself wishing you could make them
    laugh,
    You will long for their friendship.

    There will be no peace.
Fight back, then, with such courage as you have
And every unchivalrous dodge you know of,
    Clear in your conscience on this:
Their cause, if they had one, is nothing to them now;
    They hate for hate's sake.[17]

Nobody seemed to like this poem at the time. Thom Gunn
wrote that it was 'the worst of Auden's poems I have seen in
book form'. And even Edward Mendelson says it was 'perhaps
the least successful poem he had written in fifteen years', that
Auden 'did not translate or universalize the experience that
had prompted it into something accessible to a sympathetic
reader'. Auden said: 'I don't know why critics have disliked
this poem so much. However, I can't be objective about it,
since it is one of the most purely personal poems I have ever
written. It was an attempt to describe a very unpleasant dark-
night-of-the-soul sort of experience which for several months
in 1956 attacked me.'[18] And he later identified the theme as
paranoia.'
    Actually there seems to me to be something universally

appreciable in the idea that there are beings out there who hate you, people unknown to you who have a long-standing inexplicable grudge against you. If it were not so, one's heart would not miss a beat in those innumerable films when the hero comes home to find his favourite cat nailed to the door, or his house sprayed with slogans.

We can take 'There Will Be No Peace' as an evocation of the visceral dislike Auden encountered in Britain. We can also see it as a study of forces encountered within, forces which urge one to admit an unfounded guilt and to go for the humiliation of appeasement. That awareness in Auden, mentioned in Chapter 11, of the proximity of the power of the poet's rhetoric to the power of the dictator was a long-standing theme. Terrifying powers work within us, or are carrying out their work through us, Auden thought. He said in 1940: 'Jung hardly went far enough when he said "Hitler is the unconscious of every German"; he comes uncomfortably near being the unconscious of most of us . . . The shock of discovering through Freud and Marx that when we thought we were being perfectly responsible, logical, and loving we were nothing of the kind, has led us to believe that responsibility and logic and love are meaningless words; instead of bringing us to repentance, it has brought us to nihilistic despair.'

Here is a poem written at that time which was first called 'The Crisis' and is now called 'They':

Where do they come from? Those whom we so much
    dread,
as on our dearest location falls the chill
    of their crooked wing and endangers
    the melting friend, the aqueduct, the flower.

Terrible Presences that the ponds reflect
back at the famous and, when the blond boy

bites eagerly into the shining
apple, emerge in their shocking fury,

and we realise the woods are deaf and the sky
nurses no one, and we are awake and these,
    like farmers, have purpose and knowledge
    but towards us their hate is directed.

We are the barren pastures to which they bring
the resentment of outcasts; on us they work
    out their despair; they wear our weeping
    as the disgraceful badge of their exile.

We have conjured them here like a lying map;
desiring the extravagant joy of life,
    we lured with a mirage of orchards,
    fat in the lazy climate of refuge.

Our money sang like streams on the aloof peaks
of our thinking that beckoned them on like girls;
    our culture like a West of wonder
    shone a solemn promise in their faces.

We expected the beautiful or the wise,
ready to see a charm in our childish fibs,
    pleased to find nothing but stones, and
    able at once to create a garden.

But those who come are not even children with
the big indiscriminate eyes we had lost,
    occupying our narrow spaces
    with their anarchist vivid abandon.

They arrive, already adroit, having learned
restraint at the table of a father's rage;
    in a mother's distorting mirror
    they discovered the Meaning of Knowing.

For a future of marriage nevertheless
the bed is prepared; though all our whiteness shrinks

from the hairy and clumsy bridegroom
we conceive in the shuddering instant.

For the barren must wish to bear though the Spring
punish; and the crooked that dreads to be straight
 cannot alter its prayer but summons
 out of the dark a horrible rector.

The tawny and vigorous tiger can move
with style through the borough of murder; the ape
 is really at home in the parish
 of grimacing and licking: but we have

failed as their pupils. Our tears well from a love
we have never outgrown; our cities predict
 more than we hope; even our armies
 have to express our need for forgiveness.[19]

Quite a lot of 'trilling wires' here, enough to provoke E. R. Dodds's wife, Annie Dodds, to ask Auden what crisis he was referring to. He replied: 'The Crisis is just the spiritual crisis of our time, i.e. the division between reason and the heart, the individual and the collective, the liberal ineffective highbrow and the brutal practical demagogue like Hitler or Huey Long.'[20]

The powers that suddenly and terrifyingly appear are, as Mendelson glosses them,

the chthonic powers that our intellectual pride has banished from ourselves, and they exist, paradoxically, because we banished them. Evolutionary and erotic instincts were inseparable from the whole being of a lower animal; they took on separate existence only when we human beings divided ourselves into proletarian Matter and aristocratic Idea, and excluded from both the instincts that had once informed the whole.[21]

Auden believed that though we are under the illusion that we live and act, we are in fact 'lived'—unknown and irrational forces work through us.

> We are lived by powers we pretend to understand:
> They arrange our loves, it is they who direct at the end
> The enemy bullet, the sickness, or even our hand.
> It is their to-morrow hangs over the earth of the living
> And all that we wish for our friends: but existence is
>   believing
> We know for whom we mourn and who is grieving.[22]

That comes from an elegy for Ernst Toller, who had committed suicide (which explains the reference to the powers directing 'even our hand'). While Auden was contemplating these powers, and the awful way they seemed to be shaping the destiny of Europe, while he was trying to shake off one way of thinking and explore another—shake off a way of thinking based on the belief in the inevitability of human progress, explore a way of thinking suggested to him by the theologies of the time—while he was doing this, and writing the poems which came out of his contemplation of the war and its meaning—Auden would have thought that he was doing what he was set on earth to do. He had written in 1938:

> The primary function of poetry, as of all the arts, is to make us more aware of ourselves and the world around us. I do not know if such increased awareness makes us more moral or more efficient. I hope not.
>
> I think it makes us more human, and I am quite certain it makes us more difficult to deceive, which is why, perhaps, all totalitarian theories of the State, from Plato's downwards, have deeply distrusted the arts. They notice and say too much, and the neighbours start talking.[23]

So if Auden was working (as he always was), he felt that he was doing the right thing. He had a gift, and he was at this time particularly conscious of his responsibilities towards it. Mendelson quotes a stanza from one of the suppressed poems, 'Pascal':

> Yet like a lucky orphan he had been discovered
> And instantly adopted by a Gift;
> And she became his sensible protector
> Who found a passage through the caves of accusation,
> And even in the canyon of distress was able
> To use the echo of his weakness as a proof
> That joy was probable and took the place
> Of the poor lust and hunger he had never known.[24]

The Gift is your protector against your accusers.

When Golo Mann first met Auden in Switzerland in 1935, his manner was, Mann later put it,

> appealingly awkward, but at the same time self-confi-
> dent. If one studied him closer, he had the air of one who
> was used to being *primus inter pares*, one might even say
> a triumphant air, so long as this does not suggest
> anything exaggerated or theatrical.

Mann goes on to say:

> He was the most intelligent man I have known, or rather,
> because 'intelligence' only suggests insight and under-
> standing, the cleverest, with a cleverness which was
> essentially creative. He thought truths out for himself.
> Many of them could have been expanded into whole
> books. But he only presented them, in his own particu-
> lar way, unsystematically. So there is no Auden 'philoso-
> phy'.

Golo Mann later shared that famous house in Brooklyn with Auden, along with Carson McCullers, Bejamin Britten, Paul and Jane Bowles, and Gipsy Rose Lee. Mann tells us:

> Benjamin Britten soon left Brooklyn and returned to England, presumably because he did not wish to remain far away from his native country in time of war. Auden remained. This did not endear him to his countrymen, soon to be his ex-countrymen. When I showed him a hostile article in an English paper, and said it required some reply from him, he cut me short: 'There is no point.' It was another example of his independence, self-confidence and pride. He knew that he would survive such a crisis, best of all by taking no notice of it.[25]

Mann means that Auden knew he would survive being attacked in the press, not, as might at first seem, that he knew he would survive the war best by taking no notice of it. Auden's 'There is no point' might be taken to mean, 'Whatever I say in my defence will be useless.' And that has certainly proved the case, since the accusation of cowardice pursued him all his life, and afterwards too. In the first of these chapters on Auden I traced an irritating little scholarly tradition, which began by calling Auden a hypocrite and ended up detecting 'a characteristic instance of [his] cowardice'.

Ursula Niebuhr, the theologian wife of the theologian Reinhold Niebuhr, who was critical of pacifism, gives an account of Auden's commencement address at Smith College in 1940, from part of which I have already quoted. Auden called his address a sermon, but he put the text at the end. It is from Rilke's *Words to a Young Poet*:

> The only courage that is demanded of us: [is] to have courage for the most extraordinary, the most singular,

and the most inexplicable that we may encounter. . . .
Only he or she who is ready for everything . . . will live
the relation to another as something alive. . . . We must
always hold to what is difficult, then that which still
seems to us the most hostile will become what we most
trust and find most faithful . . . Perhaps all the dragons
of our lives are princesses who are only waiting to see us
once beautiful and brave. Perhaps everything terrible is
in its deepest being something helpless that wants help
from us.[26]

And Ursula Niebuhr goes on to recall how Auden

wrote sympathetically about Rilke's negative reaction to
the First World War. 'Not to understand: yes, that was my
entire occupation in those years'; and commented on
these words of Rilke, 'To be conscious but to refuse to
understand, is a positive act that calls for courage of the
highest order.' But he admitted that, 'It may be difficult
for the outsider . . . to distinguish it from selfish or
cowardly indifference.' For him, Rilke was the writer to
whom to turn, 'for strength to resist the treacherous
temptations that approach us disguised as righteous
duties.'[27]

I think of Blake's question:

> Thou hast a lap full of seed
> And this is a fine country.
> Why dost thou not cast thy seed
> And live in it merrily.[28]

To which the answer must be: if only it were as easy as that. If
only what the question supposes were true. Auden had the
greatest gifts of any of our poets in the twentieth century, the

greatest lap full of seed. And it was given him to know this, and to doubt it, to know and to doubt it. The sense of being *primus inter pares*, the sense of always being the youngest person in the room, the spirit that could say to posterity 'You did not live in our time—be sorry'—all this was given him. And then, to be conscious but to refuse to understand, to live not in a fine but in a lean country, to hold to what was most difficult, to face that which was most hostile—this too was given him. To make mistakes, to cling to impossible ideals, to fail, to find himself hated, to know humiliation—this too was given him. To find himself wronged or in the wrong, to find his courage taken for cowardice, to find himself human in short—all this was given him. 'Perhaps everything terrible is in its deepest being something helpless that wants help from us,' and perhaps that forward impulse of renunciation implied a gesture towards the terrible. This was where his Gift had brought him, to this lean country and to these caves of accusation.

Notes

1. A Lesson from Michelangelo

1. Filippo Baldinucci, *Notizie de' Professori del Disegno* . . . (Florence, 1681–8; 1845 edn.), vol. ii, 556.
2. Michael Hirst, *Michelangelo and His Drawings* (New Haven: Yale University Press, 1988), 19.
3. Vasari, *Lives of the Artists*, trans. George Bull (Harmondsworth: Penguin, 1965), 262.
4. W. R. Valentiner, *Studies of Italian Renaissance Sculpture* (London: Phaidon, 1950), 134.
5. Vasari, *Lives of the Artists*, 233.
6. Ibid. 139.
7. Ibid.
8. W. H. Auden, *Juvenilia: Poems 1922–1928*, ed. Catherine Bucknell (Princeton: Princeton University Press, 1994), xx.
9. Thomas Carlyle, *Reminiscences*, ed. C. E. Norton (London: Everyman, 1932; repr. of 1881 edn.), 360.
10. Robert Gittings, *John Keats* (Atlantic Monthly Press/Little Brown, 1968), 167.
11. Stephen Gill, *William Wordsworth: A Life* (Oxford: Clarendon Press, 1989), 326–8.
12. Gittings, *John Keats*, 167.
13. *Letters of John Keats*, ed. Robert Gittings (London: OUP, 1970), 60–1.
14. Ibid.
15. *Byron's Letters and Journals*, vii. *'Between two worlds' (1820)*, ed. Leslie A. Marchand (London: John Murray, 1977), 200, 202.
16. Ibid. 225.
17. Gittings, *John Keats*, 168.
18. Ibid. 250.
19. John Keats, letter to J. A. Hessey, 8 October 1818, in *Letters*, ed. Gittings, 156.
20. *The Letters of Gustave Flaubert 1830–1857*, ed. Francis Steegmuller (Cambridge, Mass.: Harvard University Press/Belknap Press, 1900), 100.

2. Wilfred Owen's Juvenilia

1. 'To Poesy', in Wilfred Owen, *The Complete Poems and Fragments,* ed. Jon Stallworthy (London: Chatto and Windus, 1983), 3.
2. Wardour Street in London used to sell antique furniture, some of which would have been confected on the premises.
3. Stephen Spender once asked Siegfried Sassoon about meeting Owen. Sassoon said: 'It was very embarrassing. He had a grammar-school accent'.
4. Dominic Hibberd, *Owen the Poet* (Basingstoke: Macmillan, 1986), 71.
5. Dylan Thomas, *The Collected Letters,* ed. Paul Ferris (London: J. M. Dent & Sons Ltd, 1985), 410, 411.
6. Ibid. 415.
7. Quoted by Owen in Letter 95 (28 September 1911), in Owen, *Collected Letters,* ed. Harold Owen and John Bell (London: Oxford University Press, 1967), 88.
8. Letter 314 (14 [15] January 1915), ibid. 316.
9. Letter 319 (6 February 1915), ibid. 320.
10. Letter 238 (14 February 1914), ibid. 324.
11. Letter 285 (28 August 1914), ibid. 282.
12. Letter 308 (27 December 1914), ibid. 310.
13. Letter 308 (27 December 1914), ibid. 311.
14. ['The time was aeon'], in *Complete Poems,* 75.
15. 'Perversity', ibid. 108.
16. 'A Palinode', ibid. 77.
17. ['I am the ghost of Shadwell Stair'], ibid. 183.
18. Hibberd, *Owen the Poet,* 155.
19. Id., *Wilfred Owen: The Last Year* (London: Constable, 1992), 116.
20. Letter 557 (5 November 1917), in *Collected Letters,* 504–5.
21. Ibid. 505.
22. Letter 510 (14 May 1917), ibid. 458–9.

3. Philip Larkin: Wounded by Unshrapnel

1. When I delivered this lecture, I remarked off the cuff that Larkin appears, from the formulation 'Quarterly, is it', to be uncertain how often his pay cheques arrived. This was challenged immediately after the lecture, and later, at some length, by Barbara Everett, who correctly pointed out that it is savings and investments account

statements that come quarterly. This does not alter the point I made above: How many people feel *reproached* by their savings? Is this a common experience? But see Barbara Everett, 'Larkin's Money', in James Booth (ed.) *New Larkins for Old* (Basingstoke: Macmillan, 1999).

2. Philip Larkin, 'Money', in *Collected Poems* (London: Marvell Press and Faber and Faber, 1990 edn.), 198.

3. Id., 'I Remember, I Remember', ibid. 81–2.

4. Id., *Selected Letters of Philip Larkin 1940–1985*, ed. Anthony Thwaite (London: Faber and Faber, 1992).

5. Andrew Motion, *Philip Larkin: A Writer's Life* (London: Faber and Faber, 1993), 11–12.

6. Philip Larkin, *Jill* (London: Faber and Faber, 1998 edn.), 186, 194, 196, 201.

7. Quoted in Motion, *Philip Larkin*, 48–9.

8. Philip Larkin, 'Forget What Did', in *Collected Poems*, 184.

9. Id., 'Love Again', ibid. 215.

10. Id., 'The Winter Palace', ibid. 211.

11. Id., *Selected Letters*, 7.

12. Quoted in Motion, *Philip Larkin*, 52.

13. Larkin, *Selected Letters*, 36.

14. Ibid. 53.

15. Quoted in Motion, *Philip Larkin*, 53.

16. Larkin, *Selected Letters*, 27.

17. Quoted in Motion, *Philip Larkin*, 70.

18. Quoted ibid.

19. Ibid. 72; Larkin, *Selected Letters*, 31.

20. Larkin, 'Homage to a Government', in *Collected Poems*, 171.

21. Quoted in Motion, *Philip Larkin*, 389–90.

22. Repr. in Larkin, *Required Writing: Miscellaneous Pieces 1955–1982* (Faber and Faber, 1983), 159.

23. Ibid. 163.

24. Quoted in Motion, *Philip Larkin*, 66.

25. Larkin, *All What Jazz: A Record Diary 1961–1968* (London: Faber and Faber, 1970), 12, 10.

26. Id., 'In times where nothing stood', ibid. 210.

27. Id., 'Going, Going', ibid. 189–90.

28. John Betjeman, 'Hymn', in *Collected Poems* (London: John Murray, 1958), 3.

29. Freud, 'On Transience', in *Art and Literature*, Pelican Freud Library, vol. xiv (Harmondsworth: Penguin, 1985), 287–90.

30. Philip Larkin, 'The Trees', in *Collected Poems*, 166.

31. Id., 'On Being Twenty-six', ibid. 24–5.

4. Goodbye to All That?

1. *The Works of John Dryden*, ed. Samuel Holt Monk, vol. xvii (Berkeley and Los Angeles: University of California Press, 1971), 8–9.
2. *The Diary of Samuel Pepys*, ed. Robert Latham and William Matthews, vol. vi, *1665* (London: Bell & Hyman Ltd, 1972), 116 (3 June 1665).
3. *Works of Dryden*, ed. Monk, xvii, 8–9.
4. *Diary of Pepys*, vi, 122 (8 June 1665).
5. Ibid. 122 n. 3.
6. *Works of Dryden*, ed. Monk, i, 59–60.
7. *The Works of John Dryden*, ed. Edward Niles Hooker and H. T. Swedenborg, Jr., vol. i (Berkeley and Los Angeles: University of California Press, 1961), 59. Dryden's own note reads: 'In Eastern Quarries &c. Precious stones at first are Dew, condens'd and harden'd by the warmth of the Sun, or subterranean Fires.'
8. Ibid. 62.
9. Ibid. 64.
10. *Medallic Illustrations of the History of Great Britain and Ireland*, vol. i (London: Edward Hawkins, 1885; repr. London: Spink, 1978).
11. Robert Frost, 'The Gift Outright', in *The Poetry of Robert Frost*, ed. Edward Connery Lathem (London: Jonathan Cape, 1971), 348.
12. Id., 'For John F. Kennedy His Inauguration ('Gift Outright of "The Gift Outright"'), ibid. 424.
13. Ibid. 422.
14. T. S. Eliot, 'To the Indians Who Died in Africa', in *Collected Poems 1909–1962* (London: Faber and Faber, 1963), 231.
15. Id., 'Little Gidding', ibid. 222.
16. Douglas Dunn, *Terry Street* (London: Faber and Faber, 1969), 60.
17. Id., *Barbarians* (London: Faber and Faber, 1979), 26.

5. The Orpheus of Ulster

1. Seamus Heaney, *An Open Letter*, Field Day Pamphlet No. 2 (Derry: Field Day Theatre Company, 1983).
2. Id., 'The Flight Path', 4, in *The Spirit Level* (London: Faber and Faber, 1986), 25.
3. Blake Morrison, *Seamus Heaney* (London: Methuen, 1982), 83.
4. Alvarez, in *New York Review*, 6 March 1980, 16.

5. Seamus Heaney, 'Frontiers of Writing', in *The Redress of Poetry* (London: Faber and Faber, 1995), 201–2.
6. James Simmons, 'The Trouble with Seamus', repr. in Elmer Andrews (ed.), *Seamus Heaney: A Collection of Critical Essays* (Basingstoke: Macmillan, 1992), 39.
7. Ciarán Carson, 'Escaped from the Massacre?', *Honest Ulsterman* (Winter, 1975), 183.
8. Seamus Heaney, 'Punishment', in *North* (London: Faber and Faber, 1975), 38.
9. Carson, 'Escaped from the Massacre?', 184.
10. Simmons, 'The Trouble with Seamus', 56.
11. Seamus Heaney, 'Craig's Dragoons', as quoted in Neil Corcoran, *Seamus Heaney* (London: Faber and Faber, 1986), 26–7.
12. Id., *Crediting Poetry: The Nobel Lecture* (London: Faber and Faber, 1996), 16.
13. Ibid. 15.
14. Id., 'The Errand', in *The Spirit Level*, 54.
15. Id., 'The Butter-Print', in *The Spirit Level*, 44.

6. Becoming Marianne Moore

1. Germaine Greer, *Slip-Shod Sibyls: Recognition, Rejection and the Woman Poet* (New York: Viking, 1995), xi–xiii.
2. I cannot see why the same procedure should not be followed for Moore as had been done so successfully for Auden: that the *Complete Poems* (London: Faber and Faber, 1968) remains in print as she wanted them, but other supplementary publications make available the juvenilia and uncollected work. At the very least, a facsimile printout of the 1924 *Observations* would be a welcome alternative to paying $1,600 for a first edition (the current going rate).
3. April Bernard, 'Exile's Return', *New York Review*, 13 January 1994.
4. *Encyclopedia Britannica Year Book* (1957).
5. Charles Molesworth, *Marianne Moore: A Literary Life* (New York: Atheneum, 1990). Despite the fact that Molesworth in this excellent and respectful biography was extremely sparing in his quotations from Moore's work, he was sued by the Moore estate and forced to settle out of court for $12,000. It is obvious that the estate would have been better advised to allow Molesworth to quote extensively, and to charge him the going rate. That way, his biography would have been

that much better, and Moore would have been better served. For a precise account of the lamentable early history of the Moore estate, see the February 1996 issue of the magazine *Brooklyn Bridge*.

6. 'Silence', in *Collected Poems*, 91.
7. Cited in Margaret Holley, *The Poetry of Marianne Moore: A Study in Voice and Value* (Cambridge: Cambridge University Press, 1987). This work contains a helpful chronology of Moore's published poems.
8. Bryher, *West* (London: Jonathan Cape, 1925), 101–2.
9. Robert Cantwell, article in *Sports Illustrated* (1960), February 15, 74–82.
10. Marianne Moore, 'To a Strategist', in *Observations* (1924), 16.
11. Ead., 'You Are Like the Realistic Product of an Idealistic Search for Gold at the Foot of the Rainbow', in *Poems* (London: Egoist Press, 1921), 12.
12. Ead., 'I May, I Might, I Must', in *Complete Poems*, 178.
13. Ead., 'A Jellyfish', ibid. 180.
14. Ead., 'To a Prize Bird', ibid. 31.
15. Ead., 'Picking and Choosing', versions in: *Observations* (1924), 55; *Complete Poems*, 45.
16. Ead., Review of *Ideas of Order* by Wallace Stevens, *The Complete Prose of Marianne Moore*, ed. Patricia C. Willis (London: Faber and Faber, 1987), 329.
17. Ead., in *Marianne Moore: A Collection of Critical Essays*, ed. Charles Tomlinson (Englewood Cliffs, N.J.: Prentice-Hall, 1969), 30.
18. Ead., 'Sojourn in the Whale', *Complete Poems*, 90.
19. Bryher, *West*, 148.
20. Ibid. 158.
21. Marianne Moore, 'Marriage', in *Complete Poems*, 62–70: 62.
22. Cited in David Kalstone, *Becoming a Poet: Elizabeth Bishop with Marianne Moore and Robert Lowell* (New York: Farrar, Straus and Giroux, 1990), 25.
23. Moore, 'Marriage', 63.
24. Ibid. 67.
25. Moore's own note in *Complete Poems*, 272, citing 'Miss M. Carey Thomas, Founder's address, Mount Holyoke, 1921'
26. Moore, 'Virginia Brittanica', ibid. 107–11: 109, 110.

7. The Many Arts of Elizabeth Bishop

1. April Bernard, 'Exile's Return', *New York Review*, 13 January 1994.
2. George Monteiro (ed.), *Conversations with Elizabeth Bishop* (University Press of Mississippi, 1996), 92–3.

3. Quentin Bell, *Virginia Woolf: A Biography*, vol. ii (St Alban's: Triad/Paladin, 1976), 204–5.

4. Elizabeth Bishop, 'Roosters', in *Complete Poems* (London: Chatto & Windus, 1991 edn.), 35–9: 35–6.

5. Monteiro, *Conversations with Elizabeth Bishop*, 89.

6. Marianne Moore, 'In Distrust of Merits', in *Complete Poems* (London: Faber and Faber, 1968), 136–8: 138.

7. Edith Sitwell, 'Still Falls the Rain', in *Collected Poems* (London: Sinclair-Stevenson, 1993), 272–3: 273.

8. David Kalstone, *Becoming a Poet: Elizabeth Bishop with Marianne Moore and Robert Lowell* (New York: Farrar, Straus and Giroux, 1990), 106. 'H & H poetry' must refer to Lincoln Kirstein's magazine, *Hound and Horn*, in which 'The Jerboa' appeared.

9. Elizabeth Bishop, 'Hymn to the Virgin', in *Complete Poems*, 221–2: 221.

10. Ead., 'Flannery O-Connor, 1925–1964', *New York Review*, 8 October 1964, 21.

11. Ead., *The Collected Prose*, ed. Robert Giroux (New York: Farrar, Straus and Giroux, 1984), 213–14.

12. For this incident see Kalstone, *Becoming a Poet*, ch. 4, and his appendix for the version of 'Roosters' as revised by Moore and her mother.

13. *The Selected Letters of Marianne Moore*, ed. Bonnie Costello (New York: Knopf, 1997), 391.

14. Elizabeth Bishop, *One Art: Letters*, selected and edited by Robert Giroux (London: Chatto & Windus, 1994), 68 and 108.

15. Ead., 'The Weed', in *Complete Poems*, 20–1.

16. Kalstone, *Becoming a Poet*, 14.

17. Brett C. Millier, *Elizabeth Bishop: Life and the Memory of It* (Berkeley, Ca.: University of California Press, 1993), 295.

18. Elizabeth Bishop, 'Sleeping on the Ceiling', in *Complete Poems*, 29.

19. Ead., *Collected Prose*, 46.

20. Thom Gunn, *Shelf Life: Essays, Memoirs, and an Interview* (Ann Arbor: University of Michigan Press, 1993), 78.

21. Quoted in Kalstone, *Becoming a Poet*, 20; Elizabeth Bishop, 'The Man-Moth', in *Complete Poems*, 14–15: 15.

22. Robert Lowell, *For the Union Dead* (New York: Farrar, Straus and Giroux, 1964), 9.

23. Elizabeth Bishop, 'Songs for a Colored Singer', in *Complete Poems*, 47–51: 49.

8. *Lady Lazarus*

1. See Chapter 6, above.
2. Anne Stevenson, *Bitter Fame: A Life of Sylvia Plath* (Boston: Houghton Mifflin, 1990), 163, quoting Plath's *Journals* (Dial Press, 1982), 321.
3. Stevenson, *Bitter Fame*, 126, quoting Plath's *Journals*, 211–12.
4. Sylvia Plath, *Letters Home: Correspondence 1950–1963*, selected and ed. Aurelia Schober Plath (New York: Harper and Row, 1975), 466 and 476.
5. Elizabeth Bishop, *One Art: Letters*, selected and ed. Robert Giroux (New York: Farrar, Straus and Giroux, 1994), 333.
6. Cited in Stevenson, *Bitter Fame*, 24.
7. Cited in Paul Alexander, *Rough Magic: A Biography of Sylvia Plath* (New York: Viking, 1991), 159.
8. Cited in Stevenson, *Bitter Fame*, 25.
9. Sylvia Plath, 'Edge', in *Collected Poems* (London: Faber and Faber, 1981), 272–3.
10. Plath's use of the word 'toga' is of course inappropriate, a toga being a man's garment.
11. Sylvia Plath, 'The Moon and the Yew Tree', in *Collected Poems*, 172–3.
12. Ead., 'Words heard, by accident, over the phone', ibid. 202–3.
13. Ead., *The Journals of Sylvia Plath 1950–1962*, ed. Karen V. Kukil (London: Faber and Faber, 2000), 199.
14. See Jacqueline Rose, *The Haunting of Sylvia Plath* (Cambridge, Mass.: Harvard University Press, 1991), ch. 6.
15. Sharon Olds, *The Dead and the Living* (New York: Knopf, 1984), 44 and 36.
16. Rose, *Haunting of Sylvia Plath*, 238.
17. Seamus Heaney, *The Government of the Tongue: The 1986 T. S. Eliot Memorial Lectures and Other Critical Writings* (New York: Farrar, Straus and Giroux, 1989), 165.
18. Plath, *Letters Home*, 243–4.
19. Ead., 'Firesong', in *Collected Poems*, 30.
20. Ead., 'Ode for Ted', ibid. 29.
21. Ead., 'Two Views of a Cadaver Room', ibid. 114.
22. Ead., 'Electra on Azalea Path', ibid. 116–17.
23. Ead., 'Stillborn', ibid. 142.
24. Stevenson, *Bitter Fame*, 134.
25. Bishop, *One Art: Letters*, quoted by Brett C. Millier in *Elizabeth Bishop: Life and the Memory of It* (Berkeley, Ca.: University of California Press, 1993), 460.

26. Cited from Diane Wood Middlebrook, *Anne Sexton: A Biography,* in Germaine Greer, *Slipshod Sibyls: Recognition, Rejection and the Woman Poet* (Viking, 1985), 419.
27. Greer, *Slipshod Sibyls,* 419.

9. Men, Women, and Beasts

1. D. H. Lawrence, 'The Bride', in *Complete Poems,* ed. Vivian de Sola Pinto and Warren Roberts, 2 vols. continuously paginated (London: Heinemann, 1972 edn.), 101.
2. Id., 'The Virgin Mother', MS version with marginalia by Frieda Lawrence.
3. Id., 'The Virgin Mother', published version, in *Complete Poems,* 101–2.
4. Mark Kinkead-Weekes, *D. H. Lawrence: Triumph to Exile 1912–1922* (vol. ii of the Cambridge Biography) (Cambridge: Cambridge University Press, 1996), 377–81.
5. *The Letters of D. H. Lawrence,* ed. James T. Boulton and Andrew Robertson (Cambridge: Cambridge University Press, 1984), iii, 140–1.
6. Three essays on 'Democracy', repr. in *Reflections on the Death of a Porcupine and Other Essays,* ed. Michael Herbert (Cambridge: Cambridge University Press, 1988), 63–83.
7. Lawrence, 'Whitman', *Studies in Classic American Literature* (Harmondsworth: Penguin, 1971), 171–2.
8. W. H. Auden, 'D. H. Lawrence', in *The Dyer's Hand* (London: Faber and Faber, 1963), 277–95: quotes from 287–8, 288.
9. Whitman, quoted in Charley Shively (ed.), *Calamus Lovers: Walt Whitman's Working Class Camerados* (San Francisco: Gay Sunshine Press, 1987), 28.
10. Quoted in Kinkead-Weekes, *Triumph to Exile,* 455.
11. Ezra Pound, 'A Pact', in *Collected Shorter Poems,* 2nd edn. (London: Faber and Faber, 1968), 98.
12. Lawrence, *Studies in Classic American Literature,* 180.
13. T. S. Eliot, 'Reflections on *Vers Libre'*, *Selected Prose of T. S. Eliot,* ed. Frank Kermode (London: Faber and Faber, 1975), 31 and 32.
14. Lawrence, 'Poetry of the Present' (introduction to the American edition of *New Poems,* 1918), in *Complete Poems,* 181–6: 182.
15. Pound, *Literary Essays of Ezra Pound,* ed. T. S. Eliot (London: Faber and Faber, 1954), 12.
16. Lawrence, 'Poetry of the Present', 184.

17. Pound, *Literary Essays of Ezra Pound*, 218.
18. Lawrence, 'Poetry of the Present', 184.
19. W. H. Auden, *The English Auden: Poems, Essays and Dramatic Writings, 1927–1939*, ed. Edward Mandelson (London: Faber and Faber, 1977), 49.
20. Id., 'D. H. Lawrence', 278.
21. Ibid. 280.
22. Lawrence, 'Poetry of the Present', 184.
23. Id., 'Pomegranate', in *Complete Poems*, 278–9: 278.
24. Id., 'The Turkey-Cock', ibid. 369–72: 369.
25. Auden, 'D. H. Lawrence', 28.
26. H.D., in Lawrence, *Letters*, iii. 102.
27. Lawrence, 'Argument', to *Look! We Have Come Through*, in *Complete Poems*, 191.
28. Id., 'Meeting Among the Mountains', ibid. 224–6: 225–6.
29. David Ellis, *D. H. Lawrence: Dying Game 1922–1930* (vol. iii of the Cambridge Biography) (Cambridge: Cambridge University Press, 1998), 97.

10. Auden on Shakespeare's Sonnets

1. See Charles H. Miller, *Auden: An American Friendship* (New York: Scribner's, 1983), 29, 92.
2. W. H. Auden, 'The Joker in the Pack', in *The Dyer's Hand* (London: Faber and Faber, 1963), 246–72: 266.
3. Miller, *Auden*, 61.
4. In a review of *Shakespeare* by Mark Van Doren, *The Nation*, October 21, 1939.
5. Id., 'Shakespeare's Sonnets', repr. in *Forewords and Afterwords* (London: Faber and Faber, 1973), 88–108: 89.
6. Ibid. 105.
7. Ibid. 99.
8. Joseph Pequigney, *Such Is My Love: A Study of Shakespeare's Sonnets* (Chicago: University of Chicago Press, 1985), 80.
9. Bruce R. Smith, *Homosexual Desire in Shakespeare's England: A Cultural Poetics* (Chicago: University of Chicago Press, 1991), 231.
10. Marjorie Garber, *Vice Versa: Bisexuality and the Eroticism of Everyday Life* (London: Hamish Hamilton, 1996), 510.

11. Katherine Duncan-Jones, introduction to Shakespeare, *Sonnets* (London: New Arden Shakespeare, 1997), 80–1.

12. Repr. in Auden, *Forewords and Afterwords*, 333–44: 336.

13. Michel Foucault, *The History of Sexuality* (London: Allen Lane, 1979), 43.

14. Alan Bray, *Homosexuality in Renaissance England* (Boston: Gay Men's Press, 1982), 7.

15. Ibid. 61.

16. Eve Kosofsky Sedgwick, *Between Men: English Literature and Male Homosocial Desire* (New York: Columbia University Press, 1990), 510.

17. W. H. Auden, '1929', I, in *Collected Poems*, ed. Edward Mendelson (London: Faber and Faber, 1994 edn.), 45.

18. Id., quoted in David Luke, 'Gerhart Meyer and the Vision of Eros', in Katherine Bucknell and Nicholas Jenkins (eds.) *'The Language of Learning and the Language of Love': Uncollected Writings, New Interpretations* (Oxford: Clarendon Press, 1994), 106.

19. Id., 107.

20. David Luke, 108.

21. Auden, 'Shakespeare's Sonnets', 100.

22. Howard Griffin, *Conversations with Auden* (San Francisco: Grey Fox Press, 1981), 98.

11. Blake Auden and James Auden

1. Stephen Spender, *World within World* (London: Faber and Faber Ltd, 1977), 51–2.

2. W. H. Auden, 'Prologue', in *The Dyer's Hand and Other Essays* (London: Faber and Faber Ltd, 1963), 18, 14, 10, 11.

3. Alan Ansen, The Table Talk of W. H. Auden (New York: Sea Cliff, 1989), 51.

4. Quotes from: William Blake, Notebook Poems and Fragments, c.1789–93, *The Complete Poems*, ed. Alicia Ostriker (Harmondsworth: Penguin, 1977), 152; Auden; Blake, Notebook Poems and Fragments, 153; Auden; Blake, *The Marriage of Heaven and Hell*, in *Complete Poems*, pp. 180–95, pl. 3; Auden, Shorts, in *Collected Poems*, ed. Edward Mendelson (London: Faber and Faber, 1994 edn.), 53; Blake, *Marriage*, pl. 5, in *Complete Poems*, 182; Auden, 'The Prolific and the Devourer', in *The English Auden*, ed. Edward Mendelson (London: Faber and Faber, 1986 edn.), 404; Blake, *Marriage*, pl. 16.

5. Auden, *The Dyer's Hand* (London: Faber and Faber, 1963), 18.

6. Id., 'The American Scene', in *The Dyer's Hand*, 309–23: 314.
7. Henry James, *The American Scene, Collected Travel Writings: Great Britain and America* (New York: Library of America, 1993), 677–8.
8. Auden, 'At the Grave of Henry James', in *Collected Poems*, 310–11.
9. Edward Mendelson, *Later Auden* (London: Faber and Faber, 1999), 163.
10. *New Statesman* 21 June, 1941.
11. Auden, final version of 'Spain 1937', in *English Auden*, 210–12.
12. *The Complete Works of George Orwell*, ed. Peter Davison (London: Secker & Warburg, 1998), vol. xi, 244.
13. Nicholas Jenkins, 'Auden and Spain', in Katherine Bucknell and Nicholas Jenkins (eds.), *'The Map of All My Youth': Early Works, Friends, and Influences* (Oxford: Clarendon Press, 1990), 88–93.
14. Orwell, *Complete Works*, xii, 103.
15. Monroe K. Spears, *The Poetry of W. H. Auden* (New York: Oxford University Press, 1968), 157.
16. Repr. in *By-Line* (London: Collins, 1968), 308–11: 308–9.
17. Auden, 'The Prolific and the Devourer', 404.
18. Ibid. 402–3, 403.
19. Ibid. 394, 406.
20. Id., 'Rimbaud', in *Collected Poems*, 181–2.
21. Quoted in id., *Prose 1926–1938*, ed. Edward Mendelson (London: Faber and Faber Ltd, 1996), 730.
22. Orwell, *Complete Works*, xi, 67.

12. Auden in the End

1. 'Shakespeare's Sonnets', repr. in W. H. Auden, *Forewords and Afterwords* (London: Faber and Faber Ltd, 1973), 88–108: 103.
2. Ibid.
3. Id., 'The More Loving One', in W. H. Auden, *Collected Poems*, ed. Edward Mendelson (London: Faber and Faber, 1994 edn.), 584–5.
4. Id., 'Five Songs', V, ibid. 577.
5. Id., 'The Letter', ibid. 29.
6. Id., 'This Loved One', ibid. 36.
7. T. S. Eliot, 'Burnt Norton', *Collected Poems 1909–1962* (London: Faber and Faber, 1963), 190–1.
8. Ibid.
9. Auden, 'Shorts', in *Collected Poems*, 53.

10. Id., 'Twelve Songs', IV, ibid. 137–8.

11. Id., 'Twelve Songs', VII, ibid. 140.

12. Edward Mendelson, *Later Auden* (London: Faber and Faber, 1999), 227 n.

13. Auden, 'Thanksgiving for a Habitat', ibid. 690–2.

14. Ibid. 715.

15. George Macdonald, *Lilith*, cited in John Fuller, *W. H. Auden: A Commentary* (London: Faber and Faber, 1998), 486.

16. John Fuller's commentary, ibid.

17. Auden, 'There Will Be No Peace', in *Collected Poems*, 617.

18. Mendelson, *Later Auden*, 406.

19. 'They', in *Collected Poems*, 253–5.

20. Quoted in Mendelson, *Later Auden*, 26.

21. Ibid. 25.

22. Auden, 'In Memory of Ernst Toller', in *Collected Poems*, 249–50.

23. Id., *The English Auden: Poems, Essays and Dramatic Writings, 1927–1939*, ed. Edward Mendelson (London: Faber and Faber, 1977), 371–2.

24. Id., 'Pascal', in Ibid., 449–51.

25. Golo Mann, 'A Memoir', in Stephen Spender (ed.), *W. H. Auden: A Tribute* (New York: Macmillan, 1975), 98–103.

26. Rilke cited in Spender, *W. H. Auden*, 105.

27. Ursula Niebuhr, 'Memories of the 1940s', in Spender, *W. H. Auden*, 105.

28. William Blake, Notebook Poems and Fragments, c.1789–93, *The Complete Poems*, ed. Alicia Ostriker (Harmondsworth: Penguin, 1977), 141.

Sources

The author and publishers would like to thank the following for permission to reprint copyright material in this work.

W. H. Auden: 'At the Grave of Henry James', 'Spain', 'The More Loving One', 'Five Songs V', 'The Loved One', 'Twelve Songs', 'There Will Be No Peace', 'They' from *Collected Poems*. Published by Faber and Faber. Reprinted by permission of Faber and Faber, Curtis Brown Inc, and in the US by Random House Inc. 'Rimbaud' from *The English Auden*. Published by Faber and Faber. Reprinted by permission of Faber and Faber, Curtis Brown Inc and in the US by Farrar Straus and Giroux, LLC.

Elizabeth Bishop: 'Roosters', 'Sleeping On The Ceiling' from *The Complete Poems: 1927–1979*. Copyright © 1979, 1983 by Alice Helen Methfessel. Reprinted by permission of Farrar, Straus and Giroux, LLC.

Douglas Dunn: 'Poem in Praise of the British' from *Terry Street*. Published by Faber and Faber, 1969 and 'Empires' from *Barbarians*. Published by Faber and Faber, 1979. Reprinted by permission of Faber and Faber.

T. S. Eliot: 'To The Indians Who Died in Africa' from *Collected Poems 1909–1962*. Published by Faber and Faber, 1963. Reprinted by permission of Faber and Faber and in the US by Harcourt Brace.

Robert Frost: 'The Gift Outright' from *The Poetry of Robert Frost*, edited by Edward Connery Latham. Published by Jonathan Cape. Copyright © 1942 by Robert Frost, © 1970 by Lesley Frost Ballantine, © 1969 by Henry Holt and Co. Reprinted by permission of the publisher and the Estate of Robert Frost, and in the US by Henry Holt and Company, LLC.

Seamus Heaney: 'The Butter-Print' and 'The Errand' from *The Spirit Level*. Published by Faber and Faber. Copyright © 1996 by Seamus Heaney. Reprinted by permission of Faber and Faber and in the US by Farrar, Straus and Giroux, LLC.